Robert Louis Stevenson (13 November 1850 – 3 December 1894) was a Scottish novelist and travel writer, most noted for Treasure Island, Kidnapped, Strange Case of Dr Jekyll and Mr Hyde, and A Child's Garden of Verses. Born and educated in Edinburgh, Stevenson suffered from serious bronchial trouble for much of his life, but continued to write prolifically and travel widely, in defiance of his poor health. As a young man, he mixed in London literary circles, receiving encouragement from Andrew Lang, Edmund Gosse, Leslie Stephen and W. E. Henley, the last of whom may have provided the model for Long John Silver in Treasure Island. His travels took him to France, America and Australia, before he finally settled in Samoa, where he died. A celebrity in his lifetime, Stevenson attracted a more negative critical response for much of the 20th century, though his reputation has been largely restored. He is currently ranked as the 26th most translated author in the world.(Source: Wikipedia)

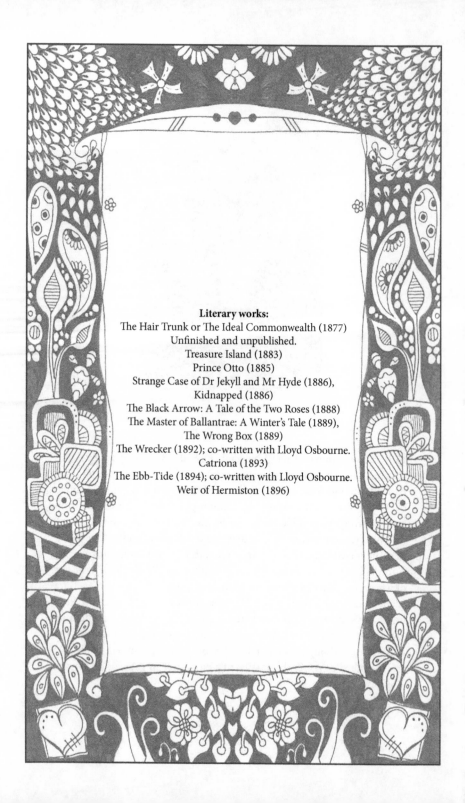

Literary works:
The Hair Trunk or The Ideal Commonwealth (1877)
Unfinished and unpublished.
Treasure Island (1883)
Prince Otto (1885)
Strange Case of Dr Jekyll and Mr Hyde (1886),
Kidnapped (1886)
The Black Arrow: A Tale of the Two Roses (1888)
The Master of Ballantrae: A Winter's Tale (1889),
The Wrong Box (1889)
The Wrecker (1892); co-written with Lloyd Osbourne.
Catriona (1893)
The Ebb-Tide (1894); co-written with Lloyd Osbourne.
Weir of Hermiston (1896)

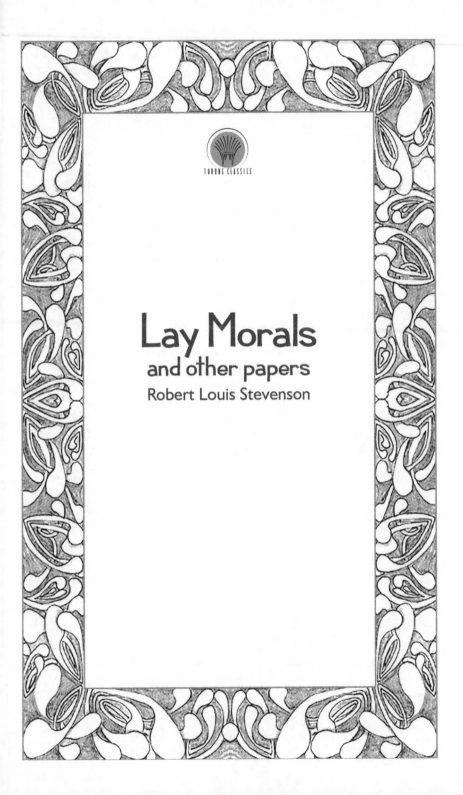

THRONE CLASSICS

Lay Morals
and other papers
Robert Louis Stevenson

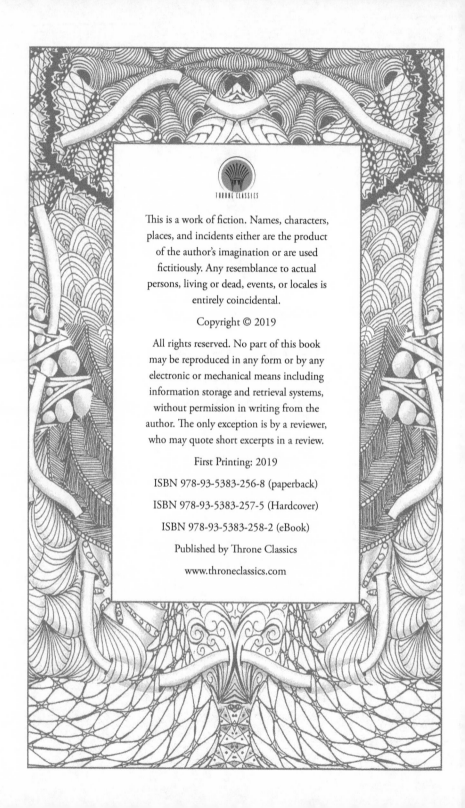

First Printing: 2019

ISBN 978-93-5383-256-8 (paperback)

ISBN 978-93-5383-257-5 (Hardcover)

ISBN 978-93-5383-258-2 (eBook)

Published by Throne Classics

www.throneclassics.com

Contents

Lay Morals
and other papers

PREFACE

BY MRS. ROBERT LOUIS STEVENSON [0]

In our long voyage on the yacht Casco, we visited many islands; I believe on every one we found the scourge of leprosy. In the Marquesas there was a regular leper settlement, though the persons living there seemed free to wander where they wished, fishing on the beach, or visiting friends in the villages. I remember one afternoon, at Anaho, when my husband and I, tired after a long quest for shells, sat down on the sand to rest awhile, a native man stepped out from under some cocoanut trees, regarding us hesitatingly as though fearful of intruding. My husband waved an invitation to the stranger to join us, offering his cigarette to the man in the island fashion. The cigarette was accepted and, after a puff or two, courteously passed back again according to native etiquette. The hand that held it was the maimed hand of a leper. To my consternation my husband took the cigarette and smoked it out. Afterwards when we were alone and I spoke of my horror he said, 'I could not mortify the man. And if you think I liked doing it—that was another reason; because I didn't want to.'

Another day, while we were still anchored in Anaho Bay, a messenger from round a distant headland came in a whale-boat with an urgent request that we go to see a young white girl who was ill with some mysterious malady. We had supposed that, with the beach-comber 'Charley the red,' we were the only white people on our side of the island. Though there was much wind that day and the sea ran high, we started at once, impelled partly by curiosity and partly by the pathetic nature of the message. Fortunately we took our luncheon with us, eating it on the beach before we went up to the house where the sick girl lay. Our hostess, the girl's mother, met us with regrets that we had already lunched, saying, 'I have a most excellent cook; here he is, now.' She turned, as she spoke, to an elderly Chinaman who was plainly in an advanced stage of leprosy. When the man was gone, my husband asked if she had no fear of contagion. 'I don't believe in contagion,' was her reply.

But there was little doubt as to what ailed her daughter. She was certainly suffering from leprosy. We could only advise that the girl be taken to the French post at Santa Maria Bay where there was a doctor.

On our return to the Casco we confessed to each other with what alarm and repugnance we touched the miserable girl. We talked long that evening of Father Damien, his sublime heroism, and his martyrdom which was already nearing its sad end. Beyond all noble qualities my husband placed courage. The more he saw of leprosy, and he saw much in the islands, the higher rose his admiration for the simple priest of Molokai. 'I must see Molokai,' he said many times. 'I must somehow manage to see Molokai.'

In January 1889, we arrived in Honolulu, settling in a pleasant cottage by the sea to rest until we were ready to return to England. The Casco we sent back to San Francisco with the captain. But the knowledge that every few days some vessel was leaving Honolulu to cruise among islands we had not seen, and now should never see, was more than we could bear. First we engaged passage on a missionary ship, but changed our minds—my husband would not be allowed to smoke on board, for one reason—and chartered the trading schooner Equator. This was thought too rough a voyage for my mother-in-law, as indeed it would have been; so she was sent, somewhat protesting, back to Scotland.

My husband was still intent on seeing Molokai. After the waste of much time and red tape, he finally received an official permission to visit the leper settlement. It did not occur to him it would be necessary to get a separate official permission to leave Molokai; hence he was nearly left behind when the vessel sailed out. He only saved himself by a prodigious leap which landed him on board the boat, whence nothing but force could dislodge him. By the doctor's orders he took gloves to wear as a precautionary measure against contagion, but they were never worn. At first he avoided shaking hands, but when he played croquet with the young leper girls he would not listen to the Mother Superior's warning that he must wear gloves. He thought it might remind them of their condition. 'What will you do if you find you have contracted leprosy?' I asked. 'Do?' he replied; 'why, you and I would spend the rest of our lives in Molokai and become humble followers of Father

Damien.' As Mr. Balfour says in the Life of Stevenson, he was as stern with his family as he was with himself, and as exacting.

He talked very little to us of the tragedy of Molokai, though I could see it lay heavy on his spirits; but of the great work begun by Father Damien and carried on by his successors he spoke fully. He had followed the life of the priest like a detective until there seemed nothing more to learn. Mother Mary Ann, the Mother Superior, he could never mention without deep emotion. One of the first things he did on his return to Honolulu was to send her a grand piano for the use of her girls—the girls with whom he had played croquet. He also sent toys, sewing materials, small tools for the younger children, and other things that I have forgotten. After his death a letter was found among his papers, of which I have only the last few lines. 'I cannot suppose you remember me, but I won't forget you, nor God won't forget you for your kindness to the blind white leper at Molokai.'

During my husband's absence I had made every preparation for our voyage on the Equator, so but little time was lost before we found ourselves on board, our sails set for the south. The Equator, which had easily lived through the great Samoan hurricane, made no such phenomenal runs as the Casco, but we could trust her, and she had no 'tricks and ways' that we did not understand. We liked the sailors, we loved the ship and her captain, so it was with heart-felt regret we said farewell in the harbour of Apia after a long and perfect cruise.

After reading the letters that awaited us in Apia, we looked over the newspapers. Our indignation may be imagined when we read in one item that, owing to the publication of a letter by a well-known Honolulu missionary, depicting Father Damien as a dirty old peasant who had contracted leprosy through his immoral habits, the project to erect a monument to his memory would be abandoned. 'I'll not believe it,' said my husband, 'unless I see it with my own eyes; for it is too damnable for belief!'

But see it he did, in spite of his incredulity, for in Sydney, a month or two later, the very journal containing the letter condemnatory of Father Damien was among the first we chanced to open. I shall never forget my husband's ferocity of indignation, his leaping stride as he paced the room holding the offending paper at arm's-length before his eyes that burned and sparkled with a peculiar flashing light. His cousin Mr. Balfour, in his Life of Robert Louis Stevenson, says: 'his eyes . . . when he was moved to anger or any fierce emotion seemed literally to blaze and glow with a burning light.' In another moment he disappeared through the doorway, and I could hear him, in his own room, pulling his chair to the table, and the sound of his inkstand being dragged towards him.

That afternoon he called us together—my son, my daughter, and myself—saying that he had something serious to lay before us. He went over the circumstances succinctly, and then we three had the incomparable experience of hearing its author read aloud the defence of Father Damien while it was still red-hot from his indignant soul.

As we sat, dazed and overcome by emotion, he pointed out to us that the subject-matter was libellous in the highest degree, and the publication of the article might cause the loss of his entire substance. Without our concurrence he would not take such a risk. There was no dissenting voice; how could there be? The paper was published with almost no change or revision, though afterwards my husband said he considered this a mistake. He thought he should have waited for his anger to cool, when he might have been more impersonal and less egotistic.

The next day he consulted an eminent lawyer, more from curiosity than from any other reason. Mr. Moses—I think that was his name—was at first inclined to be jocular. I remember his smiling question: 'Have you called him a hell-hound or an atheist? Otherwise there is no libel.' But when he looked over the manuscript his countenance changed. 'This is a serious affair,' he said; 'however, no one will publish it for you.' In that Mr. Moses was right; no one dared publish the pamphlet. But that difficulty was soon overcome. My husband hired a printer by the day, and the work was rushed through. We then, my daughter, my son, and myself, were set to work helping address the pamphlets, which were scattered far and wide.

Father Damien was vindicated by a stranger, a man of another country and another religion from his own.

F. V. de G. S.

LAY MORALS

The following chapters of a projected treatise on Ethics were drafted at Edinburgh in the spring of 1879. They are unrevised, and must not be taken as representing, either as to matter or form, their author's final thoughts; but they contain much that is essentially characteristic of his mind.

CHAPTER I

The problem of education is twofold: first to know, and then to utter. Every one who lives any semblance of an inner life thinks more nobly and profoundly than he speaks; and the best of teachers can impart only broken images of the truth which they perceive. Speech which goes from one to another between two natures, and, what is worse, between two experiences, is doubly relative. The speaker buries his meaning; it is for the hearer to dig it up again; and all speech, written or spoken, is in a dead language until it finds a willing and prepared hearer. Such, moreover, is the complexity of life, that when we condescend upon details in our advice, we may be sure we condescend on error; and the best of education is to throw out some magnanimous hints. No man was ever so poor that he could express all he has in him by words, looks, or actions; his true knowledge is eternally incommunicable, for it is a knowledge of himself; and his best wisdom comes to him by no process of the mind, but in a supreme self-dictation, which keeps varying from hour to hour in its dictates with the variation of events and circumstances.

A few men of picked nature, full of faith, courage, and contempt for others, try earnestly to set forth as much as they can grasp of this inner law; but the vast majority, when they come to advise the young, must be content to retail certain doctrines which have been already retailed to them in their own youth. Every generation has to educate another which it has brought upon the stage. People who readily accept the responsibility of parentship, having very different matters in their eye, are apt to feel rueful when that responsibility falls due. What are they to tell the child about life and conduct, subjects on which they have themselves so few and such confused opinions? Indeed, I do not know; the least said, perhaps, the soonest mended; and yet the child keeps asking, and the parent must find some words to say in his own defence. Where does he find them? and what are they when found?

As a matter of experience, and in nine hundred and ninety-nine cases out of a thousand, he will instil into his wide-eyed brat three bad things: the terror of public opinion, and, flowing from that as a fountain, the desire of wealth and applause. Besides these, or what might be deduced as corollaries from these, he will teach not much else of any effective value: some dim notions of divinity, perhaps, and book-keeping, and how to walk through a quadrille.

But, you may tell me, the young people are taught to be Christians. It may be want of penetration, but I have not yet been able to perceive it. As an honest man, whatever we teach, and be it good or evil, it is not the doctrine of Christ. What he taught (and in this he is like all other teachers worthy of the name) was not a code of rules, but a ruling spirit; not truths, but a spirit of truth; not views, but a view. What he showed us was an attitude of mind. Towards the many considerations on which conduct is built, each man stands in a certain relation. He takes life on a certain principle. He has a compass in his spirit which points in a certain direction. It is the attitude, the relation, the point of the compass, that is the whole body and gist of what he has to teach us; in this, the details are comprehended; out of this the specific precepts issue, and by this, and this only, can they be explained and applied. And thus, to learn aright from any teacher, we must first of all, like a historical artist, think ourselves into sympathy with his position and, in the technical phrase, create his character. A historian confronted with some ambiguous politician, or an actor charged with a part, have but one pre-occupation; they must search all round and upon every side, and grope for some central conception which is to explain and justify the most extreme details; until that is found, the politician is an enigma, or perhaps a quack, and the part a tissue of fustian sentiment and big words; but once that is found, all enters into a plan, a human nature appears, the politician or the stage-king is understood from point to point, from end to end. This is a degree of trouble which will be gladly taken by a very humble artist; but not even the terror of eternal fire can teach a business man to bend his imagination to such athletic efforts. Yet without this, all is vain; until we understand the whole, we shall understand none of the parts; and otherwise we have no more than broken images and scattered words; the meaning remains buried; and the language in which our prophet speaks to us is a dead language in our ears.

Take a few of Christ's sayings and compare them with our current doctrines.

'Ye cannot,' he says, 'serve God and Mammon.' Cannot? And our whole system is to teach us how we can!

'The children of this world are wiser in their generation than the children of light.' Are they? I had been led to understand the reverse: that the Christian merchant, for example, prospered exceedingly in his affairs; that honesty was the best policy; that an author of repute had written a conclusive treatise 'How to make the best of both worlds.' Of both worlds indeed! Which am I to believe then—Christ or the author of repute?

'Take no thought for the morrow.' Ask the Successful Merchant; interrogate your own heart; and you will have to admit that this is not only a silly but an immoral position. All we believe, all we hope, all we honour in ourselves or our contemporaries, stands condemned in this one sentence, or, if you take the other view, condemns the sentence as unwise and inhumane. We are not then of the 'same mind that was in Christ.' We disagree with Christ. Either Christ meant nothing, or else he or we must be in the wrong. Well says Thoreau, speaking of some texts from the New Testament, and finding a strange echo of another style which the reader may recognise: 'Let but one of these sentences be rightly read from any pulpit in the land, and there would not be left one stone of that meeting-house upon another.'

It may be objected that these are what are called 'hard sayings'; and that a man, or an education, may be very sufficiently Christian although it

19

leave some of these sayings upon one side. But this is a very gross delusion. Although truth is difficult to state, it is both easy and agreeable to receive, and the mind runs out to meet it ere the phrase be done. The universe, in relation to what any man can say of it, is plain, patent and staringly comprehensible. In itself, it is a great and travailing ocean, unsounded, unvoyageable, an eternal mystery to man; or, let us say, it is a monstrous and impassable mountain, one side of which, and a few near slopes and foothills, we can dimly study with these mortal eyes. But what any man can say of it, even in his highest utterance, must have relation to this little and plain corner, which is no less visible to us than to him. We are looking on the same map; it will go hard if we cannot follow the demonstration. The longest and most abstruse flight of a philosopher becomes clear and shallow, in the flash of a moment, when we suddenly perceive the aspect and drift of his intention. The longest argument is but a finger pointed; once we get our own finger rightly parallel, and we see what the man meant, whether it be a new star or an old street-lamp. And briefly, if a saying is hard to understand, it is because we are thinking of something else.

But to be a true disciple is to think of the same things as our prophet, and to think of different things in the same order. To be of the same mind with another is to see all things in the same perspective; it is not to agree in a few indifferent matters near at hand and not much debated; it is to follow him in his farthest flights, to see the force of his hyperboles, to stand so exactly in the centre of his vision that whatever he may express, your eyes will light at once on the original, that whatever he may see to declare, your mind will at once accept. You do not belong to the school of any philosopher, because you agree with him that theft is, on the whole, objectionable, or that the sun is overhead at noon. It is by the hard sayings that discipleship is tested. We are all agreed about the middling and indifferent parts of knowledge and morality; even the most soaring spirits too often take them tamely upon trust. But the man, the philosopher or the moralist, does not stand upon these chance adhesions; and the purpose of any system looks towards those extreme points where it steps valiantly beyond tradition and returns with some covert hint of things outside. Then only can you be certain that the words are not words of course, nor mere echoes of the past; then only are you sure that if he be indicating anything at all, it is a star and not a street-lamp; then only do you touch the heart of the mystery, since it was for these that the author wrote his book.

Now, every now and then, and indeed surprisingly often, Christ finds a word that transcends all common-place morality; every now and then he quits the beaten track to pioneer the unexpressed, and throws out a pregnant and magnanimous hyperbole; for it is only by some bold poetry of thought that men can be strung up above the level of everyday conceptions to take a broader look upon experience or accept some higher principle of conduct. To a man who is of the same mind that was in Christ, who stands at some centre not too far from his, and looks at the world and conduct from some not dissimilar or, at least, not opposing attitude—or, shortly, to a man who is of Christ's philosophy—every such saying should come home with a thrill of joy and corroboration; he should feel each one below his feet as another sure foundation in the flux of time and chance; each should be another proof that in the torrent of the years and generations, where doctrines and great armaments and empires are swept away and swallowed, he stands immovable, holding by the eternal stars. But alas! at this juncture of the ages it is not so with us; on each and every such occasion our whole fellowship of Christians falls back in disapproving wonder and implicitly denies the saying. Christians! the farce is impudently broad. Let us stand up in the sight of heaven and confess. The ethics that we hold are those of Benjamin Franklin. Honesty is the best policy, is perhaps a hard saying; it is certainly one by which a wise man of these days will not too curiously direct his steps; but I think it shows a glimmer of meaning to even our most dimmed intelligences; I think we perceive a principle behind it; I think, without hyperbole, we are of the same mind that was in Benjamin Franklin.

CHAPTER II

But, I may be told, we teach the ten commandments, where a world of morals lies condensed, the very pith and epitome of all ethics and religion; and a young man with these precepts engraved upon his mind must follow after profit with some conscience and Christianity of method. A man cannot go very far astray who neither dishonours his parents, nor kills, nor commits

21

adultery, nor steals, nor bears false witness; for these things, rightly thought out, cover a vast field of duty.

Alas! what is a precept? It is at best an illustration; it is case law at the best which can be learned by precept. The letter is not only dead, but killing; the spirit which underlies, and cannot be uttered, alone is true and helpful. This is trite to sickness; but familiarity has a cunning disenchantment; in a day or two she can steal all beauty from the mountain tops; and the most startling words begin to fall dead upon the ear after several repetitions. If you see a thing too often, you no longer see it; if you hear a thing too often, you no longer hear it. Our attention requires to be surprised; and to carry a fort by assault, or to gain a thoughtful hearing from the ruck of mankind, are feats of about an equal difficulty and must be tried by not dissimilar means. The whole Bible has thus lost its message for the common run of hearers; it has become mere words of course; and the parson may bawl himself scarlet and beat the pulpit like a thing possessed, but his hearers will continue to nod; they are strangely at peace, they know all he has to say; ring the old bell as you choose, it is still the old bell and it cannot startle their composure. And so with this byword about the letter and the spirit. It is quite true, no doubt; but it has no meaning in the world to any man of us. Alas! it has just this meaning, and neither more nor less: that while the spirit is true, the letter is eternally false.

The shadow of a great oak lies abroad upon the ground at noon, perfect, clear, and stable like the earth. But let a man set himself to mark out the boundary with cords and pegs, and were he never so nimble and never so exact, what with the multiplicity of the leaves and the progression of the shadow as it flees before the travelling sun, long ere he has made the circuit the whole figure will have changed. Life may be compared, not to a single tree, but to a great and complicated forest; circumstance is more swiftly changing than a shadow, language much more inexact than the tools of a surveyor; from day to day the trees fall and are renewed; the very essences are fleeting as we look; and the whole world of leaves is swinging tempest-tossed among the winds of time. Look now for your shadows. O man of formulæ, is this a place for you? Have you fitted the spirit to a single case? Alas, in the cycle of the ages when shall such another be proposed for the judgment of man? Now when the sun shines and the winds blow, the wood is filled with an innumerable multitude of shadows, tumultuously tossed and changing; and at every gust the whole carpet leaps and becomes new. Can you or your heart say more?

Look back now, for a moment, on your own brief experience of life; and although you lived it feelingly in your own person, and had every step of conduct burned in by pains and joys upon your memory, tell me what definite lesson does experience hand on from youth to manhood, or from both to age? The settled tenor which first strikes the eye is but the shadow of a delusion. This is gone; that never truly was; and you yourself are altered beyond recognition. Times and men and circumstances change about your changing character, with a speed of which no earthly hurricane affords an image. What was the best yesterday, is it still the best in this changed theatre of a to-morrow? Will your own Past truly guide you in your own violent and unexpected Future? And if this be questionable, with what humble, with what hopeless eyes, should we not watch other men driving beside us on their unknown careers, seeing with unlike eyes, impelled by different gales, doing and suffering in another sphere of things?

And as the authentic clue to such a labyrinth and change of scene, do you offer me these two score words? these five bald prohibitions? For the moral precepts are no more than five; the first four deal rather with matters of observance than of conduct; the tenth, Thou shalt not covet, stands upon another basis, and shall be spoken of ere long. The Jews, to whom they were first given, in the course of years began to find these precepts insufficient; and made an addition of no less than six hundred and fifty others! They hoped to make a pocket-book of reference on morals, which should stand to life in some such relation, say, as Hoyle stands in to the scientific game of whist. The comparison is just, and condemns the design; for those who play by rule will never be more than tolerable players; and you and I would like to play our game in life to the noblest and the most divine advantage. Yet if the Jews took a petty and huckstering view of conduct, what view do we take ourselves, who callously leave youth to go forth into the enchanted forest, full of spells and dire chimeras, with no guidance more complete than is afforded by these five precepts?

Honour thy father and thy mother. Yes, but does that mean to obey? and if so, how long and how far? Thou shall not kill. Yet the very intention and purport of the prohibition may be best fulfilled by killing. Thou shall not commit adultery. But some of the ugliest adulteries are committed in the bed of marriage and under the sanction of religion and law. Thou shalt not bear false witness. How? by speech or by silence also? or even by a smile? Thou shalt not steal. Ah, that indeed! But what is to steal?

To steal? It is another word to be construed; and who is to be our guide? The police will give us one construction, leaving the word only that least minimum of meaning without which society would fall in pieces; but surely we must take some higher sense than this; surely we hope more than a bare subsistence for mankind; surely we wish mankind to prosper and go on from strength to strength, and ourselves to live rightly in the eye of some more exacting potentate than a policeman. The approval or the disapproval of the police must be eternally indifferent to a man who is both valorous and good. There is extreme discomfort, but no shame, in the condemnation of the law. The law represents that modicum of morality which can be squeezed out of the ruck of mankind; but what is that to me, who aim higher and seek to be my own more stringent judge? I observe with pleasure that no brave man has ever given a rush for such considerations. The Japanese have a nobler and more sentimental feeling for this social bond into which we all are born when we come into the world, and whose comforts and protection we all indifferently share throughout our lives:—but even to them, no more than to our Western saints and heroes, does the law of the state supersede the higher law of duty. Without hesitation and without remorse, they transgress the stiffest enactments rather than abstain from doing right. But the accidental superior duty being thus fulfilled, they at once return in allegiance to the common duty of all citizens; and hasten to denounce themselves; and value at an equal rate their just crime and their equally just submission to its punishment.

The evading of the police will not long satisfy an active conscience or a thoughtful head. But to show you how one or the other may trouble a man, and what a vast extent of frontier is left unridden by this invaluable eighth commandment, let me tell you a few pages out of a young man's life.

He was a friend of mine; a young man like others; generous, flighty, as variable as youth itself, but always with some high motions and on the search for higher thoughts of life. I should tell you at once that he thoroughly agrees with the eighth commandment. But he got hold of some unsettling works, the New Testament among others, and this loosened his views of life and led him into many perplexities. As he was the son of a man in a certain position, and well off, my friend had enjoyed from the first the advantages of education, nay, he had been kept alive through a sickly childhood by constant watchfulness, comforts, and change of air; for all of which he was indebted to his father's wealth.

At college he met other lads more diligent than himself, who followed the plough in summer-time to pay their college fees in winter; and this inequality struck him with some force. He was at that age of a conversible temper, and insatiably curious in the aspects of life; and he spent much of his time scraping acquaintance with all classes of man- and woman-kind. In this way he came upon many depressed ambitions, and many intelligences stunted for want of opportunity; and this also struck him. He began to perceive that life was a handicap upon strange, wrong-sided principles; and not, as he had been told, a fair and equal race. He began to tremble that he himself had been unjustly favoured, when he saw all the avenues of wealth, and power, and comfort closed against so many of his superiors and equals, and held unwearyingly open before so idle, so desultory, and so dissolute a being as himself. There sat a youth beside him on the college benches, who had only one shirt to his back, and, at intervals sufficiently far apart, must stay at home to have it washed. It was my friend's principle to stay away as often as he dared; for I fear he was no friend to learning. But there was something that came home to him sharply, in this fellow who had to give over study till his shirt was washed, and the scores of others who had never an opportunity at all. If one of these could take his place, he thought; and the thought tore away a bandage from his eyes. He was eaten by the shame of his discoveries,

25

and despised himself as an unworthy favourite and a creature of the back-stairs of Fortune. He could no longer see without confusion one of these brave young fellows battling up-hill against adversity. Had he not filched that fellow's birthright? At best was he not coldly profiting by the injustice of society, and greedily devouring stolen goods? The money, indeed, belonged to his father, who had worked, and thought, and given up his liberty to earn it; but by what justice could the money belong to my friend, who had, as yet, done nothing but help to squander it? A more sturdy honesty, joined to a more even and impartial temperament, would have drawn from these considerations a new force of industry, that this equivocal position might be brought as swiftly as possible to an end, and some good services to mankind justify the appropriation of expense. It was not so with my friend, who was only unsettled and discouraged, and filled full of that trumpeting anger with which young men regard injustices in the first blush of youth; although in a few years they will tamely acquiesce in their existence, and knowingly profit by their complications. Yet all this while he suffered many indignant pangs. And once, when he put on his boots, like any other unripe donkey, to run away from home, it was his best consolation that he was now, at a single plunge, to free himself from the responsibility of this wealth that was not his, and do battle equally against his fellows in the warfare of life.

Some time after this, falling into ill-health, he was sent at great expense to a more favourable climate; and then I think his perplexities were thickest. When he thought of all the other young men of singular promise, upright, good, the prop of families, who must remain at home to die, and with all their possibilities be lost to life and mankind; and how he, by one more unmerited favour, was chosen out from all these others to survive; he felt as if there were no life, no labour, no devotion of soul and body, that could repay and justify these partialities. A religious lady, to whom he communicated these reflections, could see no force in them whatever. 'It was God's will,' said she. But he knew it was by God's will that Joan of Arc was burnt at Rouen, which cleared neither Bedford nor Bishop Cauchon; and again, by God's will that Christ was crucified outside Jerusalem, which excused neither the rancour of the priests nor the timidity of Pilate. He knew, moreover, that although the possibility of this favour he was now enjoying issued from his circumstances,

26

its acceptance was the act of his own will; and he had accepted it greedily, longing for rest and sunshine. And hence this allegation of God's providence did little to relieve his scruples. I promise you he had a very troubled mind. And I would not laugh if I were you, though while he was thus making mountains out of what you think molehills, he were still (as perhaps he was) contentedly practising many other things that to you seem black as hell. Every man is his own judge and mountain-guide through life. There is an old story of a mote and a beam, apparently not true, but worthy perhaps of some consideration. I should, if I were you, give some consideration to these scruples of his, and if I were he, I should do the like by yours; for it is not unlikely that there may be something under both. In the meantime you must hear how my friend acted. Like many invalids, he supposed that he would die. Now, should he die, he saw no means of repaying this huge loan which, by the hands of his father, mankind had advanced him for his sickness. In that case it would be lost money. So he determined that the advance should be as small as possible; and, so long as he continued to doubt his recovery, lived in an upper room, and grudged himself all but necessaries. But so soon as he began to perceive a change for the better, he felt justified in spending more freely, to speed and brighten his return to health, and trusted in the future to lend a help to mankind, as mankind, out of its treasury, had lent a help to him.

I do not say but that my friend was a little too curious and partial in his view; nor thought too much of himself and too little of his parents; but I do say that here are some scruples which tormented my friend in his youth, and still, perhaps, at odd times give him a prick in the midst of his enjoyments, and which after all have some foundation in justice, and point, in their confused way, to some more honourable honesty within the reach of man. And at least, is not this an unusual gloss upon the eighth commandment? And what sort of comfort, guidance, or illumination did that precept afford my friend throughout these contentions? 'Thou shalt not steal.' With all my heart! But am I stealing?

The truly quaint materialism of our view of life disables us from pursuing any transaction to an end. You can make no one understand that his bargain is anything more than a bargain, whereas in point of fact it is a link in the policy of mankind, and either a good or an evil to the world. We have a sort of blindness which prevents us from seeing anything but sovereigns. If one man agrees to give another so many shillings for so many hours' work, and then wilfully gives him a certain proportion of the price in bad money and only the remainder in good, we can see with half an eye that this man is a thief. But if the other spends a certain proportion of the hours in smoking a pipe of tobacco, and a certain other proportion in looking at the sky, or the clock, or trying to recall an air, or in meditation on his own past adventures, and only the remainder in downright work such as he is paid to do, is he, because the theft is one of time and not of money,—is he any the less a thief? The one gave a bad shilling, the other an imperfect hour; but both broke the bargain, and each is a thief. In piecework, which is what most of us do, the case is none the less plain for being even less material. If you forge a bad knife, you have wasted some of mankind's iron, and then, with unrivalled cynicism, you pocket some of mankind's money for your trouble. Is there any man so blind who cannot see that this is theft? Again, if you carelessly cultivate a farm, you have been playing fast and loose with mankind's resources against hunger; there will be less bread in consequence, and for lack of that bread somebody will die next winter: a grim consideration. And you must not hope to shuffle out of blame because you got less money for your less quantity of bread; for although a theft be partly punished, it is none the less a theft for that. You took the farm against competitors; there were others ready to shoulder the responsibility and be answerable for the tale of loaves; but it was you who took it. By the act you came under a tacit bargain with mankind to cultivate that farm with your best endeavour; you were under no superintendence, you were on parole; and you have broke your bargain, and to all who look closely, and yourself among the rest if you have moral eyesight, you are a thief. Or take the case of men of letters. Every piece of work which is not as good as you can make it, which you have palmed off imperfect, meagrely thought, niggardly in execution, upon mankind who is your paymaster on parole and in a sense your pupil, every hasty or slovenly or untrue performance, should rise up against you in the court of your own heart and condemn you for a thief. Have you a salary? If you trifle with your health, and so render

28

yourself less capable for duty, and still touch, and still greedily pocket the emolument—what are you but a thief? Have you double accounts? do you by any time-honoured juggle, deceit, or ambiguous process, gain more from those who deal with you than it you were bargaining and dealing face to face in front of God?—What are you but a thief? Lastly, if you fill an office, or produce an article, which, in your heart of hearts, you think a delusion and a fraud upon mankind, and still draw your salary and go through the sham manœuvres of this office, or still book your profits and keep on flooding the world with these injurious goods?—though you were old, and bald, and the first at church, and a baronet, what are you but a thief? These may seem hard words and mere curiosities of the intellect, in an age when the spirit of honesty is so sparingly cultivated that all business is conducted upon lies and so-called customs of the trade, that not a man bestows two thoughts on the utility or honourableness of his pursuit. I would say less if I thought less. But looking to my own reason and the right of things, I can only avow that I am a thief myself, and that I passionately suspect my neighbours of the same guilt.

Where did you hear that it was easy to be honest? Do you find that in your Bible? Easy! It is easy to be an ass and follow the multitude like a blind, besotted bull in a stampede; and that, I am well aware, is what you and Mrs. Grundy mean by being honest. But it will not bear the stress of time nor the scrutiny of conscience. Even before the lowest of all tribunals,—before a court of law, whose business it is, not to keep men right, or within a thousand miles of right, but to withhold them from going so tragically wrong that they will pull down the whole jointed fabric of society by their misdeeds—even before a court of law, as we begin to see in these last days, our easy view of following at each other's tails, alike to good and evil, is beginning to be reproved and punished, and declared no honesty at all, but open theft and swindling; and simpletons who have gone on through life with a quiet conscience may learn suddenly, from the lips of a judge, that the custom of the trade may be a custom of the devil. You thought it was easy to be honest. Did you think it was easy to be just and kind and truthful? Did you think the whole duty of aspiring man was as simple as a horn-pipe? and you could walk through life like a gentleman and a hero, with no more concern than it takes to go to church or to address a circular? And yet all this time you had the eighth commandment! and, what makes it richer, you would not have broken it for the world!

The truth is, that these commandments by themselves are of little use in private judgment. If compression is what you want, you have their whole spirit compressed into the golden rule; and yet there expressed with more significance, since the law is there spiritually and not materially stated. And in truth, four out of these ten commands, from the sixth to the ninth, are rather legal than ethical. The police-court is their proper home. A magistrate cannot tell whether you love your neighbour as yourself, but he can tell more or less whether you have murdered, or stolen, or committed adultery, or held up your hand and testified to that which was not; and these things, for rough practical tests, are as good as can be found. And perhaps, therefore, the best condensation of the Jewish moral law is in the maxims of the priests, 'neminem lædere' and 'suum cuique tribuere.' But all this granted, it becomes only the more plain that they are inadequate in the sphere of personal morality; that while they tell the magistrate roughly when to punish, they can never direct an anxious sinner what to do.

Only Polonius, or the like solemn sort of ass, can offer us a succinct proverb by way of advice, and not burst out blushing in our faces. We grant them one and all and for all that they are worth; it is something above and beyond that we desire. Christ was in general a great enemy to such a way of teaching; we rarely find him meddling with any of these plump commands but it was to open them out, and lift his hearers from the letter to the spirit. For morals are a personal affair; in the war of righteousness every man fights for his own hand; all the six hundred precepts of the Mishna cannot shake my private judgment; my magistracy of myself is an indefeasible charge, and my decisions absolute for the time and case. The moralist is not a judge of appeal, but an advocate who pleads at my tribunal. He has to show not the law, but that the law applies. Can he convince me? then he gains the cause. And thus you find Christ giving various counsels to varying people, and often jealously careful to avoid definite precept. Is he asked, for example, to divide a heritage? He refuses: and the best advice that he will offer is but a paraphrase of that tenth commandment which figures so strangely among

30

the rest. Take heed, and beware of covetousness. If you complain that this is vague, I have failed to carry you along with me in my argument. For no definite precept can be more than an illustration, though its truth were resplendent like the sun, and it was announced from heaven by the voice of God. And life is so intricate and changing, that perhaps not twenty times, or perhaps not twice in the ages, shall we find that nice consent of circumstances to which alone it can apply.

CHAPTER III

Although the world and life have in a sense become commonplace to our experience, it is but in an external torpor; the true sentiment slumbers within us; and we have but to reflect on ourselves or our surroundings to rekindle our astonishment. No length of habit can blunt our first surprise. Of the world I have but little to say in this connection; a few strokes shall suffice. We inhabit a dead ember swimming wide in the blank of space, dizzily spinning as it swims, and lighted up from several million miles away by a more horrible hell-fire than was ever conceived by the theological imagination. Yet the dead ember is a green, commodious dwelling-place; and the reverberation of this hell-fire ripens flower and fruit and mildly warms us on summer eves upon the lawn. Far off on all hands other dead embers, other flaming suns, wheel and race in the apparent void; the nearest is out of call, the farthest so far that the heart sickens in the effort to conceive the distance. Shipwrecked seamen on the deep, though they bestride but the truncheon of a boom, are safe and near at home compared with mankind on its bullet. Even to us who have known no other, it seems a strange, if not an appalling, place of residence.

But far stranger is the resident, man, a creature compact of wonders that, after centuries of custom, is still wonderful to himself. He inhabits a body which he is continually outliving, discarding and renewing. Food and sleep, by an unknown alchemy, restore his spirits and the freshness of his countenance. Hair grows on him like grass; his eyes, his brain, his sinews, thirst for action; he joys to see and touch and hear, to partake the sun and wind, to sit down and intently ponder on his astonishing attributes and situation, to rise up and run, to perform the strange and revolting round of physical functions. The sight of a flower, the note of a bird, will often move him deeply; yet he looks unconcerned on the impassable distances and portentous bonfires of the universe. He comprehends, he designs, he tames nature, rides the sea, ploughs, climbs the air in a balloon, makes vast inquiries, begins interminable labours, joins himself into federations and populous cities, spends his days to deliver the ends of the earth or to benefit unborn posterity; and yet knows himself for a piece of unsurpassed fragility and the creature of a few days. His sight, which conducts him, which takes notice of the farthest stars, which is miraculous in every way and a thing defying explanation or belief, is yet lodged in a piece of jelly, and can be extinguished with a touch. His heart, which all through life so indomitably, so athletically labours, is but a capsule, and may be stopped with a pin. His whole body, for all its savage energies, its leaping and its winged desires, may yet be tamed and conquered by a draught of air or a sprinkling of cold dew. What he calls death, which is the seeming arrest of everything, and the ruin and hateful transformation of the visible body, lies in wait for him outwardly in a thousand accidents, and grows up in secret diseases from within. He is still learning to be a man when his faculties are already beginning to decline; he has not yet understood himself or his position before he inevitably dies. And yet this mad, chimerical creature can take no thought of his last end, lives as though he were eternal, plunges with his vulnerable body into the shock of war, and daily affronts death with unconcern. He cannot take a step without pain or pleasure. His life is a tissue of sensations, which he distinguishes as they seem to come more directly from himself or his surroundings. He is conscious of himself as a joyer or a sufferer, as that which craves, chooses, and is satisfied; conscious of his surroundings as it were of an inexhaustible purveyor, the source of aspects, inspirations, wonders, cruel knocks and transporting caresses. Thus he goes on his way, stumbling among delights and agonies.

Matter is a far-fetched theory, and materialism is without a root in man. To him everything is important in the degree to which it moves him. The telegraph wires and posts, the electricity speeding from clerk to clerk, the clerks, the glad or sorrowful import of the message, and the paper on which it is finally brought to him at home, are all equally facts, all equally exist for man. A word or a thought can wound him as acutely as a knife of steel. If he thinks he is loved, he will rise up and glory to himself, although he be in a distant land and short of necessary bread. Does he think he is not loved?—he may have the woman at his beck, and there is not a joy for him in all the world. Indeed, if we are to make any account of this figment of reason, the distinction between material and immaterial, we shall conclude that the life of each man as an individual is immaterial, although the continuation and prospects of mankind as a race turn upon material conditions. The physical business of each man's body is transacted for him; like a sybarite, he has attentive valets in his own viscera; he breathes, he sweats, he digests without an effort, or so much as a consenting volition; for the most part he even eats, not with a wakeful consciousness, but as it were between two thoughts. His life is centred among other and more important considerations; touch him in his honour or his love, creatures of the imagination which attach him to mankind or to an individual man or woman; cross him in his piety which connects his soul with heaven; and he turns from his food, he loathes his breath, and with a magnanimous emotion cuts the knots of his existence and frees himself at a blow from the web of pains and pleasures.

It follows that man is twofold at least; that he is not a rounded and autonomous empire; but that in the same body with him there dwell other powers tributary but independent. If I now behold one walking in a garden, curiously coloured and illuminated by the sun, digesting his food with elaborate chemistry, breathing, circulating blood, directing himself by the sight of his eyes, accommodating his body by a thousand delicate balancings to the wind and the uneven surface of the path, and all the time, perhaps, with his mind engaged about America, or the dog-star, or the attributes of God—what am I to say, or how am I to describe the thing I see? Is that truly a man, in the rigorous meaning of the word? or is it not a man and something else? What, then, are we to count the centre-bit and axle of a being so variously compounded? It is a question much debated. Some read his history in a certain intricacy of nerve and the success of successive digestions; others find him an exiled piece of heaven blown upon and determined by the breath of God; and both schools of theorists will scream like scalded children at a word of doubt. Yet either of these views, however plausible, is beside the question; either may be right; and I care not; I ask a more particular answer, and to a more immediate point. What is the man? There is Something that was before hunger and that remains behind after a meal. It may or may not be engaged in any given act or passion, but when it is, it changes, heightens, and sanctifies. Thus it is not engaged in lust, where satisfaction ends the chapter; and it is engaged in love, where no satisfaction can blunt the edge of the desire, and where age, sickness, or alienation may deface what was desirable without diminishing the sentiment. This something, which is the man, is a permanence which abides through the vicissitudes of passion, now overwhelmed and now triumphant, now unconscious of itself in the immediate distress of appetite or pain, now rising unclouded above all. So, to the man, his own central self fades and grows clear again amid the tumult of the senses, like a revolving Pharos in the night. It is forgotten; it is hid, it seems, for ever; and yet in the next calm hour he shall behold himself once more, shining and unmoved among changes and storm.

Mankind, in the sense of the creeping mass that is born and eats, that generates and dies, is but the aggregate of the outer and lower sides of man. This inner consciousness, this lantern alternately obscured and shining, to and by which the individual exists and must order his conduct, is something special to himself and not common to the race. His joys delight, his sorrows wound him, according as this is interested or indifferent in the affair; according as they arise in an imperial war or in a broil conducted by the tributary chieftains of the mind. He may lose all, and this not suffer; he may lose what is materially a trifle, and this leap in his bosom with a cruel pang. I do not speak of it to hardened theorists: the living man knows keenly what it is I mean.

'Perceive at last that thou hast in thee something better and more divine than the things which cause the various effects, and, as it were, pull thee by the strings. What is that now in thy mind? is it fear, or suspicion, or desire, or anything of that kind?' Thus far Marcus Aurelius, in one of the most notable passages in any book. Here is a question worthy to be answered. What is in thy mind? What is the utterance of your inmost self when, in a quiet hour, it can be heard intelligibly? It is something beyond the compass of your thinking, inasmuch as it is yourself; but is it not of a higher spirit than you had dreamed betweenwhiles, and erect above all base considerations? This

34

soul seems hardly touched with our infirmities; we can find in it certainly no fear, suspicion, or desire; we are only conscious—and that as though we read it in the eyes of some one else—of a great and unqualified readiness. A readiness to what? to pass over and look beyond the objects of desire and fear, for something else. And this something else? this something which is apart from desire and fear, to which all the kingdoms of the world and the immediate death of the body are alike indifferent and beside the point, and which yet regards conduct—by what name are we to call it? It may be the love of God; or it may be an inherited (and certainly well concealed) instinct to preserve self and propagate the race; I am not, for the moment, averse to either theory; but it will save time to call it righteousness. By so doing I intend no subterfuge to beg a question; I am indeed ready, and more than willing, to accept the rigid consequence, and lay aside, as far as the treachery of the reason will permit, all former meanings attached to the word righteousness. What is right is that for which a man's central self is ever ready to sacrifice immediate or distant interests; what is wrong is what the central self discards or rejects as incompatible with the fixed design of righteousness.

To make this admission is to lay aside all hope of definition. That which is right upon this theory is intimately dictated to each man by himself, but can never be rigorously set forth in language, and never, above all, imposed upon another. The conscience has, then, a vision like that of the eyes, which is incommunicable, and for the most part illuminates none but its possessor. When many people perceive the same or any cognate facts, they agree upon a word as symbol; and hence we have such words as tree, star, love, honour, or death; hence also we have this word right, which, like the others, we all understand, most of us understand differently, and none can express succinctly otherwise. Yet even on the straitest view, we can make some steps towards comprehension of our own superior thoughts. For it is an incredible and most bewildering fact that a man, through life, is on variable terms with himself; he is aware of tiffs and reconciliations; the intimacy is at times almost suspended, at times it is renewed again with joy. As we said before, his inner self or soul appears to him by successive revelations, and is frequently obscured. It is from a study of these alternations that we can alone hope to discover, even dimly, what seems right and what seems wrong to this veiled prophet of ourself.

All that is in the man in the larger sense, what we call impression as well as what we call intuition, so far as my argument looks, we must accept. It is not wrong to desire food, or exercise, or beautiful surroundings, or the love of sex, or interest which is the food of the mind. All these are craved; all these should be craved; to none of these in itself does the soul demur; where there comes an undeniable want, we recognise a demand of nature. Yet we know that these natural demands may be superseded; for the demands which are common to mankind make but a shadowy consideration in comparison to the demands of the individual soul. Food is almost the first prerequisite; and yet a high character will go without food to the ruin and death of the body rather than gain it in a manner which the spirit disavows. Pascal laid aside mathematics; Origen doctored his body with a knife; every day some one is thus mortifying his dearest interests and desires, and, in Christ's words, entering maim into the Kingdom of Heaven. This is to supersede the lesser and less harmonious affections by renunciation; and though by this ascetic path we may get to heaven, we cannot get thither a whole and perfect man. But there is another way, to supersede them by reconciliation, in which the soul and all the faculties and senses pursue a common route and share in one desire. Thus, man is tormented by a very imperious physical desire; it spoils his rest, it is not to be denied; the doctors will tell you, not I, how it is a physical need, like the want of food or slumber. In the satisfaction of this desire, as it first appears, the soul sparingly takes part; nay, it oft unsparingly regrets and disapproves the satisfaction. But let the man learn to love a woman as far as he is capable of love; and for this random affection of the body there is substituted a steady determination, a consent of all his powers and faculties, which supersedes, adopts, and commands the other. The desire survives, strengthened, perhaps, but taught obedience and changed in scope and character. Life is no longer a tale of betrayals and regrets; for the man now lives as a whole; his consciousness now moves on uninterrupted like a river; through all the extremes and ups and downs of passion, he remains approvingly conscious of himself.

Now to me, this seems a type of that rightness which the soul demands.

It demands that we shall not live alternately with our opposing tendencies in continual see-saw of passion and disgust, but seek some path on which the tendencies shall no longer oppose, but serve each other to a common end. It demands that we shall not pursue broken ends, but great and comprehensive purposes, in which soul and body may unite like notes in a harmonious chord. That were indeed a way of peace and pleasure, that were indeed a heaven upon earth. It does not demand, however, or, to speak in measure, it does not demand of me, that I should starve my appetites for no purpose under heaven but as a purpose in itself; or, in a weak despair, pluck out the eye that I have not yet learned to guide and enjoy with wisdom. The soul demands unity of purpose, not the dismemberment of man; it seeks to roll up all his strength and sweetness, all his passion and wisdom, into one, and make of him a perfect man exulting in perfection. To conclude ascetically is to give up, and not to solve, the problem. The ascetic and the creeping hog, although they are at different poles, have equally failed in life. The one has sacrificed his crew; the other brings back his seamen in a cock-boat, and has lost the ship. I believe there are not many sea-captains who would plume themselves on either result as a success.

But if it is righteousness thus to fuse together our divisive impulses and march with one mind through life, there is plainly one thing more unrighteous than all others, and one declension which is irretrievable and draws on the rest. And this is to lose consciousness of oneself. In the best of times, it is but by flashes, when our whole nature is clear, strong and conscious, and events conspire to leave us free, that we enjoy communion with our soul. At the worst, we are so fallen and passive that we may say shortly we have none. An arctic torpor seizes upon men. Although built of nerves, and set adrift in a stimulating world, they develop a tendency to go bodily to sleep; consciousness becomes engrossed among the reflex and mechanical parts of life; and soon loses both the will and power to look higher considerations in the face. This is ruin; this is the last failure in life; this is temporal damnation, damnation on the spot and without the form of judgment. 'What shall it profit a man if he gain the whole world and lose himself?'

It is to keep a man awake, to keep him alive to his own soul and its fixed design of righteousness, that the better part of moral and religious education is directed; not only that of words and doctors, but the sharp ferule of calamity under which we are all God's scholars till we die. If, as teachers, we are to say anything to the purpose, we must say what will remind the pupil of his soul; we must speak that soul's dialect; we must talk of life and conduct as his soul would have him think of them. If, from some conformity between us and the pupil, or perhaps among all men, we do in truth speak in such a dialect and express such views, beyond question we shall touch in him a spring; beyond question he will recognise the dialect as one that he himself has spoken in his better hours; beyond question he will cry, 'I had forgotten, but now I remember; I too have eyes, and I had forgot to use them! I too have a soul of my own, arrogantly upright, and to that I will listen and conform.' In short, say to him anything that he has once thought, or been upon the point of thinking, or show him any view of life that he has once clearly seen, or been upon the point of clearly seeing; and you have done your part and may leave him to complete the education for himself.

Now, the view taught at the present time seems to me to want greatness; and the dialect in which alone it can be intelligibly uttered is not the dialect of my soul. It is a sort of postponement of life; nothing quite is, but something different is to be; we are to keep our eyes upon the indirect from the cradle to the grave. We are to regulate our conduct not by desire, but by a politic eye upon the future; and to value acts as they will bring us money or good opinion; as they will bring us, in one word, profit. We must be what is called respectable, and offend no one by our carriage; it will not do to make oneself conspicuous—who knows? even in virtue? says the Christian parent! And we must be what is called prudent and make money; not only because it is pleasant to have money, but because that also is a part of respectability, and we cannot hope to be received in society without decent possessions. Received in society! as if that were the kingdom of heaven! There is dear Mr. So-and-so;—look at him!—so much respected—so much looked up to—quite the Christian merchant! And we must cut our conduct as strictly as possible after the pattern of Mr. So-and-so; and lay our whole lives to make money and be strictly decent. Besides these holy injunctions, which form by far the greater part of a youth's training in our Christian homes, there are at least two other doctrines. We are to live just now as well as we can, but scrape at last into heaven, where we shall be good. We are to worry through the week in a lay, disreputable way, but, to make matters square, live a different life on Sunday.

The train of thought we have been following gives us a key to all these positions, without stepping aside to justify them on their own ground. It is because we have been disgusted fifty times with physical squalls, and fifty times torn between conflicting impulses, that we teach people this indirect and tactical procedure in life, and to judge by remote consequences instead of the immediate face of things. The very desire to act as our own souls would have us, coupled with a pathetic disbelief in ourselves, moves us to follow the example of others; perhaps, who knows? they may be on the right track; and the more our patterns are in number, the better seems the chance; until, if we be acting in concert with a whole civilised nation, there are surely a majority of chances that we must be acting right. And again, how true it is that we can never behave as we wish in this tormented sphere, and can only aspire to different and more favourable circumstances, in order to stand out and be ourselves wholly and rightly! And yet once more, if in the hurry and pressure of affairs and passions you tend to nod and become drowsy, here are twenty-four hours of Sunday set apart for you to hold counsel with your soul and look around you on the possibilities of life.

This is not, of course, all that is to be, or even should be, said for these doctrines. Only, in the course of this chapter, the reader and I have agreed upon a few catchwords, and been looking at morals on a certain system; it was a pity to lose an opportunity of testing the catchwords, and seeing whether, by this system as well as by others, current doctrines could show any probable justification. If the doctrines had come too badly out of the trial, it would have condemned the system. Our sight of the world is very narrow; the mind but a pedestrian instrument; there's nothing new under the sun, as Solomon says, except the man himself; and though that changes the aspect of everything else, yet he must see the same things as other people, only from a different side.

And now, having admitted so much, let us turn to criticism.

If you teach a man to keep his eyes upon what others think of him, unthinkingly to lead the life and hold the principles of the majority of his contemporaries, you must discredit in his eyes the one authoritative voice of his own soul. He may be a docile citizen; he will never be a man. It is ours, on the other hand, to disregard this babble and chattering of other men better and worse than we are, and to walk straight before us by what light we have. They may be right; but so, before heaven, are we. They may know; but we know also, and by that knowledge we must stand or fall. There is such a thing as loyalty to a man's own better self; and from those who have not that, God help me, how am I to look for loyalty to others? The most dull, the most imbecile, at a certain moment turn round, at a certain point will hear no further argument, but stand unflinching by their own dumb, irrational sense of right. It is not only by steel or fire, but through contempt and blame, that the martyr fulfils the calling of his dear soul. Be glad if you are not tried by such extremities. But although all the world ranged themselves in one line to tell you 'This is wrong,' be you your own faithful vassal and the ambassador of God—throw down the glove and answer 'This is right.' Do you think you are only declaring yourself? Perhaps in some dim way, like a child who delivers a message not fully understood, you are opening wider the straits of prejudice and preparing mankind for some truer and more spiritual grasp of truth; perhaps, as you stand forth for your own judgment, you are covering a thousand weak ones with your body; perhaps, by this declaration alone, you have avoided the guilt of false witness against humanity and the little ones unborn. It is good, I believe, to be respectable, but much nobler to respect oneself and utter the voice of God. God, if there be any God, speaks daily in a new language by the tongues of men; the thoughts and habits of each fresh generation and each new-coined spirit throw another light upon the universe and contain another commentary on the printed Bibles; every scruple, every true dissent, every glimpse of something new, is a letter of God's alphabet; and though there is a grave responsibility for all who speak, is there none for those who unrighteously keep silence and conform? Is not that also to conceal and cloak God's counsel? And how should we regard the man of science who suppressed all facts that would not tally with the orthodoxy of the hour?

Wrong? You are as surely wrong as the sun rose this morning round the revolving shoulder of the world. Not truth, but truthfulness, is the good of your endeavour. For when will men receive that first part and prerequisite of truth, that, by the order of things, by the greatness of the universe, by the darkness and partiality of man's experience, by the inviolate secrecy of God, kept close in His most open revelations, every man is, and to the end of the ages must be, wrong? Wrong to the universe; wrong to mankind; wrong to God. And yet in another sense, and that plainer and nearer, every man of men, who wishes truly, must be right. He is right to himself, and in the measure of his sagacity and candour. That let him do in all sincerity and zeal, not sparing a thought for contrary opinions; that, for what it is worth, let him proclaim. Be not afraid; although he be wrong, so also is the dead, stuffed Dagon he insults. For the voice of God, whatever it is, is not that stammering, inept tradition which the people holds. These truths survive in travesty, swamped in a world of spiritual darkness and confusion; and what a few comprehend and faithfully hold, the many, in their dead jargon, repeat, degrade, and misinterpret.

So far of Respectability; what the Covenanters used to call 'rank conformity': the deadliest gag and wet blanket that can be laid on men. And now of Profit. And this doctrine is perhaps the more redoubtable, because it harms all sorts of men; not only the heroic and self-reliant, but the obedient, cowlike squadrons. A man, by this doctrine, looks to consequences at the second, or third, or fiftieth turn. He chooses his end, and for that, with wily turns and through a great sea of tedium, steers this mortal bark. There may be political wisdom in such a view; but I am persuaded there can spring no great moral zeal. To look thus obliquely upon life is the very recipe for moral slumber. Our intention and endeavour should be directed, not on some vague end of money or applause, which shall come to us by a ricochet in a month or a year, or twenty years, but on the act itself; not on the approval of others, but on the rightness of that act. At every instant, at every step in life, the point has to be decided, our soul has to be saved, heaven has to be gained or lost. At every step our spirits must applaud, at every step we must set down the foot and sound the trumpet. 'This have I done,' we must say; 'right or wrong, this have I done, in unfeigned honour of intention, as to myself and God.' The profit of every act should be this, that it was right for us to do it. Any other profit than that, if it involved a kingdom or the woman I love, ought, if I were God's upright soldier, to leave me untempted.

It is the mark of what we call a righteous decision, that it is made directly and for its own sake. The whole man, mind and body, having come to an agreement, tyrannically dictates conduct. There are two dispositions eternally opposed: that in which we recognise that one thing is wrong and another right, and that in which, not seeing any clear distinction, we fall back on the consideration of consequences. The truth is, by the scope of our present teaching, nothing is thought very wrong and nothing very right, except a few actions which have the disadvantage of being disrespectable when found out; the more serious part of men inclining to think all things rather wrong, the more jovial to suppose them right enough for practical purposes. I will engage my head, they do not find that view in their own hearts; they have taken it up in a dark despair; they are but troubled sleepers talking in their sleep. The soul, or my soul at least, thinks very distinctly upon many points of right and wrong, and often differs flatly with what is held out as the thought of corporate humanity in the code of society or the code of law. Am I to suppose myself a monster? I have only to read books, the Christian Gospels for example, to think myself a monster no longer; and instead I think the mass of people are merely speaking in their sleep.

It is a commonplace, enshrined, if I mistake not, even in school copy-books, that honour is to be sought and not fame. I ask no other admission; we are to seek honour, upright walking with our own conscience every hour of the day, and not fame, the consequence, the far-off reverberation of our footsteps. The walk, not the rumour of the walk, is what concerns righteousness. Better disrespectable honour than dishonourable fame. Better useless or seemingly hurtful honour, than dishonour ruling empires and filling the mouths of thousands. For the man must walk by what he sees, and leave the issue with God who made him and taught him by the fortune of his life. You would not dishonour yourself for money; which is at least tangible; would you do it, then, for a doubtful forecast in politics, or another person's theory in morals?

So intricate is the scheme of our affairs, that no man can calculate the bearing of his own behaviour even on those immediately around him, how much less upon the world at large or on succeeding generations! To walk by external prudence and the rule of consequences would require, not a man, but God. All that we know to guide us in this changing labyrinth is our soul with its fixed design of righteousness, and a few old precepts which commend themselves to that. The precepts are vague when we endeavour to apply them; consequences are more entangled than a wisp of string, and their confusion is unrestingly in change; we must hold to what we know and walk by it. We must walk by faith, indeed, and not by knowledge.

You do not love another because he is wealthy or wise or eminently respectable: you love him because you love him; that is love, and any other only a derision and grimace. It should be the same with all our actions. If we were to conceive a perfect man, it should be one who was never torn between conflicting impulses, but who, on the absolute consent of all his parts and faculties, submitted in every action of his life to a self-dictation as absolute and unreasoned as that which bids him love one woman and be true to her till death. But we should not conceive him as sagacious, ascetical, playing off his appetites against each other, turning the wing of public respectable immorality instead of riding it directly down, or advancing toward his end through a thousand sinister compromises and considerations. The one man might be wily, might be adroit, might be wise, might be respectable, might be gloriously useful; it is the other man who would be good.

The soul asks honour and not fame; to be upright, not to be successful; to be good, not prosperous; to be essentially, not outwardly, respectable. Does your soul ask profit? Does it ask money? Does it ask the approval of the indifferent herd? I believe not. For my own part, I want but little money, I hope; and I do not want to be decent at all, but to be good.

CHAPTER IV

We have spoken of that supreme self-dictation which keeps varying from hour to hour in its dictates with the variation of events and circumstances. Now, for us, that is ultimate. It may be founded on some reasonable process, but it is not a process which we can follow or comprehend. And moreover the dictation is not continuous, or not continuous except in very lively and well-living natures; and between-whiles we must brush along without it. Practice is a more intricate and desperate business than the toughest theorising; life is an affair of cavalry, where rapid judgment and prompt action are alone possible and right. As a matter of fact, there is no one so upright but he is influenced by the world's chatter; and no one so headlong but he requires to consider consequences and to keep an eye on profit. For the soul adopts all affections and appetites without exception, and cares only to combine them for some common purpose which shall interest all. Now, respect for the opinion of others, the study of consequences, and the desire of power and comfort, are all undeniably factors in the nature of man; and the more undeniably since we find that, in our current doctrines, they have swallowed up the others and are thought to conclude in themselves all the worthy parts of man. These, then, must also be suffered to affect conduct in the practical domain, much or little according as they are forcibly or feebly present to the mind of each.

Now, a man's view of the universe is mostly a view of the civilised society in which he lives. Other men and women are so much more grossly and so much more intimately palpable to his perceptions, that they stand between him and all the rest; they are larger to his eye than the sun, he hears them more plainly than thunder, with them, by them, and for them, he must live and die. And hence the laws that affect his intercourse with his fellow-men, although merely customary and the creatures of a generation, are more clearly and continually before his mind than those which bind him into the eternal system of things, support him in his upright progress on this whirling ball, or keep up the fire of his bodily life. And hence it is that money stands in the first rank of considerations and so powerfully affects the choice. For our society is built with money for mortar; money is present in every joint of circumstance; it might be named the social atmosphere, since, in society, it is by that alone that men continue to live, and only through that or chance that they can reach or affect one another. Money gives us food, shelter, and privacy; it permits us to be clean in person, opens for us the doors of the theatre, gains us books for study or pleasure, enables us to help the distresses of others, and puts us above necessity so that we can choose the best in life. If we love, it enables us to meet and live with the loved one, or even to prolong her health and life; if we have scruples, it gives us an opportunity to be honest; if we have any bright designs, here is what will smooth the way to their accomplishment. Penury is the worst slavery, and will soon lead to death.

But money is only a means; it presupposes a man to use it. The rich can go where he pleases, but perhaps please himself nowhere. He can buy a library or visit the whole world, but perhaps has neither patience to read nor intelligence to see. The table may be loaded and the appetite wanting; the purse may be full, and the heart empty. He may have gained the world and lost himself; and with all his wealth around him, in a great house and spacious and beautiful demesne, he may live as blank a life as any tattered ditcher. Without an appetite, without an aspiration, void of appreciation, bankrupt of desire and hope, there, in his great house, let him sit and look upon his fingers. It is perhaps a more fortunate destiny to have a taste for collecting shells than to be born a millionaire. Although neither is to be despised, it is always better policy to learn an interest than to make a thousand pounds; for the money will soon be spent, or perhaps you may feel no joy in spending it; but the interest remains imperishable and ever new. To become a botanist, a geologist, a social philosopher, an antiquary, or an artist, is to enlarge one's possessions in the universe by an incalculably higher degree, and by a far surer sort of property, than to purchase a farm of many acres. You had perhaps two thousand a year before the transaction; perhaps you have two thousand five hundred after it. That represents your gain in the one case. But in the other, you have thrown down a barrier which concealed significance and beauty. The blind man has learned to see. The prisoner has opened up a window in his cell and beholds enchanting prospects; he will never again be a prisoner as he was; he can watch clouds and changing seasons, ships on the river, travellers on the road, and the stars at night; happy prisoner! his eyes have broken jail! And again he who has learned to love an art or science has wisely laid up riches against the day of riches; if prosperity come, he will not enter poor into his inheritance; he will not slumber and forget himself in the lap of money, or spend his hours in counting idle treasures, but be up and briskly doing; he will have the true alchemic touch, which is not that of Midas, but which transmutes dead money into living delight and satisfaction.

Être et pas avoir—to be, not to possess—that is the problem of life. To be wealthy, a rich nature is the first requisite and money but the second. To be of a quick and healthy blood, to share in all honourable curiosities, to be rich in admiration and free from envy, to rejoice greatly in the good of others, to love with such generosity of heart that your love is still a dear possession in absence or unkindness—these are the gifts of fortune which money cannot buy and without which money can buy nothing. For what can a man possess, or what can he enjoy, except himself? If he enlarge his nature, it is then that he enlarges his estates. If his nature be happy and valiant, he will enjoy the universe as if it were his park and orchard.

But money is not only to be spent; it has also to be earned. It is not merely a convenience or a necessary in social life; but it is the coin in which mankind pays his wages to the individual man. And from this side, the question of money has a very different scope and application. For no man can be honest who does not work. Service for service. If the farmer buys corn, and the labourer ploughs and reaps, and the baker sweats in his hot bakery, plainly you who eat must do something in your turn. It is not enough to take off your hat, or to thank God upon your knees for the admirable constitution of society and your own convenient situation in its upper and more ornamental stories. Neither is it enough to buy the loaf with a sixpence; for then you are only changing the point of the inquiry; and you must first have bought the sixpence. Service for service: how have you bought your sixpences? A man of spirit desires certainty in a thing of such a nature; he must see to it that there is some reciprocity between him and mankind; that he pays his expenditure in service; that he has not a lion's share in profit and a drone's in labour; and is not a sleeping partner and mere costly incubus on the great mercantile concern of mankind.

Services differ so widely with different gifts, and some are so inappreciable to external tests, that this is not only a matter for the private conscience, but one which even there must be leniently and trustfully considered. For remember how many serve mankind who do no more than meditate; and how many are precious to their friends for no more than a sweet and joyous temper. To perform the function of a man of letters it is not necessary to write; nay, it is perhaps better to be a living book. So long as we love we serve; so long as we are loved by others, I would almost say that we are indispensable; and no man is useless while he has a friend. The true services of life are inestimable in money, and are never paid. Kind words and caresses, high and wise thoughts, humane designs, tender behaviour to the weak and suffering, and all the charities of man's existence, are neither bought nor sold.

Yet the dearest and readiest, if not the most just, criterion of a man's services, is the wage that mankind pays him or, briefly, what he earns. There at least there can be no ambiguity. St. Paul is fully and freely entitled to his earnings as a tentmaker, and Socrates fully and freely entitled to his earnings as a sculptor, although the true business of each was not only something different, but something which remained unpaid. A man cannot forget that he is not superintended, and serves mankind on parole. He would like, when challenged by his own conscience, to reply: 'I have done so much work, and no less, with my own hands and brain, and taken so much profit, and no more, for my own personal delight.' And though St. Paul, if he had possessed a private fortune, would probably have scorned to waste his time in making tents, yet of all sacrifices to public opinion none can be more easily pardoned than that by which a man, already spiritually useful to the world, should restrict the field of his chief usefulness to perform services more apparent, and possess a livelihood that neither stupidity nor malice could call in question. Like all sacrifices to public opinion and mere external decency, this would certainly be wrong; for the soul should rest contented with its own approval and indissuadably pursue its own calling. Yet, so grave and delicate is the question, that a man may well hesitate before he decides it for himself; he may well fear that he sets too high a valuation on his own endeavours after good; he may well condescend upon a humbler duty, where others than himself shall judge the service and proportion the wage.

And yet it is to this very responsibility that the rich are born. They can shuffle off the duty on no other; they are their own paymasters on parole; and must pay themselves fair wages and no more. For I suppose that in the course of ages, and through reform and civil war and invasion, mankind was pursuing some other and more general design than to set one or two

Englishmen of the nineteenth century beyond the reach of needs and duties. Society was scarce put together, and defended with so much eloquence and blood, for the convenience of two or three millionaires and a few hundred other persons of wealth and position. It is plain that if mankind thus acted and suffered during all these generations, they hoped some benefit, some ease, some wellbeing, for themselves and their descendants; that if they supported law and order, it was to secure fair-play for all; that if they denied themselves in the present, they must have had some designs upon the future. Now, a great hereditary fortune is a miracle of man's wisdom and mankind's forbearance; it has not only been amassed and handed down, it has been suffered to be amassed and handed down; and surely in such a consideration as this, its possessor should find only a new spur to activity and honour, that with all this power of service he should not prove unserviceable, and that this mass of treasure should return in benefits upon the race. If he had twenty, or thirty, or a hundred thousand at his banker's, or if all Yorkshire or all California were his to manage or to sell, he would still be morally penniless, and have the world to begin like Whittington, until he had found some way of serving mankind. His wage is physically in his own hand; but, in honour, that wage must still be earned. He is only steward on parole of what is called his fortune. He must honourably perform his stewardship. He must estimate his own services and allow himself a salary in proportion, for that will be one among his functions. And while he will then be free to spend that salary, great or little, on his own private pleasures, the rest of his fortune he but holds and disposes under trust for mankind; it is not his, because he has not earned it; it cannot be his, because his services have already been paid; but year by year it is his to distribute, whether to help individuals whose birthright and outfit have been swallowed up in his, or to further public works and institutions.

At this rate, short of inspiration, it seems hardly possible to be both rich and honest; and the millionaire is under a far more continuous temptation to thieve than the labourer who gets his shilling daily for despicable toils. Are you surprised? It is even so. And you repeat it every Sunday in your churches. 'It is easier for a camel to pass through the eye of a needle than for a rich man to enter the kingdom of God.' I have heard this and similar texts ingeniously explained away and brushed from the path of the aspiring Christian by the tender Great-heart of the parish. One excellent clergyman told us that the 'eye of a needle' meant a low, Oriental postern through which camels could not pass till they were unloaded—which is very likely just; and then went on, bravely confounding the 'kingdom of God' with heaven, the future paradise, to show that of course no rich person could expect to carry his riches beyond the grave—which, of course, he could not and never did. Various greedy sinners of the congregation drank in the comfortable doctrine with relief. It was worth the while having come to church that Sunday morning! All was plain. The Bible, as usual, meant nothing in particular; it was merely an obscure and figurative school-copybook; and if a man were only respectable, he was a man after God's own heart.

Alas! I fear not. And though this matter of a man's services is one for his own conscience, there are some cases in which it is difficult to restrain the mind from judging. Thus I shall be very easily persuaded that a man has earned his daily bread; and if he has but a friend or two to whom his company is delightful at heart, I am more than persuaded at once. But it will be very hard to persuade me that any one has earned an income of a hundred thousand. What he is to his friends, he still would be if he were made penniless to-morrow; for as to the courtiers of luxury and power, I will neither consider them friends, nor indeed consider them at all. What he does for mankind there are most likely hundreds who would do the same, as effectually for the race and as pleasurably to themselves, for the merest fraction of this monstrous wage. Why it is paid, I am, therefore, unable to conceive, and as the man pays it himself, out of funds in his detention, I have a certain backwardness to think him honest.

At least, we have gained a very obvious point: that what a man spends upon himself, he shall have earned by services to the race. Thence flows a principle for the outset of life, which is a little different from that taught in the present day. I am addressing the middle and the upper classes; those who have already been fostered and prepared for life at some expense; those who have some choice before them, and can pick professions; and above all, those who are what is called independent, and need do nothing unless pushed by honour or ambition. In this particular the poor are happy; among them, when a lad comes to his strength, he must take the work that offers, and can take it with an easy conscience. But in the richer classes the question is complicated by the number of opportunities and a variety of considerations. Here, then, this principle of ours comes in helpfully. The young man has to seek, not a road to wealth, but an opportunity of service; not money, but honest work. If he has some strong propensity, some calling of nature, some over-weening interest in any special field of industry, inquiry, or art, he will do right to obey the impulse; and that for two reasons: the first external, because there he will render the best services; the second personal, because a demand of his own nature is to him without appeal whenever it can be satisfied with the consent of his other faculties and appetites. If he has no such elective taste, by the very principle on which he chooses any pursuit at all he must choose the most honest and serviceable, and not the most highly remunerated. We have here an external problem, not from or to ourself, but flowing from the constitution of society; and we have our own soul with its fixed design of righteousness. All that can be done is to present the problem in proper terms, and leave it to the soul of the individual. Now, the problem to the poor is one of necessity: to earn wherewithal to live, they must find remunerative labour. But the problem to the rich is one of honour: having the wherewithal, they must find serviceable labour. Each has to earn his daily bread: the one, because he has not yet got it to eat; the other, who has already eaten it, because he has not yet earned it.

Of course, what is true of bread is true of luxuries and comforts, whether for the body or the mind. But the consideration of luxuries leads us to a new aspect of the whole question, and to a second proposition no less true, and maybe no less startling, than the last.

At the present day, we, of the easier classes, are in a state of surfeit and disgrace after meat. Plethora has filled us with indifference; and we are covered from head to foot with the callosities of habitual opulence. Born into what is called a certain rank, we live, as the saying is, up to our station. We squander without enjoyment, because our fathers squandered. We eat of the best, not from delicacy, but from brazen habit. We do not keenly enjoy or eagerly desire the presence of a luxury; we are unaccustomed to its absence.

And not only do we squander money from habit, but still more pitifully waste it in ostentation. I can think of no more melancholy disgrace for a creature who professes either reason or pleasure for his guide, than to spend the smallest fraction of his income upon that which he does not desire; and to keep a carriage in which you do not wish to drive, or a butler of whom you are afraid, is a pathetic kind of folly. Money, being a means of happiness, should make both parties happy when it changes hands; rightly disposed, it should be twice blessed in its employment; and buyer and seller should alike have their twenty shillings worth of profit out of every pound. Benjamin Franklin went through life an altered man, because he once paid too dearly for a penny whistle. My concern springs usually from a deeper source, to wit, from having bought a whistle when I did not want one. I find I regret this, or would regret it if I gave myself the time, not only on personal but on moral and philanthropical considerations. For, first, in a world where money is wanting to buy books for eager students and food and medicine for pining children, and where a large majority are starved in their most immediate desires, it is surely base, stupid, and cruel to squander money when I am pushed by no appetite and enjoy no return of genuine satisfaction. My philanthropy is wide enough in scope to include myself; and when I have made myself happy, I have at least one good argument that I have acted rightly; but where that is not so, and I have bought and not enjoyed, my mouth is closed, and I conceive that I have robbed the poor. And, second, anything I buy or use which I do not sincerely want or cannot vividly enjoy, disturbs the balance of supply and demand, and contributes to remove industrious hands from the production of what is useful or pleasurable and to keep them busy upon ropes of sand and things that are a weariness to the flesh. That extravagance is truly sinful, and a very silly sin to boot, in which we impoverish mankind and ourselves. It is another question for each man's heart. He knows if he can enjoy what he buys and uses; if he cannot, he is a dog in the manger; nay, it he cannot, I contend he is a thief, for nothing really belongs to a man which he cannot use. Proprietor is connected with propriety; and that only is the man's which is proper to his wants and faculties.

A youth, in choosing a career, must not be alarmed by poverty. Want is a sore thing, but poverty does not imply want. It remains to be seen whether

51

with half his present income, or a third, he cannot, in the most generous sense, live as fully as at present. He is a fool who objects to luxuries; but he is also a fool who does not protest against the waste of luxuries on those who do not desire and cannot enjoy them. It remains to be seen, by each man who would live a true life to himself and not a merely specious life to society, how many luxuries he truly wants and to how many he merely submits as to a social propriety; and all these last he will immediately forswear. Let him do this, and he will be surprised to find how little money it requires to keep him in complete contentment and activity of mind and senses. Life at any level among the easy classes is conceived upon a principle of rivalry, where each man and each household must ape the tastes and emulate the display of others. One is delicate in eating, another in wine, a third in furniture or works of art or dress; and I, who care nothing for any of these refinements, who am perhaps a plain athletic creature and love exercise, beef, beer, flannel shirts and a camp bed, am yet called upon to assimilate all these other tastes and make these foreign occasions of expenditure my own. It may be cynical: I am sure I shall be told it is selfish; but I will spend my money as I please and for my own intimate personal gratification, and should count myself a nincompoop indeed to lay out the colour of a halfpenny on any fancied social decency or duty. I shall not wear gloves unless my hands are cold, or unless I am born with a delight in them. Dress is my own affair, and that of one other in the world; that, in fact and for an obvious reason, of any woman who shall chance to be in love with me. I shall lodge where I have a mind. If I do not ask society to live with me, they must be silent; and even if I do, they have no further right but to refuse the invitation! There is a kind of idea abroad that a man must live up to his station, that his house, his table, and his toilette, shall be in a ratio of equivalence, and equally imposing to the world. If this is in the Bible, the passage has eluded my inquiries. If it is not in the Bible, it is nowhere but in the heart of the fool. Throw aside this fancy. See what you want, and spend upon that; distinguish what you do not care about, and spend nothing upon that. There are not many people who can differentiate wines above a certain and that not at all a high price. Are you sure you are one of these? Are you sure you prefer cigars at sixpence each to pipes at some fraction of a farthing? Are you sure you wish to keep a gig? Do you care about where you sleep, or are you not as much at your ease in a cheap lodging as in an Elizabethan manor-house? Do you enjoy fine clothes? It is not possible to answer these questions without a trial; and there is nothing more obvious to my mind, than that a man who has not experienced some ups and downs, and been forced to live more cheaply than in his father's house, has still his education to begin. Let the experiment be made, and he will find to his surprise that he has been eating beyond his appetite up to that hour; that the cheap lodging, the cheap tobacco, the rough country clothes, the plain table, have not only no power to damp his spirits, but perhaps give him as keen pleasure in the using as the dainties that he took, betwixt sleep and waking, in his former callous and somnambulous submission to wealth.

The true Bohemian, a creature lost to view under the imaginary Bohemians of literature, is exactly described by such a principle of life. The Bohemian of the novel, who drinks more than is good for him and prefers anything to work, and wears strange clothes, is for the most part a respectable Bohemian, respectable in disrespectability, living for the outside, and an adventurer. But the man I mean lives wholly to himself, does what he wishes, and not what is thought proper, buys what he wants for himself, and not what is thought proper, works at what he believes he can do well and not what will bring him in money or favour. You may be the most respectable of men, and yet a true Bohemian. And the test is this: a Bohemian, for as poor as he may be, is always open-handed to his friends; he knows what he can do with money and how he can do without it, a far rarer and more useful knowledge; he has had less, and continued to live in some contentment; and hence he cares not to keep more, and shares his sovereign or his shilling with a friend. The poor, if they are generous, are Bohemian in virtue of their birth. Do you know where beggars go? Not to the great houses where people sit dazed among their thousands, but to the doors of poor men who have seen the world; and it was the widow who had only two mites, who cast half her fortune into the treasury.

But a young man who elects to save on dress or on lodging, or who in any way falls out of the level of expenditure which is common to his level in society, falls out of society altogether. I suppose the young man to have chosen his career on honourable principles; he finds his talents and instincts can be best contented in a certain pursuit; in a certain industry, he is sure that he is serving mankind with a healthy and becoming service; and he is not sure that he would be doing so, or doing so equally well, in any other industry within his reach. Then that is his true sphere in life; not the one in which he was born to his father, but the one which is proper to his talents and instincts. And suppose he does fall out of society, is that a cause of sorrow? Is your heart so dead that you prefer the recognition of many to the love of a few? Do you think society loves you? Put it to the proof. Decline in material expenditure, and you will find they care no more for you than for the Khan of Tartary. You will lose no friends. If you had any, you will keep them. Only those who were friends to your coat and equipage will disappear; the smiling faces will disappear as by enchantment; but the kind hearts will remain steadfastly kind. Are you so lost, are you so dead, are you so little sure of your own soul and your own footing upon solid fact, that you prefer before goodness and happiness the countenance of sundry diners-out, who will flee from you at a report of ruin, who will drop you with insult at a shadow of disgrace, who do not know you and do not care to know you but by sight, and whom you in your turn neither know nor care to know in a more human manner? Is it not the principle of society, openly avowed, that friendship must not interfere with business; which being paraphrased, means simply that a consideration of money goes before any consideration of affection known to this cold-blooded gang, that they have not even the honour of thieves, and will rook their nearest and dearest as readily as a stranger? I hope I would go as far as most to serve a friend; but I declare openly I would not put on my hat to do a pleasure to society. I may starve my appetites and control my temper for the sake of those I love; but society shall take me as I choose to be, or go without me. Neither they nor I will lose; for where there is no love, it is both laborious and unprofitable to associate.

But it is obvious that if it is only right for a man to spend money on that which he can truly and thoroughly enjoy, the doctrine applies with equal force to the rich and to the poor, to the man who has amassed many thousands as well as to the youth precariously beginning life. And it may be asked, Is not this merely preparing misers, who are not the best of company? But the principle was this: that which a man has not fairly earned, and, further, that which he cannot fully enjoy, does not belong to him, but is a part of mankind's treasure which he holds as steward on parole. To mankind, then, it must be made profitable; and how this should be done is, once more, a problem which each man must solve for himself, and about which none has a right to judge him. Yet there are a few considerations which are very obvious and may here be stated. Mankind is not only the whole in general, but every one in particular. Every man or woman is one of mankind's dear possessions; to his or her just brain, and kind heart, and active hands, mankind intrusts some of its hopes for the future; he or she is a possible well-spring of good acts and source of blessings to the race. This money which you do not need, which, in a rigid sense, you do not want, may therefore be returned not only in public benefactions to the race, but in private kindnesses. Your wife, your children, your friends stand nearest to you, and should be helped the first. There at least there can be little imposture, for you know their necessities of your own knowledge. And consider, if all the world did as you did, and according to their means extended help in the circle of their affections, there would be no more crying want in times of plenty and no more cold, mechanical charity given with a doubt and received with confusion. Would not this simple rule make a new world out of the old and cruel one which we inhabit?

[After two more sentences the fragment breaks off.]

FATHER DAMIEN

AN OPEN LETTER TO THE REVEREND DR. HYDE OF HONOLULU

SYDNEY,

February 25, 1890.

Sir,—It may probably occur to you that we have met, and visited, and conversed; on my side, with interest. You may remember that you have done me several courtesies, for which I was prepared to be grateful. But there are duties which come before gratitude, and offences which justly divide friends, far more acquaintances. Your letter to the Reverend H. B. Gage is a document which, in my sight, if you had filled me with bread when I was starving, if you had sat up to nurse my father when he lay a-dying, would yet absolve me from the bonds of gratitude. You know enough, doubtless, of the process of canonisation to be aware that, a hundred years after the death of Damien, there will appear a man charged with the painful office of the devil's advocate. After that noble brother of mine, and of all frail clay, shall have lain a century at rest, one shall accuse, one defend him. The circumstance is unusual that the devil's advocate should be a volunteer, should be a member of a sect immediately rival, and should make haste to take upon himself his ugly office ere the bones are cold; unusual, and of a taste which I shall leave my readers free to qualify; unusual, and to me inspiring. If I have at all learned the trade of using words to convey truth and to arouse emotion, you have at last furnished me with a subject. For it is in the interest of all mankind, and the cause of public decency in every quarter of the world, not only that Damien should be righted, but that you and your letter should be displayed at length, in their true colours, to the public eye.

To do this properly, I must begin by quoting you at large: I shall then proceed to criticise your utterance from several points of view, divine and human, in the course of which I shall attempt to draw again, and with more specification, the character of the dead saint whom it has pleased you to vilify:

so much being done, I shall say farewell to you for ever.

'HONOLULU,

'August 2, 1889.

'Rev. H. B. Gage.

'Dear Brother,—In answer to your inquiries about Father Damien, I can only reply that we who knew the man are surprised at the extravagant newspaper laudations, as if he was a most saintly philanthropist. The simple truth is, he was a coarse, dirty man, head-strong and bigoted. He was not sent to Molokai, but went there without orders; did not stay at the leper settlement (before he became one himself), but circulated freely over the whole island (less than half the island is devoted to the lepers), and he came often to Honolulu. He had no hand in the reforms and improvements inaugurated, which were the work of our Board of Health, as occasion required and means were provided. He was not a pure man in his relations with women, and the leprosy of which he died should be attributed to his vices and carelessness. Others have done much for the lepers, our own ministers, the government physicians, and so forth, but never with the Catholic idea of meriting eternal life.— Yours, etc.,

'C. M. Hyde.' [65]

To deal fitly with a letter so extraordinary, I must draw at the outset on my private knowledge of the signatory and his sect. It may offend others; scarcely you, who have been so busy to collect, so bold to publish, gossip on your rivals. And this is perhaps the moment when I may best explain to you the character of what you are to read: I conceive you as a man quite beyond and below the reticences of civility: with what measure you mete, with that shall it be measured you again; with you, at last, I rejoice to feel the button off the foil and to plunge home. And if in aught that I shall say I should offend others, your colleagues, whom I respect and remember with affection, I can but offer them my regret; I am not free, I am inspired by the consideration of interests far more large; and such pain as can be inflicted by anything from me must be indeed trifling when compared with the pain with which

57

they read your letter. It is not the hangman, but the criminal, that brings dishonour on the house.

You belong, sir, to a sect—I believe my sect, and that in which my ancestors laboured—which has enjoyed, and partly failed to utilise, an exceptional advantage in the islands of Hawaii. The first missionaries came; they found the land already self-purged of its old and bloody faith; they were embraced, almost on their arrival, with enthusiasm; what troubles they supported came far more from whites than from Hawaiians; and to these last they stood (in a rough figure) in the shoes of God. This is not the place to enter into the degree or causes of their failure, such as it is. One element alone is pertinent, and must here be plainly dealt with. In the course of their evangelical calling, they—or too many of them—grew rich. It may be news to you that the houses of missionaries are a cause of mocking on the streets of Honolulu. It will at least be news to you, that when I returned your civil visit, the driver of my cab commented on the size, the taste, and the comfort of your home. It would have been news certainly to myself, had any one told me that afternoon that I should live to drag such matter into print. But you see, sir, how you degrade better men to your own level; and it is needful that those who are to judge betwixt you and me, betwixt Damien and the devil's advocate, should understand your letter to have been penned in a house which could raise, and that very justly, the envy and the comments of the passers-by. I think (to employ a phrase of yours which I admire) it 'should be attributed' to you that you have never visited the scene of Damien's life and death. If you had, and had recalled it, and looked about your pleasant rooms, even your pen perhaps would have been stayed.

Your sect (and remember, as far as any sect avows me, it is mine) has not done ill in a worldly sense in the Hawaiian Kingdom. When calamity befell their innocent parishioners, when leprosy descended and took root in the Eight Islands, a quid pro quo was to be looked for. To that prosperous mission, and to you, as one of its adornments, God had sent at last an opportunity. I know I am touching here upon a nerve acutely sensitive. I know that others of your colleagues look back on the inertia of your Church, and the intrusive and decisive heroism of Damien, with something almost to be called remorse.

I am sure it is so with yourself; I am persuaded your letter was inspired by a certain envy, not essentially ignoble, and the one human trait to be espied in that performance. You were thinking of the lost chance, the past day; of that which should have been conceived and was not; of the service due and not rendered. Time was, said the voice in your ear, in your pleasant room, as you sat raging and writing; and if the words written were base beyond parallel, the rage, I am happy to repeat—it is the only compliment I shall pay you—the rage was almost virtuous. But, sir, when we have failed, and another has succeeded; when we have stood by, and another has stepped in; when we sit and grow bulky in our charming mansions, and a plain, uncouth peasant steps into the battle, under the eyes of God, and succours the afflicted, and consoles the dying, and is himself afflicted in his turn, and dies upon the field of honour—the battle cannot be retrieved as your unhappy irritation has suggested. It is a lost battle, and lost for ever. One thing remained to you in your defeat—some rags of common honour; and these you have made haste to cast away.

Common honour; not the honour of having done anything right, but the honour of not having done aught conspicuously foul; the honour of the inert: that was what remained to you. We are not all expected to be Damiens; a man may conceive his duty more narrowly, he may love his comforts better; and none will cast a stone at him for that. But will a gentleman of your reverend profession allow me an example from the fields of gallantry? When two gentlemen compete for the favour of a lady, and the one succeeds and the other is rejected, and (as will sometimes happen) matter damaging to the successful rival's credit reaches the ear of the defeated, it is held by plain men of no pretensions that his mouth is, in the circumstance, almost necessarily closed. Your Church and Damien's were in Hawaii upon a rivalry to do well: to help, to edify, to set divine examples. You having (in one huge instance) failed, and Damien succeeded, I marvel it should not have occurred to you that you were doomed to silence; that when you had been outstripped in that high rivalry, and sat inglorious in the midst of your wellbeing, in your pleasant room—and Damien, crowned with glories and horrors, toiled and rotted in that pigsty of his under the cliffs of Kalawao—you, the elect who would not, were the last man on earth to collect and propagate gossip on the volunteer who would and did.

I think I see you—for I try to see you in the flesh as I write these sentences—I think I see you leap at the word pigsty, a hyperbolical expression at the best. 'He had no hand in the reforms,' he was 'a coarse, dirty man'; these were your own words; and you may think it possible that I am come to support you with fresh evidence. In a sense, it is even so. Damien has been too much depicted with a conventional halo and conventional features; so drawn by men who perhaps had not the eye to remark or the pen to express the individual; or who perhaps were only blinded and silenced by generous admiration, such as I partly envy for myself—such as you, if your soul were enlightened, would envy on your bended knees. It is the least defect of such a method of portraiture that it makes the path easy for the devil's advocate, and leaves for the misuse of the slanderer a considerable field of truth. For the truth that is suppressed by friends is the readiest weapon of the enemy. The world, in your despite, may perhaps owe you something, if your letter be the means of substituting once for all a credible likeness for a wax abstraction. For, if that world at all remember you, on the day when Damien of Molokai shall be named Saint, it will be in virtue of one work: your letter to the Reverend H. B. Gage.

You may ask on what authority I speak. It was my inclement destiny to become acquainted, not with Damien, but with Dr. Hyde. When I visited the lazaretto, Damien was already in his resting grave. But such information as I have, I gathered on the spot in conversation with those who knew him well and long: some indeed who revered his memory; but others who had sparred and wrangled with him, who beheld him with no halo, who perhaps regarded him with small respect, and through whose unprepared and scarcely partial communications the plain, human features of the man shone on me convincingly. These gave me what knowledge I possess; and I learnt it in that scene where it could be most completely and sensitively understood— Kalawao, which you have never visited, about which you have never so much as endeavoured to inform yourself; for, brief as your letter is, you have found the means to stumble into that confession. 'Less than one-half of the island,' you say, 'is devoted to the lepers.' Molokai—'Molokai ahina,' the 'grey,' lofty, and most desolate island—along all its northern side plunges a front of precipice into a sea of unusual profundity. This range of cliff is, from east to west, the true end and frontier of the island. Only in one spot there projects into the ocean a certain triangular and rugged down, grassy, stony, windy, and rising in the midst into a hill with a dead crater: the whole bearing to the cliff that overhangs it somewhat the same relation as a bracket to a wall. With this hint you will now be able to pick out the leper station on a map; you will be able to judge how much of Molokai is thus cut off between the surf and precipice, whether less than a half, or less than a quarter, or a fifth, or a tenth—or, say, a twentieth; and the next time you burst into print you will be in a position to share with us the issue of your calculations.

I imagine you to be one of those persons who talk with cheerfulness of that place which oxen and wain-ropes could not drag you to behold. You, who do not even know its situation on the map, probably denounce sensational descriptions, stretching your limbs the while in your pleasant parlour on Beretania Street. When I was pulled ashore there one early morning, there sat with me in the boat two sisters, bidding farewell (in humble imitation of Damien) to the lights and joys of human life. One of these wept silently; I could not withhold myself from joining her. Had you been there, it is my belief that nature would have triumphed even in you; and as the boat drew but a little nearer, and you beheld the stairs crowded with abominable deformations of our common manhood, and saw yourself landing in the midst of such a population as only now and then surrounds us in the horror of a nightmare—what a haggard eye you would have rolled over your reluctant shoulder towards the house on Beretania Street! Had you gone on; had you found every fourth face a blot upon the landscape; had you visited the hospital and seen the butt-ends of human beings lying there almost unrecognisable, but still breathing, still thinking, still remembering; you would have understood that life in the lazaretto is an ordeal from which the nerves of a man's spirit shrink, even as his eye quails under the brightness of the sun; you would have felt it was (even to-day) a pitiful place to visit and a hell to dwell in. It is not the fear of possible infection. That seems a little thing when compared with the pain, the pity, and the disgust of the visitor's surroundings, and the atmosphere of affliction, disease, and physical disgrace in which he breathes. I do not think I am a man more than usually timid; but I never recall the days and nights I spent upon that island promontory (eight days and seven nights), without heartfelt thankfulness that I am somewhere else. I find in my diary that I speak of my stay as a 'grinding experience': I have once jotted in the margin, 'Harrowing is the word'; and when the Mokolii bore me at last towards the outer world, I kept repeating to myself, with a new conception of their pregnancy, those simple words of the song—

''Tis the most distressful country that ever yet was seen.'

And observe: that which I saw and suffered from was a settlement purged, bettered, beautified; the new village built, the hospital and the Bishop-Home excellently arranged; the sisters, the doctor, and the missionaries, all indefatigable in their noble tasks. It was a different place when Damien came there and made his great renunciation, and slept that first night under a tree amidst his rotting brethren: alone with pestilence; and looking forward (with what courage, with what pitiful sinkings of dread, God only knows) to a lifetime of dressing sores and stumps.

You will say, perhaps, I am too sensitive, that sights as painful abound in cancer hospitals and are confronted daily by doctors and nurses. I have long learned to admire and envy the doctors and the nurses. But there is no cancer hospital so large and populous as Kalawao and Kalaupapa; and in such a matter every fresh case, like every inch of length in the pipe of an organ, deepens the note of the impression; for what daunts the onlooker is that monstrous sum of human suffering by which he stands surrounded. Lastly, no doctor or nurse is called upon to enter once for all the doors of that gehenna; they do not say farewell, they need not abandon hope, on its sad threshold; they but go for a time to their high calling, and can look forward as they go to relief, to recreation, and to rest. But Damien shut-to with his own hand the doors of his own sepulchre.

I shall now extract three passages from my diary at Kalawao.

A. 'Damien is dead and already somewhat ungratefully remembered in the field of his labours and sufferings. "He was a good man, but very officious," says one. Another tells me he had fallen (as other priests so easily do) into something of the ways and habits of thought of a Kanaka; but he had the wit to recognise the fact, and the good sense to laugh at' [over] 'it. A plain man it seems he was; I cannot find he was a popular.'

B. 'After Ragsdale's death' [Ragsdale was a famous Luna, or overseer, of the unruly settlement] 'there followed a brief term of office by Father Damien which served only to publish the weakness of that noble man. He was rough in his ways, and he had no control. Authority was relaxed; Damien's life was threatened, and he was soon eager to resign.'

C. 'Of Damien I begin to have an idea. He seems to have been a man of the peasant class, certainly of the peasant type: shrewd, ignorant and bigoted, yet with an open mind, and capable of receiving and digesting a reproof if it were bluntly administered; superbly generous in the least thing as well as in the greatest, and as ready to give his last shirt (although not without human grumbling) as he had been to sacrifice his life; essentially indiscreet and officious, which made him a troublesome colleague; domineering in all his ways, which made him incurably unpopular with the Kanakas, but yet destitute of real authority, so that his boys laughed at him and he must carry out his wishes by the means of bribes. He learned to have a mania for doctoring; and set up the Kanakas against the remedies of his regular rivals: perhaps (if anything matter at all in the treatment of such a disease) the worst thing that he did, and certainly the easiest. The best and worst of the man appear very plainly in his dealings with Mr. Chapman's money; he had originally laid it out' [intended to lay it out] 'entirely for the benefit of Catholics, and even so not wisely; but after a long, plain talk, he admitted his error fully and revised the list. The sad state of the boys' home is in part the result of his lack of control; in part, of his own slovenly ways and false ideas of hygiene. Brother officials used to call it "Damien's Chinatown." "Well," they would say, "your China-town keeps growing." And he would laugh with perfect good-nature, and adhere to his errors with perfect obstinacy. So much I have gathered of truth about this plain, noble human brother and father of ours; his imperfections are the traits of his face, by which we know him for our fellow; his martyrdom and his example nothing can lessen or annul; and only a person here on the spot can properly appreciate their greatness.'

I have set down these private passages, as you perceive, without correction; thanks to you, the public has them in their bluntness. They are almost a list of the man's faults, for it is rather these that I was seeking: with his virtues, with the heroic profile of his life, I and the world were already sufficiently acquainted. I was besides a little suspicious of Catholic testimony; in no ill sense, but merely because Damien's admirers and disciples were the least likely to be critical. I know you will be more suspicious still; and the facts set down above were one and all collected from the lips of Protestants who had opposed the father in his life. Yet I am strangely deceived, or they build up the image of a man, with all his weaknesses, essentially heroic, and alive with rugged honesty, generosity, and mirth.

Take it for what it is, rough private jottings of the worst sides of Damien's character, collected from the lips of those who had laboured with and (in your own phrase) 'knew the man';—though I question whether Damien would have said that he knew you. Take it, and observe with wonder how well you were served by your gossips, how ill by your intelligence and sympathy; in how many points of fact we are at one, and how widely our appreciations vary. There is something wrong here; either with you or me. It is possible, for instance, that you, who seem to have so many ears in Kalawao, had heard of the affair of Mr. Chapman's money, and were singly struck by Damien's intended wrong-doing. I was struck with that also, and set it fairly down; but I was struck much more by the fact that he had the honesty of mind to be convinced. I may here tell you that it was a long business; that one of his colleagues sat with him late into the night, multiplying arguments and accusations; that the father listened as usual with 'perfect good-nature and perfect obstinacy'; but at the last, when he was persuaded—'Yes,' said he, 'I am very much obliged to you; you have done me a service; it would have been a theft.' There are many (not Catholics merely) who require their heroes and saints to be infallible; to these the story will be painful; not to the true lovers, patrons, and servants of mankind.

And I take it, this is a type of our division; that you are one of those who have an eye for faults and failures; that you take a pleasure to find and publish them; and that, having found them, you make haste to forget the overvailing virtues and the real success which had alone introduced them to your knowledge. It is a dangerous frame of mind. That you may understand how dangerous, and into what a situation it has already brought you, we will (if you please) go hand-in-hand through the different phrases of your letter, and candidly examine each from the point of view of its truth, its appositeness, and its charity.

Damien was coarse.

It is very possible. You make us sorry for the lepers, who had only a coarse old peasant for their friend and father. But you, who were so refined, why were you not there, to cheer them with the lights of culture? Or may I remind you that we have some reason to doubt if John the Baptist were genteel; and in the case of Peter, on whose career you doubtless dwell approvingly in the pulpit, no doubt at all he was a 'coarse, headstrong' fisherman! Yet even in our Protestant Bibles Peter is called Saint.

Damien was dirty.

He was. Think of the poor lepers annoyed with this dirty comrade! But the clean Dr. Hyde was at his food in a fine house.

Damien was headstrong.

I believe you are right again; and I thank God for his strong head and heart.

Damien was bigoted.

I am not fond of bigots myself, because they are not fond of me. But what is meant by bigotry, that we should regard it as a blemish in a priest? Damien believed his own religion with the simplicity of a peasant or a child; as I would I could suppose that you do. For this, I wonder at him some way off; and had that been his only character, should have avoided him in life. But the point of interest in Damien, which has caused him to be so much talked about and made him at last the subject of your pen and mine, was that, in him, his bigotry, his intense and narrow faith, wrought potently for good, and strengthened him to be one of the world's heroes and exemplars.

Damien was not sent to Molokai, but went there without orders.

Is this a misreading? or do you really mean the words for blame? I have heard Christ, in the pulpits of our Church, held up for imitation on the ground that His sacrifice was voluntary. Does Dr. Hyde think otherwise?

Damien did not stay at the settlement, etc.

It is true he was allowed many indulgences. Am I to understand that you blame the father for profiting by these, or the officers for granting them? In either case, it is a mighty Spartan standard to issue from the house on Beretania Street; and I am convinced you will find yourself with few supporters.

Damien had no hand in the reforms, etc.

I think even you will admit that I have already been frank in my description of the man I am defending; but before I take you up upon this head, I will be franker still, and tell you that perhaps nowhere in the world can a man taste a more pleasurable sense of contrast than when he passes from Damien's 'Chinatown' at Kalawao to the beautiful Bishop-Home at Kalaupapa. At this point, in my desire to make all fair for you, I will break my rule and adduce Catholic testimony. Here is a passage from my diary about my visit to the Chinatown, from which you will see how it is (even now) regarded by its own officials: 'We went round all the dormitories, refectories, etc.—dark and dingy enough, with a superficial cleanliness, which he' [Mr. Dutton, the lay-brother] 'did not seek to defend. "It is almost decent," said he; "the sisters will make that all right when we get them here."' And yet I gathered it was already better since Damien was dead, and far better than when he was there alone and had his own (not always excellent) way. I have now come far enough to meet you on a common ground of fact; and I tell you that, to a mind not prejudiced by jealousy, all the reforms of the lazaretto, and even those which he most vigorously opposed, are properly the work of Damien. They are the evidence of his success; they are what his heroism provoked from the reluctant and the careless. Many were before him in the field; Mr. Meyer, for instance, of whose faithful work we hear too little: there have been many since; and some had more worldly wisdom, though none had more devotion, than our saint. Before his day, even you will confess, they had effected little. It was his part, by one striking act of martyrdom, to direct all men's eyes on that distressful country. At a blow, and with the price of his life, he made the place illustrious and public. And that, if you will consider largely, was the one reform needful; pregnant of all that should succeed. It brought money; it brought (best individual addition of them all) the sisters; it brought supervision, for public opinion and public interest landed with the man at Kalawao. If ever any man brought reforms, and died to bring them, it was he. There is not a clean cup or towel in the Bishop-Home, but dirty Damien washed it.

Damien was not a pure man in his relations with women, etc.

How do you know that? Is this the nature of the conversation in that house on Beretania Street which the cabman envied, driving past?—racy details of the misconduct of the poor peasant priest, toiling under the cliffs of Molokai?

Many have visited the station before me; they seem not to have heard the rumour. When I was there I heard many shocking tales, for my informants were men speaking with the plainness of the laity; and I heard plenty of complaints of Damien. Why was this never mentioned? and how came it to you in the retirement of your clerical parlour?

But I must not even seem to deceive you. This scandal, when I read it in your letter, was not new to me. I had heard it once before; and I must tell you how. There came to Samoa a man from Honolulu; he, in a public-house on the beach, volunteered the statement that Damien had 'contracted the disease from having connection with the female lepers'; and I find a joy in telling you how the report was welcomed in a public-house. A man sprang to his feet; I am not at liberty to give his name, but from what I heard I doubt if you would care to have him to dinner in Beretania Street. 'You miserable little—' (here is a word I dare not print, it would so shock your ears). 'You miserable little—,' he cried, 'if the story were a thousand times true, can't you see you are a million times a lower—for daring to repeat it?' I wish it could be told of you that when the report reached you in your house, perhaps after family worship, you had found in your soul enough holy anger to receive it with the same expressions; ay, even with that one which I dare not print; it would not need to have been blotted away, like Uncle Toby's oath, by the tears of the recording angel; it would have been counted to you for your brightest righteousness. But you have deliberately chosen the part of the man from Honolulu, and you have played it with improvements of your own. The man from Honolulu—miserable, leering creature—communicated the tale to a rude knot of beach-combing drinkers in a public-house, where (I will so far agree with your temperance opinions) man is not always at his noblest; and the man from Honolulu had himself been drinking—drinking, we may charitably fancy, to excess. It was to your 'Dear Brother, the Reverend H. B. Gage,' that you chose to communicate the sickening story; and the blue ribbon which adorns your portly bosom forbids me to allow you the extenuating plea that you were drunk when it was done. Your 'dear brother'—a brother indeed—made haste to deliver up your letter (as a means of grace, perhaps) to the religious papers; where, after many months, I found and read and wondered at it; and whence I have now reproduced it for the wonder of others. And you and your dear brother have, by this cycle of operations, built up a contrast very edifying to examine in detail. The man whom you would not care to have to dinner, on the one side; on the other, the Reverend Dr. Hyde and the Reverend H. B. Gage: the Apia bar-room, the Honolulu manse.

But I fear you scarce appreciate how you appear to your fellow-men; and to bring it home to you, I will suppose your story to be true. I will suppose—and God forgive me for supposing it—that Damien faltered and stumbled in his narrow path of duty; I will suppose that, in the horror of his isolation, perhaps in the fever of incipient disease, he, who was doing so much more than he had sworn, failed in the letter of his priestly oath—he, who was so much a better man than either you or me, who did what we have never dreamed of daring—he too tasted of our common frailty. 'O, Iago, the pity of it!' The least tender should be moved to tears; the most incredulous to prayer. And all that you could do was to pen your letter to the Reverend H. B. Gage!

Is it growing at all clear to you what a picture you have drawn of your own heart? I will try yet once again to make it clearer. You had a father: suppose this tale were about him, and some informant brought it to you, proof in hand: I am not making too high an estimate of your emotional nature when I suppose you would regret the circumstance? that you would feel the tale of frailty the more keenly since it shamed the author of your days? and that the last thing you would do would be to publish it in the religious press? Well, the man who tried to do what Damien did, is my father, and the father of the man in the Apia bar, and the father of all who love goodness; and he was your father too, if God had given you grace to see it.

THE PENTLAND RISING

A PAGE OF HISTORY

1666

'A cloud of witnesses lyes here,

Who for Christ's interest did appear.'

Inscription on Battlefield at Rullion Green.

CHAPTER I—THE CAUSES OF THE REVOLT

'Halt, passenger; take heed what thou dost see,

This tomb doth show for what some men did die.'

Monument, Greyfriars' Churchyard, Edinburgh,

1661–1668. [85]

Two hundred years ago a tragedy was enacted in Scotland, the memory whereof has been in great measure lost or obscured by the deep tragedies which followed it. It is, as it were, the evening of the night of persecution—a sort of twilight, dark indeed to us, but light as the noonday when compared with the midnight gloom which followed. This fact, of its being the very threshold of persecution, lends it, however, an additional interest.

The prejudices of the people against Episcopacy were 'out of measure increased,' says Bishop Burnet, 'by the new incumbents who were put in the places of the ejected preachers, and were generally very mean and despicable in all respects. They were the worst preachers I ever heard; they were ignorant to a reproach; and many of them were openly vicious. They . . . were indeed the dreg and refuse of the northern parts. Those of them who arose above contempt or scandal were men of such violent tempers that they were as much hated as the others were despised.' [86] It was little to be wondered at, from this account that the country-folk refused to go to the parish church, and chose rather to listen to outed ministers in the fields. But this was not to be allowed, and their persecutors at last fell on the method of calling a roll of the parishioners' names every Sabbath, and marking a fine of twenty shillings Scots to the name of each absenter. In this way very large debts were incurred by persons altogether unable to pay. Besides this, landlords were fined for their tenants' absences, tenants for their landlords', masters for their servants', servants for their masters', even though they themselves were perfectly regular in their attendance. And as the curates were allowed to fine with the sanction of any common soldier, it may be imagined that often the pretexts were neither very sufficient nor well proven.

When the fines could not be paid at once, Bibles, clothes, and household utensils were seized upon, or a number of soldiers, proportionate to his wealth, were quartered on the offender. The coarse and drunken privates filled the houses with woe; snatched the bread from the children to feed their dogs; shocked the principles, scorned the scruples, and blasphemed the religion of their humble hosts; and when they had reduced them to destitution, sold the furniture, and burned down the roof-tree which was consecrated to the peasants by the name of Home. For all this attention each of these soldiers received from his unwilling landlord a certain sum of money per day—three shillings sterling, according to Naphtali. And frequently they were forced to pay quartering money for more men than were in reality 'cessed on them.' At that time it was no strange thing to behold a strong man begging for money to pay his fines, and many others who were deep in arrears, or who had attracted attention in some other way, were forced to flee from their homes, and take refuge from arrest and imprisonment among the wild mosses of the uplands. [87a]

One example in particular we may cite:

John Neilson, the Laird of Corsack, a worthy man, was, unfortunately for himself, a Nonconformist. First he was fined in four hundred pounds Scots, and then through cessing he lost nineteen hundred and ninety-three pounds Scots. He was next obliged to leave his house and flee from place to place, during which wanderings he lost his horse. His wife and children were turned out of doors, and then his tenants were fined till they too were almost ruined. As a final stroke, they drove away all his cattle to Glasgow and sold them. [87b] Surely it was time that something were done to alleviate so much sorrow, to overthrow such tyranny.

About this time too there arrived in Galloway a person calling himself Captain Andrew Gray, and advising the people to revolt. He displayed some documents purporting to be from the northern Covenanters, and stating that they were prepared to join in any enterprise commenced by their southern brethren. The leader of the persecutors was Sir James Turner, an officer afterwards degraded for his share in the matter. 'He was naturally fierce, but was mad when he was drunk, and that was very often,' said Bishop Burnet. 'He was a learned man, but had always been in armies, and knew no other rule but to obey orders. He told me he had no regard to any law, but acted, as he was commanded, in a military way.' [88]

This was the state of matters, when an outrage was committed which gave spirit and determination to the oppressed countrymen, lit the flame of insubordination, and for the time at least recoiled on those who perpetrated it with redoubled force.

CHAPTER II—THE BEGINNING

I love no warres,

I love no jarres,

Nor strife's fire.

May discord cease,

Let's live in peace:

This I desire.

If it must be

Warre we must see

(So fates conspire),

May we not feel

The force of steel:

This I desire.

T. JACKSON, 1651 [89]

Upon Tuesday, November 13th, 1666, Corporal George Deanes and three other soldiers set upon an old man in the clachan of Dalry and demanded the payment of his fines. On the old man's refusing to pay, they forced a large party of his neighbours to go with them and thresh his corn. The field was a certain distance out of the clachan, and four persons, disguised as countrymen, who had been out on the moors all night, met this mournful drove of slaves, compelled by the four soldiers to work for the ruin of their friend. However, chided to the bone by their night on the hills, and worn out by want of food, they proceeded to the village inn to refresh themselves. Suddenly some people rushed into the room where they were sitting, and told them that the soldiers were about to roast the old man, naked, on his own girdle. This was too much for them to stand, and they repaired immediately to the scene of this gross outrage, and at first merely requested that the captive should be released. On the refusal of the two soldiers who were in the front room, high words were given and taken on both sides, and the other two rushed forth from an adjoining chamber and made at the countrymen with drawn swords. One of the latter, John M'Lellan of Barscob, drew a pistol and shot the corporal in the body. The pieces of tobacco-pipe with which it was loaded, to the number of ten at least, entered him, and he was so much disturbed that he never appears to have recovered, for we find long afterwards a petition to the Privy Council requesting a pension for him. The other soldiers then laid down their arms, the old man was rescued, and the rebellion was commenced. [90]

And now we must turn to Sir James Turner's memoirs of himself; for, strange to say, this extraordinary man was remarkably fond of literary composition, and wrote, besides the amusing account of his own adventures just mentioned, a large number of essays and short biographies, and a work on war, entitled Pallas Armata. The following are some of the shorter pieces 'Magick,' 'Friendship,' 'Imprisonment,' 'Anger,' 'Revenge,' 'Duells,' 'Cruelty,'

'A Defence of some of the Ceremonies of the English Liturgie—to wit—Bowing at the Name of Jesus, The frequent repetition of the Lord's Prayer and Good Lord deliver us, Of the Doxologie, Of Surplesses, Rotchets, Canonnicall Coats,' etc. From what we know of his character we should expect 'Anger' and 'Cruelty' to be very full and instructive. But what earthly right he had to meddle with ecclesiastical subjects it is hard to see.

Upon the 12th of the month he had received some information concerning Gray's proceedings, but as it was excessively indefinite in its character, he paid no attention to it. On the evening of the 14th, Corporal Deanes was brought into Dumfries, who affirmed stoutly that he had been shot while refusing to sign the Covenant—a story rendered singularly unlikely by the after conduct of the rebels. Sir James instantly dispatched orders to the cessed soldiers either to come to Dumfries or meet him on the way to Dalry, and commanded the thirteen or fourteen men in the town with him to come at nine next morning to his lodging for supplies.

On the morning of Thursday the rebels arrived at Dumfries with 50 horse and 150 foot. Neilson of Corsack, and Gray, who commanded, with a considerable troop, entered the town, and surrounded Sir James Turner's lodging. Though it was between eight and nine o'clock, that worthy, being unwell, was still in bed, but rose at once and went to the window.

Neilson and some others cried, 'You may have fair quarter.'

'I need no quarter,' replied Sir James; 'nor can I be a prisoner, seeing there is no war declared.' On being told, however, that he must either be a prisoner or die, he came down, and went into the street in his night-shirt. Here Gray showed himself very desirous of killing him, but he was overruled by Corsack. However, he was taken away a prisoner, Captain Gray mounting him on his own horse, though, as Turner naively remarks, 'there was good reason for it, for he mounted himself on a farre better one of mine.' A large coffer containing his clothes and money, together with all his papers, were taken away by the rebels. They robbed Master Chalmers, the Episcopalian minister of Dumfries, of his horse, drank the King's health at the market cross, and then left Dumfries. [92]

CHAPTER III—THE MARCH OF THE REBELS

'Stay, passenger, take notice what thou reads,

At Edinburgh lie our bodies, here our heads;

Our right hands stood at Lanark, these we want,

Because with them we signed the Covenant.'

Epitaph on a Tombstone at Hamilton. [93]

On Friday the 16th, Bailie Irvine of Dumfries came to the Council at Edinburgh, and gave information concerning this 'horrid rebellion.' In the absence of Rothes, Sharpe presided—much to the wrath of some members; and as he imagined his own safety endangered, his measures were most energetic. Dalzell was ordered away to the West, the guards round the city were doubled, officers and soldiers were forced to take the oath of allegiance, and all lodgers were commanded to give in their names. Sharpe, surrounded with all these guards and precautions, trembled—trembled as he trembled when the avengers of blood drew him from his chariot on Magus Muir,—for he knew how he had sold his trust, how he had betrayed his charge, and he felt that against him must their chiefest hatred be directed, against him their direst thunder-bolts be forged. But even in his fear the apostate Presbyterian was unrelenting, unpityingly harsh; he published in his manifesto no promise of pardon, no inducement to submission. He said, 'If you submit not you must die,' but never added, 'If you submit you may live!' [94a]

Meantime the insurgents proceeded on their way. At Carsphairn they were deserted by Captain Gray, who, doubtless in a fit of oblivion, neglected to leave behind him the coffer containing Sir James's money. Who he was is a mystery, unsolved by any historian; his papers were evidently forgeries—that, and his final flight, appear to indicate that he was an agent of the Royalists, for either the King or the Duke of York was heard to say, 'That, if he might have his wish, he would have them all turn rebels and go to arms.' [94b]

Upon the 18th day of the month they left Carsphairn and marched onwards.

Turner was always lodged by his captors at a good inn, frequently at the best of which their halting-place could boast. Here many visits were paid to him by the ministers and officers of the insurgent force. In his description of these interviews he displays a vein of satiric severity, admitting any kindness that was done to him with some qualifying souvenir of former harshness, and gloating over any injury, mistake, or folly, which it was his chance to suffer or to hear. He appears, notwithstanding all this, to have been on pretty good terms with his cruel 'phanaticks,' as the following extract sufficiently proves:

'Most of the foot were lodged about the church or churchyard, and order given to ring bells next morning for a sermon to be preached by Mr. Welch. Maxwell of Morith, and Major M'Cullough invited me to heare "that phanatick sermon" (for soe they merrilie called it). They said that preaching might prove an effectual meane to turne me, which they heartilie wished. I answered to them that I was under guards, and that if they intended to heare that sermon, it was probable I might likewise, for it was not like my guards wold goe to church and leave me alone at my lodgeings. Bot to what they said of my conversion, I said it wold be hard to turne a Turner. Bot because I founde them in a merrie humour, I said, if I did not come to heare Mr. Welch preach, then they might fine me in fortie shillings Scots, which was double the suome of what I had exacted from the phanatics.' [95]

This took place at Ochiltree, on the 22nd day of the month. The following is recounted by this personage with malicious glee, and certainly, if authentic, it is a sad proof of how chaff is mixed with wheat, and how ignorant, almost impious, persons were engaged in this movement; nevertheless we give it, for we wish to present with impartiality all the alleged facts to the reader:

'Towards the evening Mr. Robinsone and Mr. Crukshank gaue me a visite; I called for some ale purposelie to heare one of them blesse it. It fell Mr. Robinsone to seeke the blessing, who said one of the most bombastick graces that ever I heard in my life. He summoned God Allmightie very imperiouslie to be their secondarie (for that was his language). "And if," said he, "thou wilt not be our Secondarie, we will not fight for thee at all, for it is not our cause bot thy cause; and if thou wilt not fight for our cause and thy oune cause, then we are not obliged to fight for it. They say," said he, "that Dukes, Earles, and Lords are coming with the King's General against us, bot they shall be nothing bot a threshing to us." This grace did more fullie satisfie me of the folly and injustice of their cause, then the ale did quench my thirst.' [96a]

Frequently the rebels made a halt near some roadside alehouse, or in some convenient park, where Colonel Wallace, who had now taken the command, would review the horse and foot, during which time Turner was sent either into the alehouse or round the shoulder of the hill, to prevent him from seeing the disorders which were likely to arise. He was, at last, on the 25th day of the month, between Douglas and Lanark, permitted to behold their evolutions. 'I found their horse did consist of four hundreth and fortie, and the foot of five hundreth and upwards. . . . The horsemen were armed for most part with suord and pistoll, some onlie with suord. The foot with musket, pike, sith (scythe), forke, and suord; and some with suords great and long.' He admired much the proficiency of their cavalry, and marvelled how they had attained to it in so short a time. [96b]

At Douglas, which they had just left on the morning of this great wapinshaw, they were charged—awful picture of depravity!—with the theft of a silver spoon and a nightgown. Could it be expected that while the whole country swarmed with robbers of every description, such a rare opportunity for plunder should be lost by rogues—that among a thousand men, even though fighting for religion, there should not be one Achan in the camp? At Lanark a declaration was drawn up and signed by the chief rebels. In it occurs the following:

'The just sense whereof '—the sufferings of the country—'made us choose, rather to betake ourselves to the fields for self-defence, than to stay at home, burdened daily with the calamities of others, and tortured with the fears of our own approaching misery.' [97]

The whole body, too, swore the Covenant, to which ceremony the epitaph at the head of this chapter seems to refer.

A report that Dalzell was approaching drove them from Lanark to Bathgate, where, on the evening of Monday the 26th, the wearied army stopped. But at twelve o'clock the cry, which served them for a trumpet, of 'Horse! horse!' and 'Mount the prisoner!' resounded through the night-shrouded town, and called the peasants from their well-earned rest to toil onwards in their march. The wind howled fiercely over the moorland; a close, thick, wetting rain descended. Chilled to the bone, worn out with long fatigue, sinking to the knees in mire, onward they marched to destruction. One by one the weary peasants fell off from their ranks to sleep, and die in the rain-soaked moor, or to seek some house by the wayside wherein to hide till daybreak. One by one at first, then in gradually increasing numbers, at every shelter that was seen, whole troops left the waning squadrons, and rushed to hide themselves from the ferocity of the tempest. To right and left nought could be descried but the broad expanse of the moor, and the figures of their fellow-rebels, seen dimly through the murky night, plodding onwards through the sinking moss. Those who kept together—a miserable few—often halted to rest themselves, and to allow their lagging comrades to overtake them. Then onward they went again, still hoping for assistance, reinforcement, and supplies; onward again, through the wind, and the rain, and the darkness—onward to their defeat at Pentland, and their scaffold at Edinburgh. It was calculated that they lost one half of their army on that disastrous night-march.

Next night they reached the village of Colinton, four miles from Edinburgh, where they halted for the last time. [98]

CHAPTER IV—RULLION GREEN

'From Covenanters with uplifted hands,

From Remonstrators with associate bands,

Good Lord, deliver us!'

Royalist Rhyme, KIRKTON, p. 127.

Late on the fourth night of November, exactly twenty-four days before Rullion Green, Richard and George Chaplain, merchants in Haddington, beheld four men, clad like West-country Whigamores, standing round some object on the ground. It was at the two-mile cross, and within that distance from their homes. At last, to their horror, they discovered that the recumbent figure was a livid corpse, swathed in a blood-stained winding-sheet. [99] Many thought that this apparition was a portent of the deaths connected with the Pentland Rising.

On the morning of Wednesday, the 28th of November 1666, they left Colinton and marched to Rullion Green. There they arrived about sunset. The position was a strong one. On the summit of a bare, heathery spur of the Pentlands are two hillocks, and between them lies a narrow band of flat marshy ground. On the highest of the two mounds—that nearest the Pentlands, and on the left hand of the main body—was the greater part of the cavalry, under Major Learmont; on the other Barscob and the Galloway gentlemen; and in the centre Colonel Wallace and the weak, half-armed infantry. Their position was further strengthened by the depth of the valley below, and the deep chasm-like course of the Rullion Burn.

The sun, going down behind the Pentlands, cast golden lights and blue shadows on their snow-clad summits, slanted obliquely into the rich plain before them, bathing with rosy splendour the leafless, snow-sprinkled trees, and fading gradually into shadow in the distance. To the south, too, they beheld a deep-shaded amphitheatre of heather and bracken; the course of the Esk, near Penicuik, winding about at the foot of its gorge; the broad, brown expanse of Maw Moss; and, fading into blue indistinctness in the south, the wild heath-clad Peeblesshire hills. In sooth, that scene was fair, and many a yearning glance was cast over that peaceful evening scene from the spot where the rebels awaited their defeat; and when the fight was over, many a noble fellow lifted his head from the blood-stained heather to strive with darkening eyeballs to behold that landscape, over which, as over his life and his cause, the shadows of night and of gloom were falling and thickening.

It was while waiting on this spot that the fear-inspiring cry was raised: 'The enemy! Here come the enemy!'

Unwilling to believe their own doom—for our insurgents still hoped for success in some negotiations for peace which had been carried on at Colinton—they called out, 'They are some of our own.'

'They are too blacke' (i.e. numerous), 'fie! fie! for ground to draw up on,' cried Wallace, fully realising the want of space for his men, and proving that it was not till after this time that his forces were finally arranged. [101a]

79

First of all the battle was commenced by fifty Royalist horse sent obliquely across the hill to attack the left wing of the rebels. An equal number of Learmont's men met them, and, after a struggle, drove them back. The course of the Rullion Burn prevented almost all pursuit, and Wallace, on perceiving it, dispatched a body of foot to occupy both the burn and some ruined sheep-walls on the farther side.

Dalzell changed his position, and drew up his army at the foot of the hill, on the top of which were his foes. He then dispatched a mingled body of infantry and cavalry to attack Wallace's outpost, but they also were driven back. A third charge produced a still more disastrous effect, for Dalzell had to check the pursuit of his men by a reinforcement.

These repeated checks bred a panic in the Lieutenant-General's ranks, for several of his men flung down their arms. Urged by such fatal symptoms, and by the approaching night, he deployed his men, and closed in overwhelming numbers on the centre and right flank of the insurgent army. In the increasing twilight the burning matches of the firelocks, shimmering on barrel, halbert, and cuirass, lent to the approaching army a picturesque effect, like a huge, many-armed giant breathing flame into the darkness.

Placed on an overhanging hill, Welch and Semple cried aloud, 'The God of Jacob! The God of Jacob!' and prayed with uplifted hands for victory. [101b]

But still the Royalist troops closed in.

Captain John Paton was observed by Dalzell, who determined to capture him with his own hands. Accordingly he charged forward, presenting his pistols. Paton fired, but the balls hopped off Dalzell's buff coat and fell into his boot. With the superstition peculiar to his age, the Nonconformist concluded that his adversary was rendered bullet-proof by enchantment, and, pulling some small silver coins from his pocket, charged his pistol therewith. Dalzell, seeing this, and supposing, it is likely, that Paton was putting in larger balls, hid behind his servant, who was killed. [102]

Meantime the outposts were forced, and the army of Wallace was enveloped in the embrace of a hideous boa-constrictor—tightening, closing, crushing every semblance of life from the victim enclosed in his toils. The flanking parties of horse were forced in upon the centre, and though, as even Turner grants, they fought with desperation, a general flight was the result.

But when they fell there was none to sing their coronach or wail the death-wail over them. Those who sacrificed themselves for the peace, the liberty, and the religion of their fellow-countrymen, lay bleaching in the field of death for long, and when at last they were buried by charity, the peasants dug up their bodies, desecrated their graves, and cast them once more upon the open heath for the sorry value of their winding-sheets!

Inscription on stone at Rullion Green:

HERE

AND NEAR TO

THIS PLACE LYES THE

REVEREND MR JOHN CROOKSHANK

AND MR ANDREW MCCORMICK

MINISTERS OF THE GOSPEL AND

ABOUT FIFTY OTHER TRUE COVENANTED

PRESBYTERIANS WHO WERE

KILLED IN THIS PLACE IN THEIR OWN

INOCENT SELF DEFENCE AND DEFFENCE

OF THE COVENANTED

WORK OF REFORMATION BY

THOMAS DALZEEL OF BINS

UPON THE 28 OF NOVEMBER

1666. REV. 12. 11. ERECTED

SEPT. 28 1738.

Back of stone:

A Cloud of Witnesses lyes here,

Who for Christ's Interest did appear,

For to restore true Liberty,

O'erturnèd then by tyranny.

And by proud Prelats who did Rage

Against the Lord's Own heritage.

They sacrificed were for the laws

Of Christ their king, his noble cause.

These heroes fought with great renown;

By falling got the Martyr's crown. [103]

CHAPTER V—A RECORD OF BLOOD

'They cut his hands ere he was dead,

And after that struck of his head.

His blood under the altar cries

For vengeance on Christ's enemies.'

Epitaph on Tomb at Longcross of Clermont. [104]

Master Andrew Murray, an outed minister, residing in the Potterrow, on the morning after the defeat, heard the sounds of cheering and the march of many feet beneath his window. He gazed out. With colours flying, and with music sounding, Dalzell, victorious, entered Edinburgh. But his banners were dyed in blood, and a band of prisoners were marched within his ranks. The old man knew it all. That martial and triumphant strain was the death-knell of his friends and of their cause, the rust-hued spots upon the flags were the tokens of their courage and their death, and the prisoners were the miserable remnant spared from death in battle to die upon the scaffold. Poor old man! he had outlived all joy. Had he lived longer he would have seen increasing torment and increasing woe; he would have seen the clouds, then but gathering in mist, cast a more than midnight darkness over his native hills, and have fallen a victim to those bloody persecutions which, later, sent their red memorials to the sea by many a burn. By a merciful Providence all this was spared to him—he fell beneath the first blow; and ere four days had passed since Rullion Green, the aged minister of God was gathered to is fathers. [105a]

When Sharpe first heard of the rebellion, he applied to Sir Alexander Ramsay, the Provost, for soldiers to guard his house. Disliking their occupation, the soldiers gave him an ugly time of it. All the night through they kept up a continuous series of 'alarms and incursions,' 'cries of "Stand!" "Give fire!"' etc., which forced the prelate to flee to the Castle in the morning, hoping there to find the rest which was denied him at home. [105b] Now, however, when all danger to himself was past, Sharpe came out in his true colours, and scant was the justice likely to be shown to the foes of Scottish Episcopacy when the Primate was by. The prisoners were lodged in Haddo's Hole, a part of St. Giles' Cathedral, where, by the kindness of Bishop Wishart, to his credit be it spoken, they were amply supplied with food. [105c]

Some people urged, in the Council, that the promise of quarter which had been given on the field of battle should protect the lives of the miserable men. Sir John Gilmoure, the greatest lawyer, gave no opinion—certainly a suggestive circumstance—but Lord Lee declared that this would not interfere with their legal trial, 'so to bloody executions they went.' [105d] To the number of thirty they were condemned and executed; while two of them, Hugh M'Kail, a young minister, and Neilson of Corsack, were tortured with the boots.

The goods of those who perished were confiscated, and their bodies were dismembered and distributed to different parts of the country; 'the heads of Major M'Culloch and the two Gordons,' it was resolved, says Kirkton, 'should be pitched on the gate of Kirkcudbright; the two Hamiltons and Strong's head should be affixed at Hamilton, and Captain Arnot's sett on the Watter Gate at Edinburgh. The armes of all the ten, because they hade with uplifted hands renewed the Covenant at Lanark, were sent to the people of that town to expiate that crime, by placing these arms on the top of the prison.' [106] Among these was John Neilson, the Laird of Corsack, who saved Turner's life at Dumfries; in return for which service Sir James attempted, though without success, to get the poor man reprieved. One of the condemned died of his wounds between the day of condemnation and the day of execution. 'None of them,' says Kirkton, 'would save their life by taking the declaration and renouncing the Covenant, though it was offered to them. . . . But never men died in Scotland so much lamented by the people, not only spectators, but those in the country. When Knockbreck and his brother were turned over, they clasped each other in their armes, and so endured the pangs of death. When Humphrey Colquhoun died, he spoke not like an ordinary citizen, but like a heavenly minister, relating his comfortable Christian experiences, and called for his Bible, and laid it on his wounded arm, and read John iii. 8, and spoke upon it to the admiration of all. But most of all, when Mr. M'Kail died, there was such a lamentation as was never known in Scotland before; not one dry cheek upon all the street, or in all the numberless windows in the mercate place.' [107a]

The following passage from this speech speaks for itself and its author:

'Hereafter I will not talk with flesh and blood, nor think on the world's consolations. Farewell to all my friends, whose company hath been refreshful to me in my pilgrimage. I have done with the light of the sun and the moon; welcome eternal light, eternal life, everlasting love, everlasting praise, everlasting glory. Praise to Him that sits upon the throne, and to the Lamb for ever! Bless the Lord, O my soul, that hath pardoned all my iniquities in the blood of His Son, and healed all my diseases. Bless Him, O all ye His angels that excel in strength, ye ministers of His that do His pleasure. Bless the Lord, O my soul!' [107b]

After having ascended the gallows ladder he again broke forth in the following words of touching eloquence: 'And now I leave off to speak any more to creatures, and begin my intercourse with God, which shall never be broken off. Farewell father and mother, friends and relations! Farewell the world and all delights! Farewell meat and drink! Farewell sun, moon, and stars!—Welcome God and Father! Welcome sweet Jesus Christ, the Mediator of the new covenant! Welcome blessed Spirit of grace and God of all consolation! Welcome glory! Welcome eternal life! Welcome Death!' [107c]

At Glasgow, too, where some were executed, they caused the soldiers to beat the drums and blow the trumpets on their closing ears. Hideous refinement of revenge! Even the last words which drop from the lips of a dying man—words surely the most sincere and the most unbiassed which mortal mouth can utter—even these were looked upon as poisoned and as poisonous. 'Drown their last accents,' was the cry, 'lest they should lead the crowd to take their part, or at the least to mourn their doom!' [108a] But, after all, perhaps it was more merciful than one would think—unintentionally so, of course; perhaps the storm of harsh and fiercely jubilant noises, the clanging of trumpets, the rattling of drums, and the hootings and jeerings of an unfeeling mob, which were the last they heard on earth, might, when the mortal fight was over, when the river of death was passed, add tenfold sweetness to the hymning of the angels, tenfold peacefulness to the shores which they had reached.

Not content with the cruelty of these executions, some even of the peasantry, though these were confined to the shire of Mid-Lothian, pursued, captured, plundered, and murdered the miserable fugitives who fell in their way. One strange story have we of these times of blood and persecution: Kirkton the historian and popular tradition tell us alike of a flame which often would arise from the grave, in a moss near Carnwath, of some of those poor rebels: of how it crept along the ground; of how it covered the house of their murderer; and of how it scared him with its lurid glare.

Hear Daniel Defoe: [108b]

'If the poor people were by these insupportable violences made desperate, and driven to all the extremities of a wild despair, who can justly reflect on them when they read in the Word of God "That oppression makes a wise man mad"? And therefore were there no other original of the insurrection known by the name of the Rising of Pentland, it was nothing but what the intolerable oppressions of those times might have justified to all the world, nature having dictated to all people a right of defence when illegally and arbitrarily attacked in a manner not justifiable either by laws of nature, the laws of God, or the laws of the country.'

Bear this remonstrance of Defoe's in mind, and though it is the fashion of the day to jeer and to mock, to execrate and to contemn, the noble band of Covenanters—though the bitter laugh at their old-world religious views, the curl of the lip at their merits, and the chilling silence on their bravery and their determination, are but too rife through all society—be charitable to what was evil and honest to what was good about the Pentland insurgents, who fought for life and liberty, for country and religion, on the 28th of November 1666, now just two hundred years ago.

Edinburgh, *28th November* 1866.

THE DAY AFTER TO-MORROW

History is much decried; it is a tissue of errors, we are told, no doubt correctly; and rival historians expose each other's blunders with gratification. Yet the worst historian has a clearer view of the period he studies than the best of us can hope to form of that in which we live. The obscurest epoch is to-day; and that for a thousand reasons of inchoate tendency, conflicting report, and sheer mass and multiplicity of experience; but chiefly, perhaps, by reason of an insidious shifting of landmarks. Parties and ideas continually move, but not by measurable marches on a stable course; the political soil itself steals forth by imperceptible degrees, like a travelling glacier, carrying on its bosom not only political parties but their flag-posts and cantonments; so that what appears to be an eternal city founded on hills is but a flying island of Laputa. It is for this reason in particular that we are all becoming Socialists without knowing it; by which I would not in the least refer to the acute case of Mr. Hyndman and his horn-blowing supporters, sounding their trumps of a Sunday within the walls of our individualist Jericho—but to the stealthy change that has come over the spirit of Englishmen and English legislation. A little while ago, and we were still for liberty; 'crowd a few more thousands on the bench of Government,' we seemed to cry; 'keep her head direct on liberty, and we cannot help but come to port.' This is over; laisser faire declines in favour; our legislation grows authoritative, grows philanthropical, bristles with new duties and new penalties, and casts a spawn of inspectors, who now begin, note-book in hand, to darken the face of England. It may be right or wrong, we are not trying that; but one thing it is beyond doubt: it is Socialism in action, and the strange thing is that we scarcely know it.

Liberty has served us a long while, and it may be time to seek new altars. Like all other principles, she has been proved to be self-exclusive in the long run. She has taken wages besides (like all other virtues) and dutifully served Mammon; so that many things we were accustomed to admire as the benefits of freedom and common to all were truly benefits of wealth, and took their value from our neighbours' poverty. A few shocks of logic, a few disclosures (in the journalistic phrase) of what the freedom of manufacturers, landlords, or shipowners may imply for operatives, tenants, or seamen, and we not unnaturally begin to turn to that other pole of hope, beneficent tyranny. Freedom, to be desirable, involves kindness, wisdom, and all the virtues of the free; but the free man as we have seen him in action has been, as of yore, only the master of many helots; and the slaves are still ill-fed, ill-clad, ill-taught, ill-housed, insolently treated, and driven to their mines and workshops by the lash of famine. So much, in other men's affairs, we have begun to see clearly; we have begun to despair of virtue in these other men, and from our seat in Parliament begin to discharge upon them, thick as arrows, the host of our inspectors. The landlord has long shaken his head over the manufacturer; those who do business on land have lost all trust in the virtues of the shipowner; the professions look askance upon the retail traders and have even started their co-operative stores to ruin them; and from out the smoke-wreaths of Birmingham a finger has begun to write upon the wall the condemnation of the landlord. Thus, piece by piece, do we condemn each other, and yet not perceive the conclusion, that our whole estate is somewhat damnable. Thus, piece by piece, each acting against his neighbour, each sawing away the branch on which some other interest is seated, do we apply in detail our Socialistic remedies, and yet not perceive that we are all labouring together to bring in Socialism at large. A tendency so stupid and so selfish is like to prove invincible; and if Socialism be at all a practicable rule of life, there is every chance that our grand-children will see the day and taste the pleasures of existence in something far liker an ant-heap than any previous human polity. And this not in the least because of the voice of Mr. Hyndman or the horns of his followers; but by the mere glacier movement of the political soil, bearing forward on its bosom, apparently undisturbed, the proud camps of Whig and Tory. If Mr. Hyndman were a man of keen humour, which is far from my conception of his character, he might rest from his troubling and look on: the walls of Jericho begin already to crumble and dissolve. That great servile war, the Armageddon of money and numbers, to which we looked forward when young, becomes more and more unlikely; and we may rather look to see a peaceable and blindfold evolution, the work of dull men immersed in political tactics and dead to political results.

The principal scene of this comedy lies, of course, in the House of Commons; it is there, besides, that the details of this new evolution (if it proceed) will fall to be decided; so that the state of Parliament is not only diagnostic of the present but fatefully prophetic of the future. Well, we all know what Parliament is, and we are all ashamed of it. We may pardon it some faults, indeed, on the ground of Irish obstruction—a bitter trial, which it supports with notable good humour. But the excuse is merely local; it cannot apply to similar bodies in America and France; and what are we to say of these? President Cleveland's letter may serve as a picture of the one; a glance at almost any paper will convince us of the weakness of the other. Decay appears to have seized on the organ of popular government in every land; and this just at the moment when we begin to bring to it, as to an oracle of justice, the whole skein of our private affairs to be unravelled, and ask it, like a new Messiah, to take upon itself our frailties and play for us the part that should be played by our own virtues. For that, in few words, is the case. We cannot trust ourselves to behave with decency; we cannot trust our consciences; and the remedy proposed is to elect a round number of our neighbours, pretty much at random, and say to these: 'Be ye our conscience; make laws so wise, and continue from year to year to administer them so wisely, that they shall save us from ourselves and make us righteous and happy, world without end. Amen.' And who can look twice at the British Parliament and then seriously bring it such a task? I am not advancing this as an argument against Socialism: once again, nothing is further from my mind. There are great truths in Socialism, or no one, not even Mr. Hyndman, would be found to hold it; and if it came, and did one-tenth part of what it offers, I for one should make it welcome. But if it is to come, we may as well have some notion of what it will be like; and the first thing to grasp is that our new polity will be designed and administered (to put it courteously) with something short of inspiration. It will be made, or will grow, in a human parliament; and the one thing that will not very hugely change is human nature. The Anarchists think otherwise, from which it is only plain that they have not carried to the study of history the lamp of human sympathy.

Given, then, our new polity, with its new waggon-load of laws, what headmarks must we look for in the life? We chafe a good deal at that excellent thing, the income-tax, because it brings into our affairs the prying fingers, and exposes us to the tart words, of the official. The official, in all degrees, is already something of a terror to many of us. I would not willingly have to do with even a police-constable in any other spirit than that of kindness. I still remember in my dreams the eye-glass of a certain attaché at a certain embassy—an eyeglass that was a standing indignity to all on whom it looked; and my next most disagreeable remembrance is of a bracing, Republican postman in the city of San Francisco. I lived in that city among working folk, and what my neighbours accepted at the postman's hands—nay, what I took from him myself—it is still distasteful to recall. The bourgeois, residing in the upper parts of society, has but few opportunities of tasting this peculiar bowl; but about the income-tax, as I have said, or perhaps about a patent, or in the halls of an embassy at the hands of my friend of the eye-glass, he occasionally sets his lips to it; and he may thus imagine (if he has that faculty of imagination, without which most faculties are void) how it tastes to his poorer neighbours, who must drain it to the dregs. In every contact with authority, with their employer, with the police, with the School Board officer, in the hospital, or in the workhouse, they have equally the occasion to appreciate the light-hearted civility of the man in office; and as an experimentalist in several out-of-the-way provinces of life, I may say it has but to be felt to be appreciated. Well, this golden age of which we are speaking will be the golden age of officials. In all our concerns it will be their beloved duty to meddle, with what tact, with what obliging words, analogy will aid us to imagine. It is likely these gentlemen will be periodically elected; they will therefore have their turn of being underneath, which does not always sweeten men's conditions. The laws they will have to administer will be no clearer than those we know to-day, and the body which is to regulate their administration no wiser than the British Parliament. So that upon all hands we may look for a form of servitude most galling to the blood—servitude to many and changing masters, and for all the slights that accompany the rule of jack-in-office. And if the Socialistic programme be carried out with the least fulness, we shall have lost a thing, in most respects not much to be regretted, but as a moderator of oppression, a thing nearly invaluable—the newspaper. For the independent journal is a creature of capital and competition; it stands and falls with millionaires and railway bonds and all the abuses and glories of to-day; and as soon as the State has fairly taken its bent to authority and philanthropy, and laid the least touch on private property, the days of the independent journal are numbered. State railways may be good things and so may State bakeries; but a State newspaper will never be a very trenchant critic of the State officials.

But again, these officials would have no sinecure. Crime would perhaps be less, for some of the motives of crime we may suppose would pass away. But if Socialism were carried out with any fulness, there would be more contraventions. We see already new sins ringing up like mustard—School Board sins, factory sins, Merchant Shipping Act sins—none of which I would be thought to except against in particular, but all of which, taken together, show us that Socialism can be a hard master even in the beginning. If it go on to such heights as we hear proposed and lauded, if it come actually to its ideal of the ant-heap, ruled with iron justice, the number of new contraventions will be out of all proportion multiplied. Take the case of work alone. Man is an idle animal. He is at least as intelligent as the ant; but generations of advisers have in vain recommended him the ant's example. Of those who are found truly indefatigable in business, some are misers; some are the practisers of delightful industries, like gardening; some are students, artists, inventors, or discoverers, men lured forward by successive hopes; and the rest are those who live by games of skill or hazard—financiers, billiard-players, gamblers, and the like. But in unloved toils, even under the prick of necessity, no man is continually sedulous. Once eliminate the fear of starvation, once eliminate or bound the hope of riches, and we shall see plenty of skulking and malingering. Society will then be something not wholly unlike a cotton plantation in the old days; with cheerful, careless, demoralised slaves, with elected overseers, and, instead of the planter, a chaotic popular assembly. If the blood be purposeful and the soil strong, such a plantation may succeed, and be, indeed, a busy ant-heap, with full granaries and long hours of leisure. But even then I think the whip will be in the overseer's hands, and not in vain. For, when it comes to be a question of each man doing his own share or the rest doing more, prettiness of sentiment will be forgotten. To dock the skulker's food is not enough; many will rather eat haws and starve on petty pilferings than put their shoulder to the wheel for one hour daily. For such as these, then, the whip will be in the overseer's hand; and his own sense of justice and the superintendence of a chaotic popular assembly will be the only checks on its employment. Now, you may be an industrious man and a good citizen, and yet not love, nor yet be loved by, Dr. Fell the inspector. It is admitted by private soldiers that the disfavour of a sergeant is an evil not to be combated; offend the sergeant, they say, and in a brief while you will either be disgraced or have deserted. And the sergeant can no longer appeal to the lash. But if these things go on, we shall see, or our sons shall see, what it is to have offended an inspector.

This for the unfortunate. But with the fortunate also, even those whom the inspector loves, it may not be altogether well. It is concluded that in such a state of society, supposing it to be financially sound, the level of comfort will be high. It does not follow: there are strange depths of idleness in man, a too-easily-got sufficiency, as in the case of the sago-eaters, often quenching the desire for all besides; and it is possible that the men of the richest ant-heaps may sink even into squalor. But suppose they do not; suppose our tricksy instrument of human nature, when we play upon it this new tune, should respond kindly; suppose no one to be damped and none exasperated by the new conditions, the whole enterprise to be financially sound—a vaulting supposition—and all the inhabitants to dwell together in a golden mean of comfort: we have yet to ask ourselves if this be what man desire, or if it be what man will even deign to accept for a continuance. It is certain that man loves to eat, it is not certain that he loves that only or that best. He is supposed to love comfort; it is not a love, at least, that he is faithful to. He is supposed to love happiness; it is my contention that he rather loves excitement. Danger, enterprise, hope, the novel, the aleatory, are dearer to man than regular meals. He does not think so when he is hungry, but he thinks so again as soon as he is fed; and on the hypothesis of a successful ant-heap, he would never go hungry. It would be always after dinner in that society, as, in the land of the Lotos-eaters, it was always afternoon; and food, which, when we have it not, seems all-important, drops in our esteem, as soon as we have it, to a mere prerequisite of living.

That for which man lives is not the same thing for all individuals nor in all ages; yet it has a common base; what he seeks and what he must have is that which will seize and hold his attention. Regular meals and weatherproof lodgings will not do this long. Play in its wide sense, as the artificial induction of sensation, including all games and all arts, will, indeed, go far to keep him conscious of himself; but in the end he wearies for realities. Study or experiment, to some rare natures, is the unbroken pastime of a life. These are enviable natures; people shut in the house by sickness often bitterly envy them; but the commoner man cannot continue to exist upon such altitudes: his feet itch for physical adventure; his blood boils for physical dangers, pleasures, and triumphs; his fancy, the looker after new things, cannot continue to look for them in books and crucibles, but must seek them on the breathing stage of life. Pinches, buffets, the glow of hope, the shock of disappointment, furious contention with obstacles: these are the true elixir for all vital spirits, these are what they seek alike in their romantic enterprises and their unromantic dissipations. When they are taken in some pinch closer than the common, they cry, 'Catch me here again!' and sure enough you catch them there again—perhaps before the week is out. It is as old as Robinson Crusoe; as old as man. Our race has not been strained for all these ages through that sieve of dangers that we call Natural Selection, to sit down with patience in the tedium of safety; the voices of its fathers call it forth. Already in our society as it exists, the bourgeois is too much cottoned about for any zest in living; he sits in his parlour out of reach of any danger, often out of reach of any vicissitude but one of health; and there he yawns. If the people in the next villa took pot-shots at him, he might be killed indeed, but so long as he escaped he would find his blood oxygenated and his views of the world brighter. If Mr. Mallock, on his way to the publishers, should have his skirts pinned to a wall by a javelin, it would not occur to him—at least for several hours—to ask if life were worth living; and if such peril were a daily matter, he would ask it never more; he would have other things to think about, he would be living indeed—not lying in a box with cotton, safe, but immeasurably dull. The aleatory, whether it touch life, or fortune, or renown—whether we explore Africa or only toss for halfpence—that is what I conceive men to love best, and that is what we are seeking to exclude from men's existences. Of all forms of the aleatory, that which most commonly attends our working men—the danger of misery from want of work—is the least inspiriting: it does not whip the blood, it does not evoke the glory of contest; it is tragic, but it is passive; and yet, in so far as it is aleatory, and a peril sensibly touching them, it does truly season the men's lives. Of those who fail, I do not speak—despair should be sacred; but to those who even modestly succeed, the changes of their life bring interest: a job found, a shilling saved, a dainty earned, all these are wells of pleasure springing afresh for the successful poor; and it is not from these but from the villa-dweller that we hear complaints of the unworthiness of life. Much, then, as the average of the proletariat would gain in this new state of life, they would also lose a certain something, which would not be missed in the beginning, but would be missed progressively and progressively lamented. Soon there would be a looking back: there would be tales of the old world humming in young men's ears, tales of the tramp and the pedlar, and the hopeful emigrant. And in the stall-fed life of the successful ant-heap—with its regular meals, regular duties, regular pleasures, an even course of life, and fear excluded—the vicissitudes, delights, and havens of to-day will seem of epic breadth. This may seem a shallow observation; but the springs by which men are moved lie much on the surface. Bread, I believe, has always been considered first, but the circus comes close upon its heels. Bread we suppose to be given amply; the cry for circuses will be the louder, and if the life of our descendants be such as we have conceived, there are two beloved pleasures on which they will be likely to fall back: the pleasures of intrigue and of sedition.

In all this I have supposed the ant-heap to be financially sound. I am no economist, only a writer of fiction; but even as such, I know one thing that bears on the economic question—I know the imperfection of man's faculty for business. The Anarchists, who count some rugged elements of common sense among what seem to me their tragic errors, have said upon this matter all that I could wish to say, and condemned beforehand great economical polities. So far it is obvious that they are right; they may be right also in predicting a period of communal independence, and they may even be right in thinking that desirable. But the rise of communes is none the less the end of economic equality, just when we were told it was beginning. Communes will not be all equal in extent, nor in quality of soil, nor in growth of population; nor will the surplus produce of all be equally marketable. It will be the old story of competing interests, only with a new unit; and, as it appears to me, a new, inevitable danger. For the merchant and the manufacturer, in this new world, will be a sovereign commune; it is a sovereign power that will see its crops undersold, and its manufactures worsted in the market. And all the more dangerous that the sovereign power should be small. Great powers are slow to stir; national affronts, even with the aid of newspapers, filter slowly into popular consciousness; national losses are so unequally shared, that one part of the population will be counting its gains while another sits by a cold hearth. But in the sovereign commune all will be centralised and sensitive. When jealousy springs up, when (let us say) the commune of Poole has overreached the commune of Dorchester, irritation will run like quicksilver throughout the body politic; each man in Dorchester will have to suffer directly in his diet and his dress; even the secretary, who drafts the official correspondence, will sit down to his task embittered, as a man who has dined ill and may expect to dine worse; and thus a business difference between communes will take on much the same colour as a dispute between diggers in the lawless West, and will lead as directly to the arbitrament of blows. So that the establishment of the communal system will not only reintroduce all the injustices and heart-burnings of economic inequality, but will, in all human likelihood, inaugurate a world of hedgerow warfare. Dorchester will march on Poole, Sherborne on Dorchester, Wimborne on both; the waggons will be fired on as they follow the highway, the trains wrecked on the lines, the ploughman will go armed into the field of tillage; and if we have not a return of ballad literature, the local press at least will celebrate in a high vein the victory of Cerne Abbas or the reverse of Toller Porcorum. At least this will not be dull; when I was younger, I could have welcomed such a world with relief; but it is the New-Old with a vengeance, and irresistibly suggests the growth of military powers and the foundation of new empires.

COLLEGE PAPERS

CHAPTER I—EDINBURGH STUDENTS IN 1824

On the 2nd of January 1824 was issued the prospectus of the Lapsus Linguæ; or, the College Tatler; and on the 7th the first number appeared. On Friday the 2nd of April 'Mr. Tatler became speechless.' Its history was not all one success; for the editor (who applies to himself the words of Iago, 'I am nothing if I am not critical') overstepped the bounds of caution, and found himself seriously embroiled with the powers that were. There appeared in No. xvi. a most bitter satire upon Sir John Leslie, in which he was compared to Falstaff, charged with puffing himself, and very prettily censured for publishing only the first volume of a class-book, and making all purchasers pay for both. Sir John Leslie took up the matter angrily, visited Carfrae the publisher, and threatened him with an action, till he was forced to turn the hapless Lapsus out of doors. The maltreated periodical found shelter in the shop of Huie, Infirmary Street; and No. xvii. was duly issued from the new office. No. xvii. beheld Mr. Tatler's humiliation, in which, with fulsome apology and not very credible assurances of respect and admiration, he disclaims the article in question, and advertises a new issue of No. xvi. with all objectionable matter omitted. This, with pleasing euphemism, he terms in a later advertisement, 'a new and improved edition.' This was the only remarkable adventure of Mr. Tatler's brief existence; unless we consider as such a silly Chaldee manuscript in imitation of Blackwood, and a letter of reproof from a divinity student on the impiety of the same dull effusion. He laments the near approach of his end in pathetic terms. 'How shall we summon up sufficient courage,' says he, 'to look for the last time on our beloved little devil and his inestimable proof-sheet? How shall we be able to pass No. 14 Infirmary Street and feel that all its attractions are over? How shall we bid farewell for ever to that excellent man, with the long greatcoat, wooden leg and wooden board, who acts as our representative at the gate of Alma Mater?' But alas! he had no choice: Mr. Tatler, whose career, he says himself, had been successful, passed peacefully away, and has ever since dumbly implored 'the bringing home of bell and burial.'

Alter et idem. A very different affair was the Lapsus Linguæ from the Edinburgh University Magazine. The two prospectuses alone, laid side by side, would indicate the march of luxury and the repeal of the paper duty. The penny bi-weekly broadside of session 1828–4 was almost wholly dedicated to Momus. Epigrams, pointless letters, amorous verses, and University grievances are the continual burthen of the song. But Mr. Tatler was not without a vein of hearty humour; and his pages afford what is much better: to wit, a good picture of student life as it then was. The students of those polite days insisted on retaining their hats in the class-room. There was a cab-stance in front of the College; and 'Carriage Entrance' was posted above the main arch, on what the writer pleases to call 'coarse, unclassic boards.' The benches of the 'Speculative' then, as now, were red; but all other Societies (the 'Dialectic' is the only survivor) met downstairs, in some rooms of which it is pointedly said that 'nothing else could conveniently be made of them.' However horrible these dungeons may have been, it is certain that they were paid for, and that far too heavily for the taste of session 1823–4, which found enough calls upon its purse for porter and toasted cheese at Ambrose's, or cranberry tarts and ginger-wine at Doull's. Duelling was still a possibility; so much so that when two medicals fell to fisticuffs in Adam Square, it was seriously hinted that single combat would be the result. Last and most wonderful of all, Gall and Spurzheim were in every one's mouth; and the Law student, after having exhausted Byron's poetry and Scott's novels, informed the ladies of his belief in phrenology. In the present day he would dilate on 'Red as a rose is she,' and then mention that he attends Old Greyfriars', as a tacit claim to intellectual superiority. I do not know that the advance is much.

But Mr. Tatler's best performances were three short papers in which he hit off pretty smartly the idiosyncrasies of the 'Divinity,' the 'Medical,' and the 'Law' of session 1823–4. The fact that there was no notice of the 'Arts' seems to suggest that they stood in the same intermediate position as they do now—the epitome of student-kind. Mr. Tatler's satire is, on the whole, good-humoured, and has not grown superannuated in all its limbs. His descriptions may limp at some points, but there are certain broad traits that apply equally well to session 1870–1. He shows us the Divinity of the period—tall, pale, and slender—his collar greasy, and his coat bare about the seams—'his white neckcloth serving four days, and regularly turned the third'—'the rim of his hat deficient in wool'—and 'a weighty volume of theology under his arm.' He was the man to buy cheap 'a snuff-box, or a dozen of pencils, or a six-bladed knife, or a quarter of a hundred quills,' at any of the public sale-rooms. He was noted for cheap purchases, and for exceeding the legal tender in halfpence. He haunted 'the darkest and remotest corner of the Theatre Gallery.' He was to be seen issuing from 'aerial lodging-houses.' Withal, says mine author, 'there were many good points about him: he paid his landlady's bill, read his Bible, went twice to church on Sunday, seldom swore, was not often tipsy, and bought the Lapsus Linguæ.'

The Medical, again, 'wore a white greatcoat, and consequently talked loud'—(there is something very delicious in that consequently). He wore his hat on one side. He was active, volatile, and went to the top of Arthur's Seat on the Sunday forenoon. He was as quiet in a debating society as he was loud in the streets. He was reckless and imprudent: yesterday he insisted on your sharing a bottle of claret with him (and claret was claret then, before the cheap-and-nasty treaty), and to-morrow he asks you for the loan of a penny to buy the last number of the Lapsus.

The student of Law, again, was a learned man. 'He had turned over the leaves of Justinian's Institutes, and knew that they were written in Latin. He was well acquainted with the title-page of Blackstone's Commentaries, and argal (as the gravedigger in Hamlet says) he was not a person to be laughed at.' He attended the Parliament House in the character of a critic, and could give you stale sneers at all the celebrated speakers. He was the terror of essayists at the Speculative or the Forensic. In social qualities he seems to have stood unrivalled. Even in the police-office we find him shining with undiminished lustre. 'If a Charlie should find him rather noisy at an untimely hour, and venture to take him into custody, he appears next morning like a Daniel come to judgment. He opens his mouth to speak, and the divine precepts

98

of unchanging justice and Scots law flow from his tongue. The magistrate listens in amazement, and fines him only a couple of guineas.'

Such then were our predecessors and their College Magazine. Barclay, Ambrose, Young Amos, and Fergusson were to them what the Café, the Rainbow, and Rutherford's are to us. An hour's reading in these old pages absolutely confuses us, there is so much that is similar and so much that is different; the follies and amusements are so like our own, and the manner of frolicking and enjoying are so changed, that one pauses and looks about him in philosophic judgment. The muddy quadrangle is thick with living students; but in our eyes it swarms also with the phantasmal white greatcoats and tilted hats of 1824. Two races meet: races alike and diverse. Two performances are played before our eyes; but the change seems merely of impersonators, of scenery, of costume. Plot and passion are the same. It is the fall of the spun shilling whether seventy-one or twenty-four has the best of it.

In a future number we hope to give a glance at the individualities of the present, and see whether the cast shall be head or tail—whether we or the readers of the Lapsus stand higher in the balance.

CHAPTER II—THE MODERN STUDENT CONSIDERED GENERALLY

We have now reached the difficult portion of our task. Mr. Tatler, for all that we care, may have been as virulent as he liked about the students of a former; but for the iron to touch our sacred selves, for a brother of the Guild to betray its most privy infirmities, let such a Judas look to himself as he passes on his way to the Scots Law or the Diagnostic, below the solitary lamp at the corner of the dark quadrangle. We confess that this idea alarms us. We enter a protest. We bind ourselves over verbally to keep the peace. We hope, moreover, that having thus made you secret to our misgivings, you will excuse us if we be dull, and set that down to caution which you might before have charged to the account of stupidity.

The natural tendency of civilisation is to obliterate those distinctions which are the best salt of life. All the fine old professional flavour in language has evaporated. Your very gravedigger has forgotten his avocation in his electorship, and would quibble on the Franchise over Ophelia's grave, instead of more appropriately discussing the duration of bodies under ground. From this tendency, from this gradual attrition of life, in which everything pointed and characteristic is being rubbed down, till the whole world begins to slip between our fingers in smooth undistinguishable sands, from this, we say, it follows that we must not attempt to join Mr. Taller in his simple division of students into Law, Divinity, and Medical. Nowadays the Faculties may shake hands over their follies; and, like Mrs. Frail and Mrs. Foresight (in Love for Love) they may stand in the doors of opposite class-rooms, crying: 'Sister, Sister—Sister everyway!' A few restrictions, indeed, remain to influence the followers of individual branches of study. The Divinity, for example, must be an avowed believer; and as this, in the present day, is unhappily considered by many as a confession of weakness, he is fain to choose one of two ways of gilding the distasteful orthodox bolus. Some swallow it in a thin jelly of metaphysics; for it is even a credit to believe in God on the evidence of some crack-jaw philosopher, although it is a decided slur to believe in Him on His own authority. Others again (and this we think the worst method), finding German grammar a somewhat dry morsel, run their own little heresy as a proof of independence; and deny one of the cardinal doctrines that they may hold the others without being laughed at.

Besides, however, such influences as these, there is little more distinction between the faculties than the traditionary ideal, handed down through a long sequence of students, and getting rounder and more featureless at each successive session. The plague of uniformity has descended on the College. Students (and indeed all sorts and conditions of men) now require their faculty and character hung round their neck on a placard, like the scenes in Shakespeare's theatre. And in the midst of all this weary sameness, not the least common feature is the gravity of every face. No more does the merry medical run eagerly in the clear winter morning up the rugged sides of Arthur's Seat, and hear the church bells begin and thicken and die away below him among the gathered smoke of the city. He will not break Sunday to so little purpose. He no longer finds pleasure in the mere output of his surplus energy. He husbands his strength, and lays out walks, and reading, and amusement with deep consideration, so that he may get as much work and pleasure out of his body as he can, and waste none of his energy on mere impulse, or such flat enjoyment as an excursion in the country.

See the quadrangle in the interregnum of classes, in those two or three minutes when it is full of passing students, and we think you will admit that, if we have not made it 'an habitation of dragons,' we have at least transformed it into 'a court for owls.' Solemnity broods heavily over the enclosure; and wherever you seek it, you will find a dearth of merriment, an absence of real youthful enjoyment. You might as well try

'To move wild laughter in the throat of death'

as to excite any healthy stir among the bulk of this staid company.

The studious congregate about the doors of the different classes, debating the matter of the lecture, or comparing note-books. A reserved rivalry sunders them. Here are some deep in Greek particles: there, others are already inhabitants of that land

'Where entity and quiddity,

'Like ghosts of defunct bodies fly—

Where Truth in person does appear

Like words congealed in northern air.'

But none of them seem to find any relish for their studies—no pedantic love of this subject or that lights up their eyes—science and learning are only means for a livelihood, which they have considerately embraced and which they solemnly pursue. 'Labour's pale priests,' their lips seem incapable of laughter, except in the way of polite recognition of professorial wit. The stains of ink are chronic on their meagre fingers. They walk like Saul among the asses.

The dandies are not less subdued. In 1824 there was a noisy dapper dandyism abroad. Vulgar, as we should now think, but yet genial—a matter of white greatcoats and loud voices—strangely different from the stately frippery that is rife at present. These men are out of their element in the quadrangle. Even the small remains of boisterous humour, which still clings to any collection of young men, jars painfully on their morbid sensibilities; and they beat a hasty retreat to resume their perfunctory march along Princes Street. Flirtation is to them a great social duty, a painful obligation, which they perform on every occasion in the same chill official manner, and with the same commonplace advances, the same dogged observance of traditional behaviour. The shape of their raiment is a burden almost greater than they can bear, and they halt in their walk to preserve the due adjustment of their trouser-knees, till one would fancy he had mixed in a procession of Jacobs. We speak, of course, for ourselves; but we would as soon associate with a herd of sprightly apes as with these gloomy modern beaux. Alas, that our Mirabels, our Valentines, even our Brummels, should have left their mantles upon nothing more amusing!

Nor are the fast men less constrained. Solemnity, even in dissipation, is the order of the day; and they go to the devil with a perverse seriousness, a systematic rationalism of wickedness that would have surprised the simpler sinners of old. Some of these men whom we see gravely conversing on the steps have but a slender acquaintance with each other. Their intercourse consists principally of mutual bulletins of depravity; and, week after week, as they meet they reckon up their items of transgression, and give an abstract of their downward progress for approval and encouragement. These folk form a freemasonry of their own. An oath is the shibboleth of their sinister fellowship. Once they hear a man swear, it is wonderful how their tongues loosen and their bashful spirits take enlargement, under the consciousness of brotherhood. There is no folly, no pardoning warmth of temper about them; they are as steady-going and systematic in their own way as the studious in theirs.

Not that we are without merry men. No. We shall not be ungrateful to those, whose grimaces, whose ironical laughter, whose active feet in the 'College Anthem' have beguiled so many weary hours and added a pleasant variety to the strain of close attention. But even these are too evidently professional in their antics. They go about cogitating puns and inventing tricks. It is their vocation, Hal. They are the gratuitous jesters of the class-room; and, like the clown when he leaves the stage, their merriment too often sinks as the bell rings the hour of liberty, and they pass forth by the Post-Office, grave and sedate, and meditating fresh gambols for the morrow.

This is the impression left on the mind of any observing student by too many of his fellows. They seem all frigid old men; and one pauses to think how such an unnatural state of matters is produced. We feel inclined to blame for it the unfortunate absence of University feeling which is so marked a characteristic of our Edinburgh students. Academical interests are so few and far between—students, as students, have so little in common, except a peevish rivalry—there is such an entire want of broad college sympathies and ordinary college friendships, that we fancy that no University in the kingdom is in so poor a plight. Our system is full of anomalies. A, who cut B whilst he was a shabby student, curries sedulously up to him and cudgels his memory for anecdotes about him when he becomes the great so-and-so. Let there be an end of this shy, proud reserve on the one hand, and this shuddering fine ladyism on the other; and we think we shall find both ourselves and the College bettered. Let it be a sufficient reason for intercourse that two men sit together on the same benches. Let the great A be held excused for nodding to the shabby B in Princes Street, if he can say, 'That fellow is a student.' Once this could be brought about, we think you would find the whole heart of the University beat faster. We think you would find a fusion among the students, a growth of common feelings, an increasing sympathy between class and class, whose influence (in such a heterogeneous company as ours) might be of incalculable value in all branches of politics and social progress. It would do more than this. If we could find some method of making the University a real mother to her sons—something beyond a building of class-rooms, a Senatus and a lottery of somewhat shabby prizes—we should strike a death-blow at the constrained and unnatural attitude of our Society. At present we are not a united body, but a loose gathering of individuals, whose inherent attraction is allowed to condense them into little knots and coteries. Our last snowball riot read us a plain lesson on our condition. There was no party spirit—no unity of interests. A few, who were mischievously inclined, marched off to the College of Surgeons in a pretentious file; but even before they reached their destination the feeble inspiration had died out in many, and their numbers were sadly thinned. Some followed strange gods in the direction of Drummond Street, and others slunk back to meek good-boyism at the feet of the Professors. The same is visible in better things. As you send a man to an English University that he may have his prejudices rubbed off, you might send him to Edinburgh that he may have them ingrained—rendered indelible—fostered by sympathy into living principles of his spirit. And the reason of it is quite plain. From this absence of University feeling it comes that a man's friendships are always the direct and immediate results of these very prejudices. A common weakness is the best master of ceremonies in our quadrangle: a mutual vice is the readiest introduction. The studious associate with the studious alone—the dandies with the dandies. There is nothing to force them to rub shoulders with the others; and so they grow day by day more wedded to their own original opinions and affections. They see through the same spectacles continually. All broad sentiments, all real catholic humanity expires; and the mind gets gradually stiffened into one position—becomes so habituated to a contracted atmosphere, that it shudders and withers under the least draught of the free air that circulates in the general field of mankind.

Specialism in Society then is, we think, one cause of our present state. Specialism in study is another. We doubt whether this has ever been a good thing since the world began; but we are sure it is much worse now than it was. Formerly, when a man became a specialist, it was out of affection for his subject. With a somewhat grand devotion he left all the world of Science to follow his true love; and he contrived to find that strange pedantic interest which inspired the man who

> 'Settled Hoti's business—let it be—
>
> Properly based Oun—
>
> Gave us the doctrine of the enclitic De,
>
> Dead from the waist down.'

Nowadays it is quite different. Our pedantry wants even the saving clause of Enthusiasm. The election is now matter of necessity and not of choice. Knowledge is now too broad a field for your Jack-of-all-Trades; and, from beautifully utilitarian reasons, he makes his choice, draws his pen through a dozen branches of study, and behold—John the Specialist. That this is the way to be wealthy we shall not deny; but we hold that it is not the way to be healthy or wise. The whole mind becomes narrowed and circumscribed to one 'punctual spot' of knowledge. A rank unhealthy soil breeds a harvest of prejudices. Feeling himself above others in his one little branch—in the classification of toadstools, or Carthaginian history—he waxes great in his own eyes and looks down on others. Having all his sympathies educated in one way, they die out in every other; and he is apt to remain a peevish, narrow, and intolerant bigot. Dilettante is now a term of reproach; but there is a certain form of dilettantism to which no one can object. It is this that we want among our students. We wish them to abandon no subject until they have seen and felt its merit—to act under a general interest in all branches of knowledge, not a commercial eagerness to excel in one.

In both these directions our sympathies are constipated. We are apostles of our own caste and our own subject of study, instead of being, as we should, true men and loving students. Of course both of these could be corrected by the students themselves; but this is nothing to the purpose: it is more important to ask whether the Senatus or the body of alumni could do nothing towards the growth of better feeling and wider sentiments. Perhaps in another paper we may say something upon this head.

One other word, however, before we have done. What shall we be when we grow really old? Of yore, a man was thought to lay on restrictions and acquire new deadweight of mournful experience with every year, till he looked back on his youth as the very summer of impulse and freedom. We please ourselves with thinking that it cannot be so with us. We would fain hope that, as we have begun in one way, we may end in another; and that when we are in fact the octogenarians that we seem at present, there shall be no merrier men on earth. It is pleasant to picture us, sunning ourselves in Princes Street of a morning, or chirping over our evening cups, with all the merriment that we wanted in youth.

CHAPTER III—DEBATING SOCIETIES

A debating society is at first somewhat of a disappointment. You do not often find the youthful Demosthenes chewing his pebbles in the same room with you; or, even if you do, you will probably think the performance little to be admired. As a general rule, the members speak shamefully ill. The subjects of debate are heavy; and so are the fines. The Ballot Question—oldest of dialectic nightmares—is often found astride of a somnolent sederunt. The Greeks and Romans, too, are reserved as sort of general-utility men, to do all the dirty work of illustration; and they fill as many functions as the famous waterfall scene at the 'Princess's,' which I found doing duty on one evening as a gorge in Peru, a haunt of German robbers, and a peaceful vale in the Scottish borders. There is a sad absence of striking argument or real lively discussion. Indeed, you feel a growing contempt for your fellow-members; and it is not until you rise yourself to hawk and hesitate and sit shamefully down again, amid eleemosynary applause, that you begin to find your level and value others rightly. Even then, even when failure has damped your critical ardour, you will see many things to be laughed at in the deportment of your rivals.

Most laughable, perhaps, are your indefatigable strivers after eloquence. They are of those who 'pursue with eagerness the phantoms of hope,' and who, since they expect that 'the deficiencies of last sentence will be supplied by the next,' have been recommended by Dr. Samuel Johnson to 'attend to the History of Rasselas, Prince of Abyssinia.' They are characterised by a hectic hopefulness. Nothing damps them. They rise from the ruins of one abortive sentence, to launch forth into another with unabated vigour. They have all the manner of an orator. From the tone of their voice, you would expect a splendid period—and lo! a string of broken-backed, disjointed clauses, eked out with stammerings and throat-clearings. They possess the art (learned from the pulpit) of rounding an uneuphonious sentence by dwelling on a single syllable—of striking a balance in a top-heavy period by lengthening out a word into a melancholy quaver. Withal, they never cease to hope. Even at last, even when they have exhausted all their ideas, even after the would-be peroration has finally refused to perorate, they remain upon their feet with their mouths open, waiting for some further inspiration, like Chaucer's widow's son in the dung-hole, after

'His throat was kit unto the nekké bone,'

in vain expectation of that seed that was to be laid upon his tongue, and give him renewed and clearer utterance.

These men may have something to say, if they could only say it—indeed they generally have; but the next class are people who, having nothing to say, are cursed with a facility and an unhappy command of words, that makes them the prime nuisances of the society they affect. They try to cover their absence of matter by an unwholesome vitality of delivery. They look triumphantly round the room, as if courting applause, after a torrent of diluted truism. They talk in a circle, harping on the same dull round of argument, and returning again and again to the same remark with the same sprightliness, the same irritating appearance of novelty.

After this set, any one is tolerable; so we shall merely hint at a few other varieties. There is your man who is pre-eminently conscientious, whose face beams with sincerity as he opens on the negative, and who votes on the affirmative at the end, looking round the room with an air of chastened pride. There is also the irrelevant speaker, who rises, emits a joke or two, and then sits down again, without ever attempting to tackle the subject of debate. Again, we have men who ride pick-a-back on their family reputation, or, if their family have none, identify themselves with some well-known statesman, use his opinions, and lend him their patronage on all occasions. This is a dangerous plan, and serves oftener, I am afraid, to point a difference than to adorn a speech.

But alas! a striking failure may be reached without tempting Providence by any of these ambitious tricks. Our own stature will be found high enough for shame. The success of three simple sentences lures us into a fatal parenthesis in the fourth, from whose shut brackets we may never disentangle the thread of our discourse. A momentary flush tempts us into a quotation; and we may be left helpless in the middle of one of Pope's couplets, a white film gathering before our eyes, and our kind friends charitably trying to cover our disgrace by a feeble round of applause. Amis lecteurs, this is a painful topic. It is possible that we too, we, the 'potent, grave, and reverend' editor, may have suffered these things, and drunk as deep as any of the cup of shameful failure. Let us dwell no longer on so delicate a subject.

In spite, however, of these disagreeables, I should recommend any student to suffer them with Spartan courage, as the benefits he receives should repay him an hundredfold for them all. The life of the debating society is a handy antidote to the life of the classroom and quadrangle. Nothing could be conceived more excellent as a weapon against many of those peccant humours that we have been railing against in the jeremiad of our last 'College Paper'— particularly in the field of intellect. It is a sad sight to see our heather-scented students, our boys of seventeen, coming up to College with determined views—roués in speculation—having gauged the vanity of philosophy or learned to shun it as the middle-man of heresy—a company of determined, deliberate opinionists, not to be moved by all the sleights of logic. What have such men to do with study? If their minds are made up irrevocably, why burn the 'studious lamp' in search of further confirmation? Every set opinion I hear a student deliver I feel a certain lowering of my regard. He who studies, he who is yet employed in groping for his premises, should keep his mind fluent and sensitive, keen to mark flaws, and willing to surrender untenable positions. He should keep himself teachable, or cease the expensive farce of being taught. It is to further this docile spirit that we desire to press the claims of debating societies. It is as a means of melting down this museum of premature petrifactions into living and impressionable soul that we insist on their utility. If we could once prevail on our students to feel no shame in avowing an uncertain attitude towards any subject, if we could teach them that it was unnecessary for every lad to have his opinionette on every topic, we should have gone a far way towards bracing the intellectual tone of the coming race of thinkers; and this it is which debating societies are so well fitted to perform.

We there meet people of every shade of opinion, and make friends with them. We are taught to rail against a man the whole session through, and then hob-a-nob with him at the concluding entertainment. We find men of talent far exceeding our own, whose conclusions are widely different from ours; and we are thus taught to distrust ourselves. But the best means of all towards catholicity is that wholesome rule which some folk are most inclined to condemn—I mean the law of obliged speeches. Your senior member commands; and you must take the affirmative or the negative, just as suits his best convenience. This tends to the most perfect liberality. It is no good hearing the arguments of an opponent, for in good verity you rarely follow them; and even if you do take the trouble to listen, it is merely in a captious search for weaknesses. This is proved, I fear, in every debate; when you hear each speaker arguing out his own prepared spécialité (he never intended speaking, of course, until some remarks of, etc.), arguing out, I say, his own coached-up subject without the least attention to what has gone before, as utterly at sea about the drift of his adversary's speech as Panurge when he argued with Thaumaste, and merely linking his own prelection to the last by a few flippant criticisms. Now, as the rule stands, you are saddled with the side you disapprove, and so you are forced, by regard for your own fame, to argue out, to feel with, to elaborate completely, the case as it stands against yourself; and what a fund of wisdom do you not turn up in this idle digging of the vineyard! How many new difficulties take form before your eyes? how many superannuated arguments cripple finally into limbo, under the glance of your enforced eclecticism!

Nor is this the only merit of Debating Societies. They tend also to foster taste, and to promote friendship between University men. This last, as we have had occasion before to say, is the great requirement of our student life; and it will therefore be no waste of time if we devote a paragraph to this subject in its connection with Debating Societies. At present they partake too much of the nature of a clique. Friends propose friends, and mutual friends second them, until the society degenerates into a sort of family party. You may confirm old acquaintances, but you can rarely make new ones. You find yourself in the atmosphere of your own daily intercourse. Now, this is an unfortunate circumstance, which it seems to me might readily be rectified. Our Principal has shown himself so friendly towards all College improvements that I cherish the hope of seeing shortly realised a certain suggestion, which is not a new one with me, and which must often have been proposed and canvassed heretofore—I mean, a real University Debating Society, patronised by the Senatus, presided over by the Professors, to which every one might gain ready admittance on sight of his matriculation ticket, where it would be a favour and not a necessity to speak, and where the obscure student might have another object for attendance besides the mere desire to save his fines: to wit, the chance of drawing on himself the favourable consideration of his teachers. This would be merely following in the good tendency, which has been so noticeable during all this session, to increase and multiply student societies and clubs of every sort. Nor would it be a matter of much difficulty. The united societies would form a nucleus: one of the class-rooms at first, and perhaps afterwards the great hall above the library, might be the place of meeting. There would be no want of attendance or enthusiasm, I am sure; for it is a very different thing to speak under the bushel of a private club on the one hand, and, on the other, in a public place, where a happy period or a subtle argument may do the speaker permanent service in after life. Such a club might end, perhaps, by rivalling the 'Union' at Cambridge or the 'Union' at Oxford.

CHAPTER IV—THE PHILOSOPHY OF UMBRELLAS [151]

It is wonderful to think what a turn has been given to our whole Society by the fact that we live under the sign of Aquarius—that our climate is essentially wet. A mere arbitrary distinction, like the walking-swords of yore, might have remained the symbol of foresight and respectability, had not the raw mists and dropping showers of our island pointed the inclination of Society to another exponent of those virtues. A ribbon of the Legion of Honour or a string of medals may prove a person's courage; a title may prove his birth; a professorial chair his study and acquirement; but it is the habitual carriage of the umbrella that is the stamp of Respectability. The umbrella has become the acknowledged index of social position.

Robinson Crusoe presents us with a touching instance of the hankering after them inherent in the civilised and educated mind. To the superficial, the hot suns of Juan Fernandez may sufficiently account for his quaint choice of a luxury; but surely one who had borne the hard labour of a seaman under the tropics for all these years could have supported an excursion after goats or a peaceful constitutional arm in arm with the nude Friday. No, it was not this: the memory of a vanished respectability called for some outward manifestation, and the result was—an umbrella. A pious castaway might have rigged up a belfry and solaced his Sunday mornings with the mimicry of church-bells; but Crusoe was rather a moralist than a pietist, and his leaf-umbrella is as fine an example of the civilised mind striving to express itself

110

under adverse circumstances as we have ever met with.

It is not for nothing, either, that the umbrella has become the very foremost badge of modern civilisation—the Urim and Thummim of respectability. Its pregnant symbolism has taken its rise in the most natural manner. Consider, for a moment, when umbrellas were first introduced into this country, what manner of men would use them, and what class would adhere to the useless but ornamental cane. The first, without doubt, would be the hypochondriacal, out of solicitude for their health, or the frugal, out of care for their raiment; the second, it is equally plain, would include the fop, the fool, and the Bobadil. Any one acquainted with the growth of Society, and knowing out of what small seeds of cause are produced great revolutions, and wholly new conditions of intercourse, sees from this simple thought how the carriage of an umbrella came to indicate frugality, judicious regard for bodily welfare, and scorn for mere outward adornment, and, in one word, all those homely and solid virtues implied in the term respectability. Not that the umbrella's costliness has nothing to do with its great influence. Its possession, besides symbolising (as we have already indicated) the change from wild Esau to plain Jacob dwelling in tents, implies a certain comfortable provision of fortune. It is not every one that can expose twenty-six shillings' worth of property to so many chances of loss and theft. So strongly do we feel on this point, indeed, that we are almost inclined to consider all who possess really well-conditioned umbrellas as worthy of the Franchise. They have a qualification standing in their lobbies; they carry a sufficient stake in the common-weal below their arm. One who bears with him an umbrella—such a complicated structure of whalebone, of silk, and of cane, that it becomes a very microcosm of modern industry—is necessarily a man of peace. A half-crown cane may be applied to an offender's head on a very moderate provocation; but a six-and-twenty shilling silk is a possession too precious to be adventured in the shock of war.

These are but a few glances at how umbrellas (in the general) came to their present high estate. But the true Umbrella-Philosopher meets with far stranger applications as he goes about the streets.

Umbrellas, like faces, acquire a certain sympathy with the individual who carries them: indeed, they are far more capable of betraying his trust; for whereas a face is given to us so far ready made, and all our power over it is in frowning, and laughing, and grimacing, during the first three or four decades of life, each umbrella is selected from a whole shopful, as being most consonant to the purchaser's disposition. An undoubted power of diagnosis rests with the practised Umbrella-Philosopher. O you who lisp, and amble, and change the fashion of your countenances—you who conceal all these, how little do you think that you left a proof of your weakness in our umbrella-stand—that even now, as you shake out the folds to meet the thickening snow, we read in its ivory handle the outward and visible sign of your snobbery, or from the exposed gingham of its cover detect, through coat and waistcoat, the hidden hypocrisy of the 'dickey'! But alas! even the umbrella is no certain criterion. The falsity and the folly of the human race have degraded that graceful symbol to the ends of dishonesty; and while some umbrellas, from carelessness in selection, are not strikingly characteristic (for it is only in what a man loves that he displays his real nature), others, from certain prudential motives, are chosen directly opposite to the person's disposition. A mendacious umbrella is a sign of great moral degradation. Hypocrisy naturally shelters itself below a silk; while the fast youth goes to visit his religious friends armed with the decent and reputable gingham. May it not be said of the bearers of these inappropriate umbrellas that they go about the streets 'with a lie in their right hand'?

The kings of Siam, as we read, besides having a graduated social scale of umbrellas (which was a good thing), prevented the great bulk of their subjects from having any at all, which was certainly a bad thing. We should be sorry to believe that this Eastern legislator was a fool—the idea of an aristocracy of umbrellas is too philosophic to have originated in a nobody—and we have accordingly taken exceeding pains to find out the reason of this harsh restriction. We think we have succeeded; but, while admiring the principle at which he aimed, and while cordially recognising in the Siamese potentate the only man before ourselves who had taken a real grasp of the umbrella, we must be allowed to point out how unphilosophically the great man acted in this particular. His object, plainly, was to prevent any unworthy persons from bearing the sacred symbol of domestic virtues. We cannot excuse his limiting these virtues to the circle of his court. We must only remember that such was the feeling of the age in which he lived. Liberalism had not yet raised the war-cry of the working classes. But here was his mistake: it was a needless regulation. Except in a very few cases of hypocrisy joined to a powerful intellect, men, not by nature umbrellarians, have tried again and again to become so by art, and yet have failed—have expended their patrimony in the purchase of umbrella after umbrella, and yet have systematically lost them, and have finally, with contrite spirits and shrunken purses, given up their vain struggle, and relied on theft and borrowing for the remainder of their lives. This is the most remarkable fact that we have had occasion to notice; and yet we challenge the candid reader to call it in question. Now, as there cannot be any moral selection in a mere dead piece of furniture— as the umbrella cannot be supposed to have an affinity for individual men equal and reciprocal to that which men certainly feel toward individual umbrellas—we took the trouble of consulting a scientific friend as to whether there was any possible physical explanation of the phenomenon. He was unable to supply a plausible theory, or even hypothesis; but we extract from his letter the following interesting passage relative to the physical peculiarities of umbrellas: 'Not the least important, and by far the most curious property of the umbrella, is the energy which it displays in affecting the atmospheric strata. There is no fact in meteorology better established—indeed, it is almost the only one on which meteorologists are agreed—than that the carriage of an umbrella produces desiccation of the air; while if it be left at home, aqueous vapour is largely produced, and is soon deposited in the form of rain. No theory,' my friend continues, 'competent to explain this hygrometric law has been given (as far as I am aware) by Herschel, Dove, Glaisher, Tait, Buchan, or any other writer; nor do I pretend to supply the defect. I venture, however, to throw out the conjecture that it will be ultimately found to belong to the same class of natural laws as that agreeable to which a slice of toast always descends with the buttered surface downwards.'

But it is time to draw to a close. We could expatiate much longer upon this topic, but want of space constrains us to leave unfinished these few desultory remarks—slender contributions towards a subject which has fallen sadly backward, and which, we grieve to say, was better understood by the king of Siam in 1686 than by all the philosophers of to-day. If, however, we have awakened in any rational mind an interest in the symbolism of umbrellas—in any generous heart a more complete sympathy with the dumb companion of his daily walk—or in any grasping spirit a pure notion of respectability strong enough to make him expend his six-and-twenty shillings—we shall have deserved well of the world, to say nothing of the many industrious persons employed in the manufacture of the article.

CHAPTER V—THE PHILOSOPHY OF NOMENCLATURE

'How many Cæsars and Pompeys, by mere inspirations of the names, have been rendered worthy of them? And how many are there, who might have done exceeding well in the world, had not their characters and spirits been totally depressed and Nicodemus'd into nothing?'— Tristram Shandy, vol. i. chap xix.

Such were the views of the late Walter Shandy, Esq., Turkey merchant. To the best of my belief, Mr. Shandy is the first who fairly pointed out the incalculable influence of nomenclature upon the whole life—who seems first to have recognised the one child, happy in an heroic appellation, soaring upwards on the wings of fortune, and the other, like the dead sailor in his shotted hammock, haled down by sheer weight of name into the abysses of social failure. Solomon possibly had his eye on some such theory when he said that 'a good name is better than precious ointment'; and perhaps we may trace a similar spirit in the compilers of the English Catechism, and the affectionate interest with which they linger round the catechumen's name at the very threshold of their work. But, be these as they may, I think no one can censure me for appending, in pursuance of the expressed wish of his son, the Turkey merchant's name to his system, and pronouncing, without further preface, a short epitome of the 'Shandean Philosophy of Nomenclature.'

To begin, then: the influence of our name makes itself felt from the very cradle. As a schoolboy I remember the pride with which I hailed Robin Hood, Robert Bruce, and Robert le Diable as my name-fellows; and the feeling of sore disappointment that fell on my heart when I found a freebooter or a general who did not share with me a single one of my numerous prænomina. Look at the delight with which two children find they have the same name.

They are friends from that moment forth; they have a bond of union stronger than exchange of nuts and sweetmeats. This feeling, I own, wears off in later life. Our names lose their freshness and interest, become trite and indifferent. But this, dear reader, is merely one of the sad effects of those 'shades of the prison-house' which come gradually betwixt us and nature with advancing years; it affords no weapon against the philosophy of names.

In after life, although we fail to trace its working, that name which careless godfathers lightly applied to your unconscious infancy will have been moulding your character, and influencing with irresistible power the whole course of your earthly fortunes. But the last name, overlooked by Mr. Shandy, is no whit less important as a condition of success. Family names, we must recollect, are but inherited nicknames; and if the sobriquet were applicable to the ancestor, it is most likely applicable to the descendant also. You would not expect to find Mr. M'Phun acting as a mute, or Mr. M'Lumpha excelling as a professor of dancing. Therefore, in what follows, we shall consider names, independent of whether they are first or last. And to begin with, look what a pull Cromwell had over Pym—the one name full of a resonant imperialism, the other, mean, pettifogging, and unheroic to a degree. Who would expect eloquence from Pym—who would read poems by Pym—who would bow to the opinion of Pym? He might have been a dentist, but he should never have aspired to be a statesman. I can only wonder that he succeeded as he did. Pym and Habakkuk stand first upon the roll of men who have triumphed, by sheer force of genius, over the most unfavourable appellations. But even these have suffered; and, had they been more fitly named, the one might have been Lord Protector, and the other have shared the laurels with Isaiah. In this matter we must not forget that all our great poets have borne great names. Chaucer, Spenser, Shakespeare, Milton, Pope, Wordsworth, Shelley—what a constellation of lordly words! Not a single common-place name among them—not a Brown, not a Jones, not a Robinson; they are all names that one would stop and look at on a door-plate. Now, imagine if Pepys had tried to clamber somehow into the enclosure of poetry, what a blot would that word have made upon the list! The thing was impossible. In the first place a certain natural consciousness that men would have held him down to the level of his name, would have prevented him from rising above the Pepsine standard, and so haply withheld him altogether from attempting verse. Next, the booksellers would refuse to publish, and the world to read them, on the mere evidence of the fatal appellation. And now, before I close this section, I must say one word as to punnable names, names that stand alone, that have a significance and life apart from him that bears them. These are the bitterest of all. One friend of mine goes bowed and humbled through life under the weight of this misfortune; for it is an awful thing when a man's name is a joke, when he cannot be mentioned without exciting merriment, and when even the intimation of his death bids fair to carry laughter into many a home.

So much for people who are badly named. Now for people who are too well named, who go top-heavy from the font, who are baptized into a false position, and find themselves beginning life eclipsed under the fame of some of the great ones of the past. A man, for instance, called William Shakespeare could never dare to write plays. He is thrown into too humbling an apposition with the author of Hamlet. Its own name coming after is such an anti-climax. 'The plays of William Shakespeare'? says the reader—'O no! The plays of William Shakespeare Cockerill,' and he throws the book aside. In wise pursuance of such views, Mr. John Milton Hengler, who not long since delighted us in this favoured town, has never attempted to write an epic, but has chosen a new path, and has excelled upon the tight-rope. A marked example of triumph over this is the case of Mr. Dante Gabriel Rossetti. On the face of the matter, I should have advised him to imitate the pleasing modesty of the last-named gentleman, and confine his ambition to the sawdust. But Mr. Rossetti has triumphed. He has even dared to translate from his mighty name-father; and the voice of fame supports him in his boldness.

Dear readers, one might write a year upon this matter. A lifetime of comparison and research could scarce suffice for its elucidation. So here, if it please you, we shall let it rest. Slight as these notes have been, I would that the great founder of the system had been alive to see them. How he had warmed and brightened, how his persuasive eloquence would have fallen on the ears of Toby; and what a letter of praise and sympathy would not the editor have received before the month was out! Alas, the thing was not to be. Walter

116

Shandy died and was duly buried, while yet his theory lay forgotten and neglected by his fellow-countrymen. But, reader, the day will come, I hope, when a paternal government will stamp out, as seeds of national weakness, all depressing patronymics, and when godfathers and godmothers will soberly and earnestly debate the interest of the nameless one, and not rush blindfold to the christening. In these days there shall be written a 'Godfather's Assistant,' in shape of a dictionary of names, with their concomitant virtues and vices; and this book shall be scattered broadcast through the land, and shall be on the table of every one eligible for godfathership, until such a thing as a vicious or untoward appellation shall have ceased from off the face of the earth.

CRITICISMS

CHAPTER I—LORD LYTTON'S 'FABLES IN SONG'

It seems as if Lord Lytton, in this new book of his, had found the form most natural to his talent. In some ways, indeed, it may be held inferior to Chronicles and Characters; we look in vain for anything like the terrible intensity of the night-scene in Irene, or for any such passages of massive and memorable writing as appeared, here and there, in the earlier work, and made it not altogether unworthy of its model, Hugo's Legend of the Ages. But it becomes evident, on the most hasty retrospect, that this earlier work was a step on the way towards the later. It seems as if the author had been feeling about for his definite medium, and was already, in the language of the child's game, growing hot. There are many pieces in Chronicles and Characters that might be detached from their original setting, and embodied, as they stand, among the Fables in Song.

For the term Fable is not very easy to define rigorously. In the most typical form some moral precept is set forth by means of a conception purely fantastic, and usually somewhat trivial into the bargain; there is something playful about it, that will not support a very exacting criticism, and the lesson must be apprehended by the fancy at half a hint. Such is the great mass of the old stories of wise animals or foolish men that have amused our childhood. But we should expect the fable, in company with other and more important literary forms, to be more and more loosely, or at least largely, comprehended as time went on, and so to degenerate in conception from this original type. That depended for much of its piquancy on the very fact that it was fantastic: the point of the thing lay in a sort of humorous inappropriateness; and it is natural enough that pleasantry of this description should become less common, as men learn to suspect some serious analogy underneath. Thus a comical story of an ape touches us quite differently after the proposition of Mr. Darwin's theory. Moreover, there lay, perhaps, at the bottom of this primitive sort of fable, a humanity, a tenderness of rough truths; so that at the end of some story, in which vice or folly had met with its destined punishment, the fabulist might be able to assure his auditors, as we have often to assure tearful children on the like occasions, that they may dry their eyes, for none of it was true.

But this benefit of fiction becomes lost with more sophisticated hearers and authors: a man is no longer the dupe of his own artifice, and cannot deal playfully with truths that are a matter of bitter concern to him in his life. And hence, in the progressive centralisation of modern thought, we should expect the old form of fable to fall gradually into desuetude, and be gradually succeeded by another, which is a fable in all points except that it is not altogether fabulous. And this new form, such as we should expect, and such as we do indeed find, still presents the essential character of brevity; as in any other fable also, there is, underlying and animating the brief action, a moral idea; and as in any other fable, the object is to bring this home to the reader through the intellect rather than through the feelings; so that, without being very deeply moved or interested by the characters of the piece, we should recognise vividly the hinges on which the little plot revolves. But the fabulist now seeks analogies where before he merely sought humorous situations. There will be now a logical nexus between the moral expressed and the machinery employed to express it. The machinery, in fact, as this change is developed, becomes less and less fabulous. We find ourselves in presence of quite a serious, if quite a miniature division of creative literature; and sometimes we have the lesson embodied in a sober, everyday narration, as in the parables of the New Testament, and sometimes merely the statement or, at most, the collocation of significant facts in life, the reader being left to resolve for himself the vague, troublesome, and not yet definitely moral sentiment which has been thus created. And step by step with the development of this change, yet another is developed: the moral tends to become more indeterminate and large. It ceases to be possible to append it, in a tag, to the bottom of the piece, as one might write the name below a caricature; and the fable begins to take rank with all other forms of creative literature, as something too ambitious, in spite of its miniature dimensions, to be resumed in any succinct formula without the loss of all that is deepest and most suggestive in it.

Now it is in this widest sense that Lord Lytton understands the term; there are examples in his two pleasant volumes of all the forms already mentioned, and even of another which can only be admitted among fables by the utmost possible leniency of construction. 'Composure,' 'Et Cætera,' and several more, are merely similes poetically elaborated. So, too, is the pathetic story of the grandfather and grandchild: the child, having treasured away an icicle and forgotten it for ten minutes, comes back to find it already nearly melted, and no longer beautiful: at the same time, the grandfather has just remembered and taken out a bundle of love-letters, which he too had stored away in years gone by, and then long neglected; and, behold! the letters are as faded and sorrowfully disappointing as the icicle. This is merely a simile poetically worked out; and yet it is in such as these, and some others, to be mentioned further on, that the author seems at his best. Wherever he has really written after the old model, there is something to be deprecated: in spite of all the spirit and freshness, in spite of his happy assumption of that cheerful acceptation of things as they are, which, rightly or wrongly, we come to attribute to the ideal fabulist, there is ever a sense as of something a little out of place. A form of literature so very innocent and primitive looks a little over-written in Lord Lytton's conscious and highly-coloured style. It may be bad taste, but sometimes we should prefer a few sentences of plain prose narration, and a little Bewick by way of tail-piece. So that it is not among those fables that conform most nearly to the old model, but one had nearly said among those that most widely differ from it, that we find the most satisfactory examples of the author's manner.

In the mere matter of ingenuity, the metaphysical fables are the most remarkable; such as that of the windmill who imagined that it was he who raised the wind; or that of the grocer's balance ('Cogito ergo sum') who considered himself endowed with free-will, reason, and an infallible practical judgment; until, one fine day, the police made a descent upon the shop, and find the weights false and the scales unequal; and the whole thing is broken up for old iron. Capital fables, also, in the same ironical spirit, are 'Prometheus

Unbound,' the tale of the vainglorying of a champagne-cork, and 'Teleology,' where a nettle justifies the ways of God to nettles while all goes well with it, and, upon a change of luck, promptly changes its divinity.

In all these there is still plenty of the fabulous if you will, although, even here, there may be two opinions possible; but there is another group, of an order of merit perhaps still higher, where we look in vain for any such playful liberties with Nature. Thus we have 'Conservation of Force'; where a musician, thinking of a certain picture, improvises in the twilight; a poet, hearing the music, goes home inspired, and writes a poem; and then a painter, under the influence of this poem, paints another picture, thus lineally descended from the first. This is fiction, but not what we have been used to call fable. We miss the incredible element, the point of audacity with which the fabulist was wont to mock at his readers. And still more so is this the case with others. 'The Horse and the Fly' states one of the unanswerable problems of life in quite a realistic and straightforward way. A fly startles a cab-horse, the coach is overset; a newly-married pair within and the driver, a man with a wife and family, are all killed. The horse continues to gallop off in the loose traces, and ends the tragedy by running over an only child; and there is some little pathetic detail here introduced in the telling, that makes the reader's indignation very white-hot against some one. It remains to be seen who that some one is to be: the fly? Nay, but on closer inspection, it appears that the fly, actuated by maternal instinct, was only seeking a place for her eggs: is maternal instinct, then, 'sole author of these mischiefs all'? 'Who's in the Right?' one of the best fables in the book, is somewhat in the same vein. After a battle has been won, a group of officers assemble inside a battery, and debate together who should have the honour of the success; the Prince, the general staff, the cavalry, the engineer who posted the battery in which they then stand talking, are successively named: the sergeant, who pointed the guns, sneers to himself at the mention of the engineer; and, close by, the gunner, who had applied the match, passes away with a smile of triumph, since it was through his hand that the victorious blow had been dealt. Meanwhile, the cannon claims the honour over the gunner; the cannon-ball, who actually goes forth on the dread mission, claims it over the cannon, who remains idly behind; the powder reminds the cannon-ball that, but for him, it would still

121

be lying on the arsenal floor; and the match caps the discussion; powder, cannon-ball, and cannon would be all equally vain and ineffectual without fire. Just then there comes on a shower of rain, which wets the powder and puts out the match, and completes this lesson of dependence, by indicating the negative conditions which are as necessary for any effect, in their absence, as is the presence of this great fraternity of positive conditions, not any one of which can claim priority over any other. But the fable does not end here, as perhaps, in all logical strictness, it should. It wanders off into a discussion as to which is the truer greatness, that of the vanquished fire or that of the victorious rain. And the speech of the rain is charming:

> 'Lo, with my little drops I bless again
>
> And beautify the fields which thou didst blast!
>
> Rend, wither, waste, and ruin, what thou wilt,
>
> But call not Greatness what the Gods call Guilt.
>
> Blossoms and grass from blood in battle spilt,
>
> And poppied corn, I bring.
>
> 'Mid mouldering Babels, to oblivion built,
>
> My violets spring.
>
> Little by little my small drops have strength
>
> To deck with green delights the grateful earth.'

And so forth, not quite germane (it seems to me) to the matter in hand, but welcome for its own sake.

Best of all are the fables that deal more immediately with the emotions. There is, for instance, that of 'The Two Travellers,' which is profoundly moving in conception, although by no means as well written as some others. In this, one of the two, fearfully frost-bitten, saves his life out of the snow at the cost of all that was comely in his body; just as, long before, the other, who has now quietly resigned himself to death, had violently freed himself

122

from Love at the cost of all that was finest and fairest in his character. Very graceful and sweet is the fable (if so it should be called) in which the author sings the praises of that 'kindly perspective,' which lets a wheat-stalk near the eye cover twenty leagues of distant country, and makes the humble circle about a man's hearth more to him than all the possibilities of the external world. The companion fable to this is also excellent. It tells us of a man who had, all his life through, entertained a passion for certain blue hills on the far horizon, and had promised himself to travel thither ere he died, and become familiar with these distant friends. At last, in some political trouble, he is banished to the very place of his dreams. He arrives there overnight, and, when he rises and goes forth in the morning, there sure enough are the blue hills, only now they have changed places with him, and smile across to him, distant as ever, from the old home whence he has come. Such a story might have been very cynically treated; but it is not so done, the whole tone is kindly and consolatory, and the disenchanted man submissively takes the lesson, and understands that things far away are to be loved for their own sake, and that the unattainable is not truly unattainable, when we can make the beauty of it our own. Indeed, throughout all these two volumes, though there is much practical scepticism, and much irony on abstract questions, this kindly and consolatory spirit is never absent. There is much that is cheerful and, after a sedate, fireside fashion, hopeful. No one will be discouraged by reading the book; but the ground of all this hopefulness and cheerfulness remains to the end somewhat vague. It does not seem to arise from any practical belief in the future either of the individual or the race, but rather from the profound personal contentment of the writer. This is, I suppose, all we must look for in the case. It is as much as we can expect, if the fabulist shall prove a shrewd and cheerful fellow-wayfarer, one with whom the world does not seem to have gone much amiss, but who has yet laughingly learned something of its evil. It will depend much, of course, upon our own character and circumstances, whether the encounter will be agreeable and bracing to the spirits, or offend us as an ill-timed mockery. But where, as here, there is a little tincture of bitterness along with the good-nature, where it is plainly not the humour of a man cheerfully ignorant, but of one who looks on, tolerant and superior and smilingly attentive, upon the good and bad of our existence, it will go hardly if we do not catch some reflection of the same spirit to help us on our way. There is here no impertinent and lying proclamation of peace—none of the cheap optimism of the well-to-do; what we find here is a view of life that would be even grievous, were it not enlivened with this abiding cheerfulness, and ever and anon redeemed by a stroke of pathos.

It is natural enough, I suppose, that we should find wanting in this book some of the intenser qualities of the author's work; and their absence is made up for by much happy description after a quieter fashion. The burst of jubilation over the departure of the snow, which forms the prelude to 'The Thistle,' is full of spirit and of pleasant images. The speech of the forest in 'Sans Souci' is inspired by a beautiful sentiment for nature of the modern sort, and pleases us more, I think, as poetry should please us, than anything in Chronicles and Characters. There are some admirable felicities of expression here and there; as that of the hill, whose summit

> 'Did print

> The azure air with pines.'

Moreover, I do not recollect in the author's former work any symptom of that sympathetic treatment of still life, which is noticeable now and again in the fables; and perhaps most noticeably, when he sketches the burned letters as they hover along the gusty flue, 'Thin, sable veils, wherein a restless spark Yet trembled.' But the description is at its best when the subjects are unpleasant, or even grisly. There are a few capital lines in this key on the last spasm of the battle before alluded to. Surely nothing could be better, in its own way, than the fish in 'The Last Cruise of the Arrogant,' 'the shadowy, side-faced, silent things,' that come butting and staring with lidless eyes at the sunken steam-engine. And although, in yet another, we are told, pleasantly enough, how the water went down into the valleys, where it set itself gaily to saw wood, and on into the plains, where it would soberly carry grain to town; yet the real strength of the fable is when it dealt with the shut pool in which certain unfortunate raindrops are imprisoned among slugs and snails, and in the company of an old toad. The sodden contentment of the fallen acorn is strangely significant; and it is astonishing how unpleasantly we are startled by the appearance of her horrible lover, the maggot.

And now for a last word, about the style. This is not easy to criticise. It is impossible to deny to it rapidity, spirit, and a full sound; the lines are never lame, and the sense is carried forward with an uninterrupted, impetuous rush. But it is not equal. After passages of really admirable versification, the author falls back upon a sort of loose, cavalry manner, not unlike the style of some of Mr. Browning's minor pieces, and almost inseparable from wordiness, and an easy acceptation of somewhat cheap finish. There is nothing here of that compression which is the note of a really sovereign style. It is unfair, perhaps, to set a not remarkable passage from Lord Lytton side by side with one of the signal masterpieces of another, and a very perfect poet; and yet it is interesting, when we see how the portraiture of a dog, detailed through thirty odd lines, is frittered down and finally almost lost in the mere laxity of the style, to compare it with the clear, simple, vigorous delineation that Burns, in four couplets, has given us of the ploughman's collie. It is interesting, at first, and then it becomes a little irritating; for when we think of other passages so much more finished and adroit, we cannot help feeling, that with a little more ardour after perfection of form, criticism would have found nothing left for her to censure. A similar mark of precipitate work is the number of adjectives tumultuously heaped together, sometimes to help out the sense, and sometimes (as one cannot but suspect) to help out the sound of the verses. I do not believe, for instance, that Lord Lytton himself would defend the lines in which we are told how Laocoön 'Revealed to Roman crowds, now Christian grown, That Pagan anguish which, in Parian stone, The Rhodian artist,' and so on. It is not only that this is bad in itself; but that it is unworthy of the company in which it is found; that such verses should not have appeared with the name of a good versifier like Lord Lytton. We must take exception, also, in conclusion, to the excess of alliteration. Alliteration is so liable to be abused that we can scarcely be too sparing of it; and yet it is a trick that seems to grow upon the author with years. It is a pity to see fine verses, such as some in 'Demos,' absolutely spoiled by the recurrence of one wearisome consonant.

CHAPTER II—SALVINI'S MACBETH

Salvini closed his short visit to Edinburgh by a performance of Macbeth. It was, perhaps, from a sentiment of local colour that he chose to play the Scottish usurper for the first time before Scotsmen; and the audience were not insensible of the privilege. Few things, indeed, can move a stronger interest than to see a great creation taking shape for the first time. If it is not purely artistic, the sentiment is surely human. And the thought that you are before all the world, and have the start of so many others as eager as yourself, at least keeps you in a more unbearable suspense before the curtain rises, if it does not enhance the delight with which you follow the performance and see the actor 'bend up each corporal agent' to realise a masterpiece of a few hours' duration. With a player so variable as Salvini, who trusts to the feelings of the moment for so much detail, and who, night after night, does the same thing differently but always well, it can never be safe to pass judgment after a single hearing. And this is more particularly true of last week's Macbeth; for the whole third act was marred by a grievously humorous misadventure. Several minutes too soon the ghost of Banquo joined the party, and after having sat helpless a while at a table, was ignominiously withdrawn. Twice was this ghostly Jack-in-the-box obtruded on the stage before his time; twice removed again; and yet he showed so little hurry when he was really wanted, that, after an awkward pause, Macbeth had to begin his apostrophe to empty air. The arrival of the belated spectre in the middle, with a jerk that made him nod all over, was the last accident in the chapter, and worthily topped the whole. It may be imagined how lamely matters went throughout these cross purposes.

In spite of this, and some other hitches, Salvini's Macbeth had an emphatic success. The creation is worthy of a place beside the same artist's Othello and Hamlet. It is the simplest and most unsympathetic of the three; but the absence of the finer lineaments of Hamlet is redeemed by gusto, breadth, and a headlong unity. Salvini sees nothing great in Macbeth beyond the royalty of muscle, and that courage which comes of strong and copious circulation. The moral smallness of the man is insisted on from the first, in the shudder of uncontrollable jealousy with which he sees Duncan embracing Banquo. He may have some northern poetry of speech, but he has not much logical understanding. In his dealings with the supernatural powers he is like a savage with his fetich, trusting them beyond bounds while all goes well, and whenever he is crossed, casting his belief aside and calling 'fate into the list.' For his wife, he is little more than an agent, a frame of bone and sinew for her fiery spirit to command. The nature of his feeling towards her is rendered with a most precise and delicate touch. He always yields to the woman's fascination; and yet his caresses (and we know how much meaning Salvini can give to a caress) are singularly hard and unloving. Sometimes he lays his hand on her as he might take hold of any one who happened to be nearest to him at a moment of excitement. Love has fallen out of this marriage by the way, and left a curious friendship. Only once—at the very moment when she is showing herself so little a woman and so much a high-spirited man—only once is he very deeply stirred towards her; and that finds expression in the strange and horrible transport of admiration, doubly strange and horrible on Salvini's lips—'Bring forth men-children only!'

The murder scene, as was to be expected, pleased the audience best. Macbeth's voice, in the talk with his wife, was a thing not to be forgotten; and when he spoke of his hangman's hands he seemed to have blood in his utterance. Never for a moment, even in the very article of the murder, does he possess his own soul. He is a man on wires. From first to last it is an exhibition of hideous cowardice. For, after all, it is not here, but in broad daylight, with the exhilaration of conflict, where he can assure himself at every blow he has the longest sword and the heaviest hand, that this man's physical bravery can keep him up; he is an unwieldy ship, and needs plenty of way on before he will steer.

In the banquet scene, while the first murderer gives account of what he has done, there comes a flash of truculent joy at the 'twenty trenchèd gashes' on Banquo's head. Thus Macbeth makes welcome to his imagination those very details of physical horror which are so soon to turn sour in him. As he runs out to embrace these cruel circumstances, as he seeks to realise to his mind's eye the reassuring spectacle of his dead enemy, he is dressing out the phantom to terrify himself; and his imagination, playing the part of justice, is to 'commend to his own lips the ingredients of his poisoned chalice.' With the recollection of Hamlet and his father's spirit still fresh upon him, and the holy awe with which that good man encountered things not dreamt of in his philosophy, it was not possible to avoid looking for resemblances between the two apparitions and the two men haunted. But there are none to be found. Macbeth has a purely physical dislike for Banquo's spirit and the 'twenty trenchèd gashes.' He is afraid of he knows not what. He is abject, and again blustering. In the end he so far forgets himself, his terror, and the nature of what is before him, that he rushes upon it as he would upon a man. When his wife tells him he needs repose, there is something really childish in the way he looks about the room, and, seeing nothing, with an expression of almost sensual relief, plucks up heart enough to go to bed. And what is the upshot of the visitation? It is written in Shakespeare, but should be read with the commentary of Salvini's voice and expression:—'O! siam nell' opra ancor fanciulli'—'We are yet but young in deed.' Circle below circle. He is looking with horrible satisfaction into the mouth of hell. There may still be a prick to-day; but to-morrow conscience will be dead, and he may move untroubled in this element of blood.

In the fifth act we see this lowest circle reached; and it is Salvini's finest moment throughout the play. From the first he was admirably made up, and looked Macbeth to the full as perfectly as ever he looked Othello. From the first moment he steps upon the stage you can see this character is a creation to the fullest meaning of the phrase; for the man before you is a type you know well already. He arrives with Banquo on the heath, fair and red-bearded, sparing of gesture, full of pride and the sense of animal wellbeing, and satisfied after the battle like a beast who has eaten his fill. But in the fifth act there is a change. This is still the big, burly, fleshly, handsome-looking Thane; here is still the same face which in the earlier acts could be superficially good-humoured and sometimes royally courteous. But now the atmosphere of blood, which pervades the whole tragedy, has entered into the man and subdued him to its own nature; and an indescribable degradation, a slackness and puffiness, has overtaken his features. He has breathed the air of carnage, and supped full of horrors. Lady Macbeth complains of the smell of blood on her hand: Macbeth makes no complaint—he has ceased to notice it now; but the same smell is in his nostrils. A contained fury and disgust possesses him. He taunts the messenger and the doctor as people would taunt their mortal enemies. And, indeed, as he knows right well, every one is his enemy now, except his wife. About her he questions the doctor with something like a last human anxiety; and, in tones of grisly mystery, asks him if he can 'minister to a mind diseased.' When the news of her death is brought him, he is staggered and falls into a seat; but somehow it is not anything we can call grief that he displays. There had been two of them against God and man; and now, when there is only one, it makes perhaps less difference than he had expected. And so her death is not only an affliction, but one more disillusion; and he redoubles in bitterness. The speech that follows, given with tragic cynicism in every word, is a dirge, not so much for her as for himself. From that time forth there is nothing human left in him, only 'the fiend of Scotland,' Macduff's 'hell-hound,' whom, with a stern glee, we see baited like a bear and hunted down like a wolf. He is inspired and set above fate by a demoniacal energy, a lust of wounds and slaughter. Even after he meets Macduff his courage does not fail; but when he hears the Thane was not born of woman, all virtue goes out of him; and though he speaks sounding words of defiance, the last combat is little better than a suicide.

The whole performance is, as I said, so full of gusto and a headlong unity; the personality of Macbeth is so sharp and powerful; and within these somewhat narrow limits there is so much play and saliency that, so far as concerns Salvini himself, a third great success seems indubitable. Unfortunately, however, a great actor cannot fill more than a very small fraction of the boards; and though Banquo's ghost will probably be more seasonable in his future apparitions, there are some more inherent difficulties in the piece. The company at large did not distinguish themselves. Macduff, to the huge delight of the gallery, out-Macduff'd the average ranter. The lady who filled the principal female part has done better on other occasions, but I fear she has not metal for what she tried last week. Not to succeed in the sleep-walking scene is to make a memorable failure. As it was given, it succeeded in being wrong in art without being true to nature.

And there is yet another difficulty, happily easy to reform, which somewhat interfered with the success of the performance. At the end of the incantation scene the Italian translator has made Macbeth fall insensible upon the stage. This is a change of questionable propriety from a psychological point of view; while in point of view of effect it leaves the stage for some moments empty of all business. To remedy this, a bevy of green ballet-girls came forth and pointed their toes about the prostrate king. A dance of High

Church curates, or a hornpipe by Mr. T. P. Cooke, would not be more out of the key; though the gravity of a Scots audience was not to be overcome, and they merely expressed their disapprobation by a round of moderate hisses, a similar irruption of Christmas fairies would most likely convulse a London theatre from pit to gallery with inextinguishable laughter. It is, I am told, the Italian tradition; but it is one more honoured in the breach than the observance. With the total disappearance of these damsels, with a stronger Lady Macbeth, and, if possible, with some compression of those scenes in which Salvini does not appear, and the spectator is left at the mercy of Macduffs and Duncans, the play would go twice as well, and we should be better able to follow and enjoy an admirable work of dramatic art.

CHAPTER III—BAGSTER'S 'PILGRIM'S PROGRESS'

I have here before me an edition of the Pilgrim's Progress, bound in green, without a date, and described as 'illustrated by nearly three hundred engravings, and memoir of Bunyan.' On the outside it is lettered 'Bagster's Illustrated Edition,' and after the author's apology, facing the first page of the tale, a folding pictorial 'Plan of the Road' is marked as 'drawn by the late Mr. T. Conder,' and engraved by J. Basire. No further information is anywhere vouchsafed; perhaps the publishers had judged the work too unimportant; and we are still left ignorant whether or not we owe the woodcuts in the body of the volume to the same hand that drew the plan. It seems, however, more than probable. The literal particularity of mind which, in the map, laid down the flower-plots in the devil's garden, and carefully introduced the court-house in the town of Vanity, is closely paralleled in many of the cuts; and in both, the architecture of the buildings and the disposition of the gardens have a kindred and entirely English air. Whoever he was, the author of these wonderful little pictures may lay claim to be the best illustrator of Bunyan. [183] They are not only good illustrations, like so many others; but they are like so few, good illustrations of Bunyan. Their spirit, in defect and quality, is still the same as his own. The designer also has lain down and dreamed a dream, as literal, as quaint, and almost as apposite as Bunyan's; and text and pictures make but the two sides of the same homespun yet impassioned story. To do justice to the designs, it will be necessary to say, for the hundredth time, a word or two about the masterpiece which they adorn.

All allegories have a tendency to escape from the purpose of their creators; and as the characters and incidents become more and more interesting in themselves, the moral, which these were to show forth, falls more and more into neglect. An architect may command a wreath of vine-leaves round the cornice of a monument; but if, as each leaf came from the chisel, it took proper life and fluttered freely on the wall, and if the vine grew, and the building were hidden over with foliage and fruit, the architect would stand in much the same situation as the writer of allegories. The Faëry Queen was an allegory, I am willing to believe; but it survives as an imaginative tale in incomparable verse. The case of Bunyan is widely different; and yet in this also Allegory, poor nymph, although never quite forgotten, is sometimes rudely thrust against the wall. Bunyan was fervently in earnest; with 'his fingers in his ears, he ran on,' straight for his mark. He tells us himself, in the conclusion to the first part, that he did not fear to raise a laugh; indeed, he feared nothing, and said anything; and he was greatly served in this by a certain rustic privilege of his style, which, like the talk of strong uneducated men, when it does not impress by its force, still charms by its simplicity. The mere story and the allegorical design enjoyed perhaps his equal favour. He believed in both with an energy of faith that was capable of moving mountains. And we have to remark in him, not the parts where inspiration fails and is supplied by cold and merely decorative invention, but the parts where faith has grown to be credulity, and his characters become so real to him that he forgets the end of their creation. We can follow him step by step into the trap which he lays for himself by his own entire good faith and triumphant literality of vision, till the trap closes and shuts him in an inconsistency. The allegories of the Interpreter and of the Shepherds of the Delectable Mountains are all actually performed, like stage-plays, before the pilgrims. The son of Mr. Great-grace visibly 'tumbles hills about with his words.' Adam the First has his condemnation written visibly on his forehead, so that Faithful reads it. At the very instant the net closes round the pilgrims, 'the white robe falls from the black man's body.' Despair 'getteth him a grievous crab-tree cudgel'; it was in 'sunshiny weather' that he had his fits; and the birds in the grove about the House Beautiful, 'our country birds,' only sing their little pious verses 'at the spring, when the flowers appear and the sun shines warm.' 'I often,' says Piety, 'go out to hear them; we also ofttimes keep them tame on our house.' The post between Beulah and the Celestial City sounds his horn, as you may yet hear in country places. Madam Bubble, that 'tall, comely dame, something of a swarthy complexion, in very pleasant attire, but old,' 'gives you a smile at the end of each sentence'—a real woman she; we all know her. Christiana dying 'gave Mr. Stand-fast a ring,' for no possible reason in the allegory, merely because the touch was human and affecting. Look at Great-heart, with his soldierly ways, garrison ways, as I had almost called them; with his taste in weapons; his delight in any that 'he found to be a man of his hands'; his chivalrous point of honour, letting Giant Maul get up again when he was down, a thing fairly flying in the teeth of the moral; above all, with his language in the inimitable tale of Mr. Fearing: 'I thought I should have lost my man'—'chicken-hearted'—'at last he came in, and I will say that for my lord, he carried it wonderful lovingly to him.' This is no Independent minister; this is a stout, honest, big-busted ancient, adjusting his shoulder-belts, twirling his long moustaches as he speaks. Last and most remarkable, 'My sword,' says the dying Valiant-for-Truth, he in whom Great-heart delighted, 'my sword I give to him that shall succeed me in my pilgrimage, and my courage and skill to him that can get it.' And after this boast, more arrogantly unorthodox than was ever dreamed of by the rejected Ignorance, we are told that 'all the trumpets sounded for him on the other side.'

In every page the book is stamped with the same energy of vision and the same energy of belief. The quality is equally and indifferently displayed in the spirit of the fighting, the tenderness of the pathos, the startling vigour and strangeness of the incidents, the natural strain of the conversations, and the humanity and charm of the characters. Trivial talk over a meal, the dying words of heroes, the delights of Beulah or the Celestial City, Apollyon and my Lord Hate-good, Great-heart, and Mr. Worldly-Wiseman, all have been imagined with the same clearness, all written of with equal gusto and precision, all created in the same mixed element, of simplicity that is almost comical, and art that, for its purpose, is faultless.

It was in much the same spirit that our artist sat down to his drawings. He is by nature a Bunyan of the pencil. He, too, will draw anything, from a butcher at work on a dead sheep, up to the courts of Heaven. 'A Lamb for Supper' is the name of one of his designs, 'Their Glorious Entry' of another. He has the same disregard for the ridiculous, and enjoys somewhat of the same privilege of style, so that we are pleased even when we laugh the most. He is literal to the verge of folly. If dust is to be raised from the unswept parlour, you may be sure it will 'fly abundantly' in the picture. If Faithful is to lie 'as dead' before Moses, dead he shall lie with a warrant—dead and stiff like granite; nay (and here the artist must enhance upon the symbolism of the author), it is with the identical stone tables of the law that Moses fells the sinner. Good and bad people, whom we at once distinguish in the text by their names, Hopeful, Honest, and Valiant-for-Truth, on the one hand, as against By-ends, Sir Having Greedy, and the Lord Old-man on the other, are in these drawings as simply distinguished by their costume. Good people, when not armed cap-à-pie, wear a speckled tunic girt about the waist, and low hats, apparently of straw. Bad people swagger in tail-coats and chimney-pots, a few with knee-breeches, but the large majority in trousers, and for all the world like guests at a garden-party. Worldly-Wiseman alone, by some inexplicable quirk, stands before Christian in laced hat, embroidered waistcoat, and trunk-hose. But above all examples of this artist's intrepidity, commend me to the print entitled 'Christian Finds it Deep.' 'A great darkness and horror,' says the text, have fallen on the pilgrim; it is the comfortless deathbed with which Bunyan so strikingly concludes the sorrows and conflicts of his hero. How to represent this worthily the artist knew not; and yet he was determined to represent it somehow. This was how he did: Hopeful is still shown to his neck above the water of death; but Christian has bodily disappeared, and a blot of solid blackness indicates his place.

As you continue to look at these pictures, about an inch square for the most part, sometimes printed three or more to the page, and each having a printed legend of its own, however trivial the event recorded, you will soon become aware of two things: first, that the man can draw, and, second, that he possesses the gift of an imagination. 'Obstinate reviles,' says the legend; and you should see Obstinate reviling. 'He warily retraces his steps'; and there is Christian, posting through the plain, terror and speed in every muscle. 'Mercy yearns to go' shows you a plain interior with packing going forward, and, right in the middle, Mercy yearning to go—every line of the girl's figure yearning. In 'The Chamber called Peace' we see a simple English room, bed with white curtains, window valance and door, as may be found in many thousand unpretentious houses; but far off, through the open window, we behold the sun uprising out of a great plain, and Christian hails it with his hand:

'Where am I now! is this the love and care

Of Jesus, for the men that pilgrims are!

Thus to provide! That I should be forgiven!

And dwell already the next door to heaven!'

A page or two further, from the top of the House Beautiful, the damsels point his gaze toward the Delectable Mountains: 'The Prospect,' so the cut is ticketed—and I shall be surprised, if on less than a square inch of paper you can show me one so wide and fair. Down a cross road on an English plain, a cathedral city outlined on the horizon, a hazel shaw upon the left, comes Madam Wanton dancing with her fair enchanted cup, and Faithful, book in hand, half pauses. The cut is perfect as a symbol; the giddy movement of the sorceress, the uncertain poise of the man struck to the heart by a temptation, the contrast of that even plain of life whereon he journeys with the bold, ideal bearing of the wanton—the artist who invented and portrayed this had not merely read Bunyan, he had also thoughtfully lived. The Delectable Mountains—I continue skimming the first part—are not on the whole happily rendered. Once, and once only, the note is struck, when Christian and Hopeful are seen coming, shoulder-high, through a thicket of green shrubs—box, perhaps, or perfumed nutmeg; while behind them, domed or pointed, the hills stand ranged against the sky. A little further, and we come to that masterpiece of Bunyan's insight into life, the Enchanted Ground; where, in a few traits, he has set down the latter end of such a number of the would-be good; where his allegory goes so deep that, to people looking seriously on life, it cuts like satire. The true significance of this invention lies, of course, far out of the way of drawing; only one feature, the great tedium of the land, the growing weariness in well-doing, may be somewhat represented in a symbol.

The pilgrims are near the end: 'Two Miles Yet,' says the legend. The road goes ploughing up and down over a rolling heath; the wayfarers, with outstretched arms, are already sunk to the knees over the brow of the nearest hill; they have just passed a milestone with the cipher two; from overhead a great, piled, summer cumulus, as of a slumberous summer afternoon, beshadows them: two miles! it might be hundreds. In dealing with the Land of Beulah the artist lags, in both parts, miserably behind the text, but in the distant prospect of the Celestial City more than regains his own. You will remember when Christian and Hopeful 'with desire fell sick.' 'Effect of the Sunbeams' is the artist's title. Against the sky, upon a cliffy mountain, the radiant temple beams upon them over deep, subjacent woods; they, behind a mound, as if seeking shelter from the splendour—one prostrate on his face, one kneeling, and with hands ecstatically lifted—yearn with passion after that immortal city. Turn the page, and we behold them walking by the very shores of death; Heaven, from this nigher view, has risen half-way to the zenith, and sheds a wider glory; and the two pilgrims, dark against that brightness, walk and sing out of the fulness of their hearts. No cut more thoroughly illustrates at once the merit and the weakness of the artist. Each pilgrim sings with a book in his grasp—a family Bible at the least for bigness; tomes so recklessly enormous that our second, impulse is to laughter. And yet that is not the first thought, nor perhaps the last. Something in the attitude of the manikins—faces they have none, they are too small for that—something in the way they swing these monstrous volumes to their singing, something perhaps borrowed from the text, some subtle differentiation from the cut that went before and the cut that follows after—something, at least, speaks clearly of a fearful joy, of Heaven seen from the deathbed, of the horror of the last passage no less than of the glorious coming home. There is that in the action of one of them which always reminds me, with a difference, of that haunting last glimpse of Thomas Idle, travelling to Tyburn in the cart. Next come the Shining Ones, wooden and trivial enough; the pilgrims pass into the river; the blot already mentioned settles over and obliterates Christian. In two more cuts we behold them drawing nearer to the other shore; and then, between two radiant angels, one of whom points upward, we see them mounting in new weeds, their former lendings left behind them on the inky river. More angels meet them; Heaven is displayed, and if no better, certainly no worse, than it has been shown by others—a place, at least, infinitely populous and glorious with light—a place that haunts solemnly the hearts of children. And then this symbolic draughtsman once more strikes into his proper vein. Three cuts conclude the first part. In the first the gates close, black against the glory struggling from within. The second shows us Ignorance—alas! poor Arminian!—hailing, in a sad twilight, the ferryman Vain-Hope; and in the third we behold him, bound hand and foot, and black already with the hue of his eternal fate, carried high over the mountain-tops of the world by two angels of the anger of the Lord. 'Carried to Another Place,' the artist enigmatically names his plate—a terrible design.

Wherever he touches on the black side of the supernatural his pencil grows more daring and incisive. He has many true inventions in the perilous and diabolic; he has many startling nightmares realised. It is not easy to select the best; some may like one and some another; the nude, depilated devil bounding and casting darts against the Wicket Gate; the scroll of flying horrors that hang over Christian by the Mouth of Hell; the horned shade that comes behind him whispering blasphemies; the daylight breaking through that rent cave-mouth of the mountains and falling chill adown the haunted tunnel; Christian's further progress along the causeway, between the two black pools, where, at every yard or two, a gin, a pitfall, or a snare awaits the passer-by—loathsome white devilkins harbouring close under the bank to work the springes, Christian himself pausing and pricking with his sword's point at the nearest noose, and pale discomfortable mountains rising on the farther side; or yet again, the two ill-favoured ones that beset the first of Christian's journey, with the frog-like structure of the skull, the frog-like limberness of limbs—crafty, slippery, lustful-looking devils, drawn always in outline as though possessed of a dim, infernal luminosity. Horrid fellows are they, one and all; horrid fellows and horrific scenes. In another spirit that Good-Conscience 'to whom Mr. Honest had spoken in his lifetime,' a cowled, grey, awful figure, one hand pointing to the heavenly shore, realises, I will not say all, but some at least of the strange impressiveness of Bunyan's words. It is no easy nor pleasant thing to speak in one's lifetime with Good-Conscience; he is an austere, unearthly friend, whom maybe Torquemada knew; and the folds of his raiment are not merely claustral, but have something of the horror of the pall. Be not afraid, however; with the hand of that appearance Mr. Honest will get safe across.

Yet perhaps it is in sequences that this artist best displays himself. He loves to look at either side of a thing: as, for instance, when he shows us both sides of the wall—'Grace Inextinguishable' on the one side, with the devil vainly pouring buckets on the flame, and 'The Oil of Grace' on the other, where the Holy Spirit, vessel in hand, still secretly supplies the fire. He loves, also, to show us the same event twice over, and to repeat his instantaneous photographs at the interval of but a moment. So we have, first, the whole troop of pilgrims coming up to Valiant, and Great-heart to the front, spear in hand and parleying; and next, the same cross-roads, from a more distant view, the convoy now scattered and looking safely and curiously on, and Valiant handing over for inspection his 'right Jerusalem blade.' It is true that this designer has no great care after consistency: Apollyon's spear is laid by, his quiver of darts will disappear, whenever they might hinder the designer's freedom; and the fiend's tail is blobbed or forked at his good pleasure. But this is not unsuitable to the illustration of the fervent Bunyan, breathing hurry and momentary inspiration. He, with his hot purpose, hunting sinners with a lasso, shall himself forget the things that he has written yesterday. He shall first slay Heedless in the Valley of the Shadow, and then take leave of him talking in his sleep, as if nothing had happened, in an arbour on the Enchanted Ground. And again, in his rhymed prologue, he shall assign some of the glory of the siege of Doubting Castle to his favourite Valiant-for-the-Truth, who did not meet with the besiegers till long after, at that dangerous corner by Deadman's Lane. And, with all inconsistencies and freedoms, there is a power shown in these sequences of cuts: a power of joining on one action or one humour to another; a power of following out the moods, even of the dismal subterhuman fiends engendered by the artist's fancy; a power of sustained continuous realisation, step by step, in nature's order, that can tell a story, in all its ins and outs, its pauses and surprises, fully and figuratively, like the art of words.

One such sequence is the fight of Christian and Apollyon—six cuts, weird and fiery, like the text. The pilgrim is throughout a pale and stockish figure; but the devil covers a multitude of defects. There is no better devil of the conventional order than our artist's Apollyon, with his mane, his wings, his bestial legs, his changing and terrifying expression, his infernal energy to slay. In cut the first you see him afar off, still obscure in form, but already formidable in suggestion. Cut the second, 'The Fiend in Discourse,' represents him, not reasoning, railing rather, shaking his spear at the pilgrim, his shoulder advanced, his tail writhing in the air, his foot ready for a spring, while Christian stands back a little, timidly defensive. The third illustrates these magnificent words: 'Then Apollyon straddled quite over the whole breadth of the way, and said, I am void of fear in this matter: prepare thyself to die; for I swear by my infernal den that thou shalt go no farther: here will I spill thy soul! And with that he threw a flaming dart at his breast.' In the cut he throws a dart with either hand, belching pointed flames out of his mouth, spreading his broad vans, and straddling the while across the path, as only a fiend can straddle who has just sworn by his infernal den. The defence will not be long against such vice, such flames, such red-hot nether energy. And in the fourth cut, to be sure, he has leaped bodily upon his victim, sped by foot and pinion, and roaring as he leaps. The fifth shows the climacteric of the battle; Christian has reached nimbly out and got his sword, and dealt that deadly home-thrust, the fiend still stretched upon him, but 'giving back, as one that had received his mortal wound.' The raised head, the bellowing mouth, the paw clapped upon the sword, the one wing relaxed in agony, all realise vividly these words of the text. In the sixth and last, the trivial armed figure of the pilgrim is seen kneeling with clasped hands on the betrodden scene of contest and among the shivers of the darts; while just at the margin the hinder quarters and the tail of Apollyon are whisking off, indignant and discounted.

In one point only do these pictures seem to be unworthy of the text, and that point is one rather of the difference of arts than the difference of artists. Throughout his best and worst, in his highest and most divine imaginations as in the narrowest sallies of his sectarianism, the human-hearted piety of Bunyan touches and ennobles, convinces, accuses the reader. Through no art beside the art of words can the kindness of a man's affections be expressed. In the cuts you shall find faithfully parodied the quaintness and the power, the triviality and the surprising freshness of the author's fancy; there you shall find him out-stripped in ready symbolism and the art of bringing things essentially invisible before the eyes: but to feel the contact of essential goodness, to be made in love with piety, the book must be read and not the prints examined.

Farewell should not be taken with a grudge; nor can I dismiss in any other words than those of gratitude a series of pictures which have, to one at least, been the visible embodiment of Bunyan from childhood up, and shown him, through all his years, Great-heart lungeing at Giant Maul, and Apollyon breathing fire at Christian, and every turn and town along the road to the Celestial City, and that bright place itself, seen as to a stave of music, shining afar off upon the hill-top, the candle of the world.

SKETCHES

I. THE SATIRIST

My companion enjoyed a cheap reputation for wit and insight. He was by habit and repute a satirist. If he did occasionally condemn anything or anybody who richly deserved it, and whose demerits had hitherto escaped, it was simply because he condemned everything and everybody. While I was with him he disposed of St. Paul with an epigram, shook my reverence for Shakespeare in a neat antithesis, and fell foul of the Almighty Himself, on the score of one or two out of the ten commandments. Nothing escaped his blighting censure. At every sentence he overthrew an idol, or lowered my estimation of a friend. I saw everything with new eyes, and could only marvel at my former blindness. How was it possible that I had not before observed A's false hair, B's selfishness, or C's boorish manners? I and my companion, methought, walked the streets like a couple of gods among a swarm of vermin; for every one we saw seemed to bear openly upon his brow the mark of the apocalyptic beast. I half expected that these miserable beings, like the people of Lystra, would recognise their betters and force us to the altar; in which case, warned by the late of Paul and Barnabas, I do not know that my modesty would have prevailed upon me to decline. But there was no need for such churlish virtue. More blinded than the Lycaonians, the people saw no divinity in our gait; and as our temporary godhead lay more in the way of observing than healing their infirmities, we were content to pass them by in scorn.

I could not leave my companion, not from regard or even from interest, but from a very natural feeling, inseparable from the case. To understand it, let us take a simile. Suppose yourself walking down the street with a man who continues to sprinkle the crowd out of a flask of vitriol. You would be much diverted with the grimaces and contortions of his victims; and at the same time you would fear to leave his arm until his bottle was empty, knowing that, when once among the crowd, you would run a good chance yourself of baptism with his biting liquor. Now my companion's vitriol was inexhaustible.

It was perhaps the consciousness of this, the knowledge that I was being anointed already out of the vials of his wrath, that made me fall to criticising the critic, whenever we had parted.

After all, I thought, our satirist has just gone far enough into his neighbours to find that the outside is false, without caring to go farther and discover what is really true. He is content to find that things are not what they seem, and broadly generalises from it that they do not exist at all. He sees our virtues are not what they pretend they are; and, on the strength of that, he denies us the possession of virtue altogether. He has learnt the first lesson, that no man is wholly good; but he has not even suspected that there is another equally true, to wit, that no man is wholly bad. Like the inmate of a coloured star, he has eyes for one colour alone. He has a keen scent after evil, but his nostrils are plugged against all good, as people plugged their nostrils before going about the streets of the plague-struck city.

Why does he do this? It is most unreasonable to flee the knowledge of good like the infection of a horrible disease, and batten and grow fat in the real atmosphere of a lazar-house. This was my first thought; but my second was not like unto it, and I saw that our satirist was wise, wise in his generation, like the unjust steward. He does not want light, because the darkness is more pleasant. He does not wish to see the good, because he is happier without it. I recollect that when I walked with him, I was in a state of divine exaltation, such as Adam and Eve must have enjoyed when the savour of the fruit was still unfaded between their lips; and I recognise that this must be the man's habitual state. He has the forbidden fruit in his waist-coat pocket, and can make himself a god as often and as long as he likes. He has raised himself upon a glorious pedestal above his fellows; he has touched the summit of ambition; and he envies neither King nor Kaiser, Prophet nor Priest, content in an elevation as high as theirs, and much more easily attained. Yes, certes, much more easily attained. He has not risen by climbing himself, but by pushing others down. He has grown great in his own estimation, not by blowing himself out, and risking the fate of Æsop's frog, but simply by the habitual use of a diminishing glass on everybody else. And I think altogether that his is a better, a safer, and a surer recipe than most others.

After all, however, looking back on what I have written, I detect a spirit suspiciously like his own. All through, I have been comparing myself with our satirist, and all through, I have had the best of the comparison. Well, well, contagion is as often mental as physical; and I do not think my readers, who have all been under his lash, will blame me very much for giving the headsman a mouthful of his own sawdust.

II. NUITS BLANCHES

If any one should know the pleasure and pain of a sleepless night, it should be I. I remember, so long ago, the sickly child that woke from his few hours' slumber with the sweat of a nightmare on his brow, to lie awake and listen and long for the first signs of life among the silent streets. These nights of pain and weariness are graven on my mind; and so when the same thing happened to me again, everything that I heard or saw was rather a recollection than a discovery.

Weighed upon by the opaque and almost sensible darkness, I listened eagerly for anything to break the sepulchral quiet. But nothing came, save, perhaps, an emphatic crack from the old cabinet that was made by Deacon Brodie, or the dry rustle of the coals on the extinguished fire. It was a calm; or I know that I should have heard in the roar and clatter of the storm, as I have not heard it for so many years, the wild career of a horseman, always scouring up from the distance and passing swiftly below the window; yet always returning again from the place whence first he came, as though, baffled by some higher power, he had retraced his steps to gain impetus for another and another attempt.

As I lay there, there arose out of the utter stillness the rumbling of a carriage a very great way off, that drew near, and passed within a few streets of the house, and died away as gradually as it had arisen. This, too, was as a reminiscence.

I rose and lifted a corner of the blind. Over the black belt of the garden I saw the long line of Queen Street, with here and there a lighted window. How often before had my nurse lifted me out of bed and pointed them out to me, while we wondered together if, there also, there were children that could not sleep, and if these lighted oblongs were signs of those that waited like us for the morning.

I went out into the lobby, and looked down into the great deep well of the staircase. For what cause I know not, just as it used to be in the old days that the feverish child might be the better served, a peep of gas illuminated a narrow circle far below me. But where I was, all was darkness and silence, save the dry monotonous ticking of the clock that came ceaselessly up to my ear.

The final crown of it all, however, the last touch of reproduction on the pictures of my memory, was the arrival of that time for which, all night through, I waited and longed of old. It was my custom, as the hours dragged on, to repeat the question, 'When will the carts come in?' and repeat it again and again until at last those sounds arose in the street that I have heard once more this morning. The road before our house is a great thoroughfare for early carts. I know not, and I never have known, what they carry, whence they come, or whither they go. But I know that, long ere dawn, and for hours together, they stream continuously past, with the same rolling and jerking of wheels and the same clink of horses' feet. It was not for nothing that they made the burthen of my wishes all night through. They are really the first throbbings of life, the harbingers of day; and it pleases you as much to hear them as it must please a shipwrecked seaman once again to grasp a hand of flesh and blood after years of miserable solitude. They have the freshness of the daylight life about them. You can hear the carters cracking their whips and crying hoarsely to their horses or to one another; and sometimes even a peal of healthy, harsh horse-laughter comes up to you through the darkness. There is now an end of mystery and fear. Like the knocking at the door in Macbeth, [205] or the cry of the watchman in the Tour de Nesle, they show that the horrible cæsura is over and the nightmares have fled away, because the day is breaking and the ordinary life of men is beginning to bestir itself

143

among the streets.

In the middle of it all I fell asleep, to be wakened by the officious knocking at my door, and I find myself twelve years older than I had dreamed myself all night.

III. THE WREATH OF IMMORTELLES

It is all very well to talk of death as 'a pleasant potion of immortality', but the most of us, I suspect, are of 'queasy stomachs,' and find it none of the sweetest. [206a] The graveyard may be cloak-room to Heaven; but we must admit that it is a very ugly and offensive vestibule in itself, however fair may be the life to which it leads. And though Enoch and Elias went into the temple through a gate which certainly may be called Beautiful, the rest of us have to find our way to it through Ezekiel's low-bowed door and the vault full of creeping things and all manner of abominable beasts. Nevertheless, there is a certain frame of mind to which a cemetery is, if not an antidote, at least an alleviation. If you are in a fit of the blues, go nowhere else. It was in obedience to this wise regulation that the other morning found me lighting my pipe at the entrance to Old Greyfriars', thoroughly sick of the town, the country, and myself.

Two of the men were talking at the gate, one of them carrying a spade in hands still crusted with the soil of graves. Their very aspect was delightful to me; and I crept nearer to them, thinking to pick up some snatch of sexton gossip, some 'talk fit for a charnel,' [206b] something, in fine, worthy of that fastidious logician, that adept in coroner's law, who has come down to us as the patron of Yaughan's liquor, and the very prince of gravediggers. Scots people in general are so much wrapped up in their profession that I had a good chance of overhearing such conversation: the talk of fish-mongers running usually on stockfish and haddocks; while of the Scots sexton I could repeat stories and speeches that positively smell of the graveyard. But on this occasion I was doomed to disappointment. My two friends were far into the region of generalities. Their profession was forgotten in their electorship. Politics had engulfed the narrower economy of grave-digging. 'Na, na,' said the one, 'ye're a' wrang.' 'The English and Irish Churches,' answered the other, in a tone as if he had made the remark before, and it had been called in question—'The English and Irish Churches have impoverished the country.'

'Such are the results of education,' thought I as I passed beside them and came fairly among the tombs. Here, at least, there were no commonplace politics, no diluted this-morning's leader, to distract or offend me. The old shabby church showed, as usual, its quaint extent of roofage and the relievo skeleton on one gable, still blackened with the fire of thirty years ago. A chill dank mist lay over all. The Old Greyfriars' churchyard was in perfection that morning, and one could go round and reckon up the associations with no fear of vulgar interruption. On this stone the Covenant was signed. In that vault, as the story goes, John Knox took hiding in some Reformation broil. From that window Burke the murderer looked out many a time across the tombs, and perhaps o' nights let himself down over the sill to rob some new-made grave. Certainly he would have a selection here. The very walks have been carried over forgotten resting-places; and the whole ground is uneven, because (as I was once quaintly told) 'when the wood rots it stands to reason the soil should fall in,' which, from the law of gravitation, is certainly beyond denial. But it is round the boundary that there are the finest tombs. The whole irregular space is, as it were, fringed with quaint old monuments, rich in death's-heads and scythes and hour-glasses, and doubly rich in pious epitaphs and Latin mottoes—rich in them to such an extent that their proper space has run over, and they have crawled end-long up the shafts of columns and ensconced themselves in all sorts of odd corners among the sculpture. These tombs raise their backs against the rabble of squalid dwelling-houses, and every here and there a clothes-pole projects between two monuments its fluttering trophy of white and yellow and red. With a grim irony they recall the banners in the Invalides, banners as appropriate perhaps over the sepulchres of tailors and weavers as these others above the dust of armies. Why they put things out to dry on that particular morning it was hard to imagine. The grass was grey with drops of rain, the headstones black with moisture. Yet, in despite of weather and common sense, there they hung between the tombs; and beyond them I could see through open windows into miserable rooms where whole families were born and fed, and slept and died. At one a girl sat singing merrily with her back to the graveyard; and from another came the shrill tones of a scolding woman. Every here and there was a town garden full of sickly flowers, or a pile of crockery inside upon the window-seat. But you do not grasp the full connection between these houses of the dead and the living, the unnatural marriage of stately sepulchres and squalid houses, till, lower down, where the road has sunk far below the surface of the cemetery, and the very roofs are scarcely on a level with its wall, you observe that a proprietor has taken advantage of a tall monument and trained a chimney-stack against its back. It startles you to see the red, modern pots peering over the shoulder of the tomb.

A man was at work on a grave, his spade clinking away the drift of bones that permeates the thin brown soil; but my first disappointment had taught me to expect little from Greyfriars' sextons, and I passed him by in silence. A slater on the slope of a neighbouring roof eyed me curiously. A lean black cat, looking as if it had battened on strange meats, slipped past me. A little boy at a window put his finger to his nose in so offensive a manner that I was put upon my dignity, and turned grandly off to read old epitaphs and peer through the gratings into the shadow of vaults.

Just then I saw two women coming down a path, one of them old, and the other younger, with a child in her arms. Both had faces eaten with famine and hardened with sin, and both had reached that stage of degradation, much lower in a woman than a man, when all care for dress is lost. As they came down they neared a grave, where some pious friend or relative had laid a wreath of immortelles, and put a bell glass over it, as is the custom. The effect of that ring of dull yellow among so many blackened and dusty sculptures was more pleasant than it is in modern cemeteries, where every second mound can boast a similar coronal; and here, where it was the exception and not the rule, I could even fancy the drops of moisture that dimmed the covering were the tears of those who laid it where it was. As the two women came up to it, one of them kneeled down on the wet grass and looked long and silently through the clouded shade, while the second stood above her, gently oscillating to and fro to lull the muling baby. I was struck a great way off with something religious in the attitude of these two unkempt and haggard women; and I drew near faster, but still cautiously, to hear what they were saying. Surely on them the spirit of death and decay had descended; I had no education to dread here: should I not have a chance of seeing nature? Alas! a pawnbroker could not have been more practical and commonplace, for this was what the kneeling woman said to the woman upright—this and nothing more: 'Eh, what extravagance!'

O nineteenth century, wonderful art thou indeed—wonderful, but wearisome in thy stale and deadly uniformity. Thy men are more like numerals than men. They must bear their idiosyncrasies or their professions written on a placard about their neck, like the scenery in Shakespeare's theatre. Thy precepts of economy have pierced into the lowest ranks of life; and there is now a decorum in vice, a respectability among the disreputable, a pure spirit of Philistinism among the waifs and strays of thy Bohemia. For lo! thy very gravediggers talk politics; and thy castaways kneel upon new graves, to discuss the cost of the monument and grumble at the improvidence of love.

Such was the elegant apostrophe that I made as I went out of the gates again, happily satisfied in myself, and feeling that I alone of all whom I had seen was able to profit by the silent poem of these green mounds and blackened headstones.

IV. NURSES

I knew one once, and the room where, lonely and old, she waited for death. It was pleasant enough, high up above the lane, and looking forth upon a hill-side, covered all day with sheets and yellow blankets, and with long lines of underclothing fluttering between the battered posts. There were any number of cheap prints, and a drawing by one of 'her children,' and there were flowers in the window, and a sickly canary withered into consumption in an ornamental cage. The bed, with its checked coverlid, was in a closet. A great Bible lay on the table; and her drawers were full of 'scones,' which it was her pleasure to give to young visitors such as I was then.

You may not think this a melancholy picture; but the canary, and the cat, and the white mouse that she had for a while, and that died, were all indications of the want that ate into her heart. I think I know a little of what that old woman felt; and I am as sure as if I had seen her, that she sat many an hour in silent tears, with the big Bible open before her clouded eyes.

147

If you could look back upon her life, and feel the great chain that had linked her to one child after another, sometimes to be wrenched suddenly through, and sometimes, which is infinitely worse, to be torn gradually off through years of growing neglect, or perhaps growing dislike! She had, like the mother, overcome that natural repugnance—repugnance which no man can conquer—towards the infirm and helpless mass of putty of the earlier stage. She had spent her best and happiest years in tending, watching, and learning to love like a mother this child, with which she has no connection and to which she has no tie. Perhaps she refused some sweetheart (such things have been), or put him off and off, until he lost heart and turned to some one else, all for fear of leaving this creature that had wound itself about her heart. And the end of it all—her month's warning, and a present perhaps, and the rest of the life to vain regret. Or, worse still, to see the child gradually forgetting and forsaking her, fostered in disrespect and neglect on the plea of growing manliness, and at last beginning to treat her as a servant whom he had treated a few years before as a mother. She sees the Bible or the Psalm-book, which with gladness and love unutterable in her heart she had bought for him years ago out of her slender savings, neglected for some newer gift of his father, lying in dust in the lumber-room or given away to a poor child, and the act applauded for its unfeeling charity. Little wonder if she becomes hurt and angry, and attempts to tyrannise and to grasp her old power back again. We are not all patient Grizzels, by good fortune, but the most of us human beings with feelings and tempers of our own.

And so, in the end, behold her in the room that I described. Very likely and very naturally, in some fling of feverish misery or recoil of thwarted love, she has quarrelled with her old employers and the children are forbidden to see her or to speak to her; or at best she gets her rent paid and a little to herself, and now and then her late charges are sent up (with another nurse, perhaps) to pay her a short visit. How bright these visits seem as she looks forward to them on her lonely bed! How unsatisfactory their realisation, when the forgetful child, half wondering, checks with every word and action the outpouring of her maternal love! How bitter and restless the memories that they leave behind! And for the rest, what else has she?—to watch them with eager eyes as they go to school, to sit in church where she can see them

148

every Sunday, to be passed some day unnoticed in the street, or deliberately cut because the great man or the great woman are with friends before whom they are ashamed to recognise the old woman that loved them.

When she goes home that night, how lonely will the room appear to her! Perhaps the neighbours may hear her sobbing to herself in the dark, with the fire burnt out for want of fuel, and the candle still unlit upon the table.

And it is for this that they live, these quasi-mothers—mothers in everything but the travail and the thanks. It is for this that they have remained virtuous in youth, living the dull life of a household servant. It is for this that they refused the old sweetheart, and have no fireside or offspring of their own.

I believe in a better state of things, that there will be no more nurses, and that every mother will nurse her own offspring; for what can be more hardening and demoralising than to call forth the tenderest feelings of a woman's heart and cherish them yourself as long as you need them, as long as your children require a nurse to love them, and then to blight and thwart and destroy them, whenever your own use for them is at an end. This may be Utopian; but it is always a little thing if one mother or two mothers can be brought to feel more tenderly to those who share their toil and have no part in their reward.

V. A CHARACTER

The man has a red, bloated face, and his figure is short and squat. So far there is nothing in him to notice, but when you see his eyes, you can read in these hard and shallow orbs a depravity beyond measure depraved, a thirst after wickedness, the pure, disinterested love of Hell for its own sake. The other night, in the street, I was watching an omnibus passing with lit-up windows, when I heard some one coughing at my side as though he would cough his soul out; and turning round, I saw him stopping under a lamp, with a brown greatcoat buttoned round him and his whole face convulsed. It seemed as if he could not live long; and so the sight set my mind upon a train of thought, as I finished my cigar up and down the lighted streets.

He is old, but all these years have not yet quenched his thirst for evil, and his eyes still delight themselves in wickedness. He is dumb; but he will not let that hinder his foul trade, or perhaps I should say, his yet fouler amusement, and he has pressed a slate into the service of corruption. Look at him, and he will sign to you with his bloated head, and when you go to him in answer to the sign, thinking perhaps that the poor dumb man has lost his way, you will see what he writes upon his slate. He haunts the doors of schools, and shows such inscriptions as these to the innocent children that come out. He hangs about picture-galleries, and makes the noblest pictures the text for some silent homily of vice. His industry is a lesson to ourselves. Is it not wonderful how he can triumph over his infirmities and do such an amount of harm without a tongue? Wonderful industry—strange, fruitless, pleasureless toil? Must not the very devil feel a soft emotion to see his disinterested and laborious service? Ah, but the devil knows better than this: he knows that this man is penetrated with the love of evil and that all his pleasure is shut up in wickedness: he recognises him, perhaps, as a fit type for mankind of his satanic self, and watches over his effigy as we might watch over a favourite likeness. As the business man comes to love the toil, which he only looked upon at first as a ladder towards other desires and less unnatural gratifications, so the dumb man has felt the charm of his trade and fallen captivated before the eyes of sin. It is a mistake when preachers tell us that vice is hideous and loathsome; for even vice has her Hörsel and her devotees, who love her for her own sake.

THE GREAT NORTH ROAD

CHAPTER I—NANCE AT THE 'GREEN DRAGON'

Nance Holdaway was on her knees before the fire blowing the green wood that voluminously smoked upon the dogs, and only now and then shot forth a smothered flame; her knees already ached and her eyes smarted, for she had been some while at this ungrateful task, but her mind was gone far away to meet the coming stranger. Now she met him in the wood, now at the castle gate, now in the kitchen by candle-light; each fresh presentment eclipsed the one before; a form so elegant, manners so sedate, a countenance so brave and comely, a voice so winning and resolute—sure such a man was never seen! The thick-coming fancies poured and brightened in her head like the smoke and flames upon the hearth.

Presently the heavy foot of her uncle Jonathan was heard upon the stair, and as he entered the room she bent the closer to her work. He glanced at the green fagots with a sneer, and looked askance at the bed and the white sheets, at the strip of carpet laid, like an island, on the great expanse of the stone floor, and at the broken glazing of the casement clumsily repaired with paper.

'Leave that fire a-be,' he cried. 'What, have I toiled all my life to turn innkeeper at the hind end? Leave it a-be, I say.'

'La, uncle, it doesn't burn a bit; it only smokes,' said Nance, looking up from her position.

'You are come of decent people on both sides,' returned the old man. 'Who are you to blow the coals for any Robin-run-agate? Get up, get on your hood, make yourself useful, and be off to the "Green Dragon."'

'I thought you was to go yourself,' Nance faltered.

'So did I,' quoth Jonathan; 'but it appears I was mistook.'

The very excess of her eagerness alarmed her, and she began to hang back. 'I think I would rather not, dear uncle,' she said. 'Night is at hand, and I think, dear, I would rather not.'

'Now you look here,' replied Jonathan, 'I have my lord's orders, have I not? Little he gives me, but it's all my livelihood. And do you fancy, if I disobey my lord, I'm likely to turn round for a lass like you? No, I've that hell-fire of pain in my old knee, I wouldn't walk a mile, not for King George upon his bended knees.' And he walked to the window and looked down the steep scarp to where the river foamed in the bottom of the dell.

Nance stayed for no more bidding. In her own room, by the glimmer of the twilight, she washed her hands and pulled on her Sunday mittens; adjusted her black hood, and tied a dozen times its cherry ribbons; and in less than ten minutes, with a fluttering heart and excellently bright eyes, she passed forth under the arch and over the bridge, into the thickening shadows of the groves. A well-marked wheel-track conducted her. The wood, which upon both sides of the river dell was a mere scrambling thicket of hazel, hawthorn, and holly, boasted on the level of more considerable timber. Beeches came to a good growth, with here and there an oak; and the track now passed under a high arcade of branches, and now ran under the open sky in glades. As the girl proceeded these glades became more frequent, the trees began again to decline in size, and the wood to degenerate into furzy coverts. Last of all there was a fringe of elders; and beyond that the track came forth upon an open, rolling moorland, dotted with wind-bowed and scanty bushes, and all golden brown with the winter, like a grouse. Right over against the girl the last red embers of the sunset burned under horizontal clouds; the night fell clear and still and frosty, and the track in low and marshy passages began to crackle under foot with ice.

Some half a mile beyond the borders of the wood the lights of the 'Green Dragon' hove in sight, and running close beside them, very faint in the dying dusk, the pale ribbon of the Great North Road. It was the back of the post-house that was presented to Nance Holdaway; and as she continued to draw near and the night to fall more completely, she became aware of an unusual brightness and bustle. A post-chaise stood in the yard, its lamps

152

already lighted: light shone hospitably in the windows and from the open door; moving lights and shadows testified to the activity of servants bearing lanterns. The clank of pails, the stamping of hoofs on the firm causeway, the jingle of harness, and, last of all, the energetic hissing of a groom, began to fall upon her ear. By the stir you would have thought the mail was at the door, but it was still too early in the night. The down mail was not due at the 'Green Dragon' for hard upon an hour; the up mail from Scotland not before two in the black morning.

Nance entered the yard somewhat dazzled. Sam, the tall ostler, was polishing a curb-chain wit sand; the lantern at his feet letting up spouts of candle-light through the holes with which its conical roof was peppered.

'Hey, miss,' said he jocularly, 'you won't look at me any more, now you have gentry at the castle.'

Her cheeks burned with anger.

'That's my lord's chay,' the man continued, nodding at the chaise, 'Lord Windermoor's. Came all in a fluster—dinner, bowl of punch, and put the horses to. For all the world like a runaway match, my dear—bar the bride. He brought Mr. Archer in the chay with him.'

'Is that Holdaway?' cried the landlord from the lighted entry, where he stood shading his eyes.

'Only me, sir,' answered Nance.

'O, you, Miss Nance,' he said. 'Well, come in quick, my pretty. My lord is waiting for your uncle.'

And he ushered Nance into a room cased with yellow wainscot and lighted by tall candles, where two gentlemen sat at a table finishing a bowl of punch. One of these was stout, elderly, and irascible, with a face like a full moon, well dyed with liquor, thick tremulous lips, a short, purple hand, in which he brandished a long pipe, and an abrupt and gobbling utterance. This was my Lord Windermoor. In his companion Nance beheld a younger man, tall, quiet, grave, demurely dressed, and wearing his own hair. Her glance but lighted on him, and she flushed, for in that second she made sure that she had twice betrayed herself—betrayed by the involuntary flash of her black eyes her secret impatience to behold this new companion, and, what was far worse, betrayed her disappointment in the realisation of her dreams. He, meanwhile, as if unconscious, continued to regard her with unmoved decorum.

'O, a man of wood,' thought Nance.

'What—what?' said his lordship. 'Who is this?'

'If you please, my lord, I am Holdaway's niece,' replied Nance, with a curtsey.

'Should have been here himself,' observed his lordship. 'Well, you tell Holdaway that I'm aground, not a stiver—not a stiver. I'm running from the beagles—going abroad, tell Holdaway. And he need look for no more wages: glad of 'em myself, if I could get 'em. He can live in the castle if he likes, or go to the devil. O, and here is Mr. Archer; and I recommend him to take him in—a friend of mine—and Mr. Archer will pay, as I wrote. And I regard that in the light of a precious good thing for Holdaway, let me tell you, and a set-off against the wages.'

'But O, my lord!' cried Nance, 'we live upon the wages, and what are we to do without?'

'What am I to do?—what am I to do?' replied Lord Windermoor with some exasperation. 'I have no wages. And there is Mr. Archer. And if Holdaway doesn't like it, he can go to the devil, and you with him!—and you with him!'

'And yet, my lord,' said Mr. Archer, 'these good people will have as keen a sense of loss as you or I; keener, perhaps, since they have done nothing to deserve it.'

'Deserve it?' cried the peer. 'What? What? If a rascally highwayman comes up to me with a confounded pistol, do you say that I've deserved it? How often am I to tell you, sir, that I was cheated—that I was cheated?'

154

'You are happy in the belief,' returned Mr. Archer gravely.

'Archer, you would be the death of me!' exclaimed his lordship. 'You know you're drunk; you know it, sir; and yet you can't get up a spark of animation.'

'I have drunk fair, my lord,' replied the younger man; 'but I own I am conscious of no exhilaration.'

'If you had as black a look-out as me, sir,' cried the peer, 'you would be very glad of a little innocent exhilaration, let me tell you. I am glad of it—glad of it, and I only wish I was drunker. For let me tell you it's a cruel hard thing upon a man of my time of life and my position, to be brought down to beggary because the world is full of thieves and rascals—thieves and rascals. What? For all I know, you may be a thief and a rascal yourself; and I would fight you for a pinch of snuff—a pinch of snuff,' exclaimed his lordship.

Here Mr. Archer turned to Nance Holdaway with a pleasant smile, so full of sweetness, kindness, and composure that, at one bound, her dreams returned to her. 'My good Miss Holdaway,' said he, 'if you are willing to show me the road, I am even eager to be gone. As for his lordship and myself, compose yourself; there is no fear; this is his lordship's way.'

'What? what?' cried his lordship. 'My way? Ish no such a thing, my way.'

'Come, my lord,' cried Archer; 'you and I very thoroughly understand each other; and let me suggest, it is time that both of us were gone. The mail will soon be due. Here, then, my lord, I take my leave of you, with the most earnest assurance of my gratitude for the past, and a sincere offer of any services I may be able to render in the future.'

'Archer,' exclaimed Lord Windermoor, 'I love you like a son. Le' 's have another bowl.'

'My lord, for both our sakes, you will excuse me,' replied Mr. Archer. 'We both require caution; we must both, for some while at least, avoid the chance of a pursuit.'

'Archer,' quoth his lordship, 'this is a rank ingratishood. What? I'm to go firing away in the dark in the cold po'chaise, and not so much as a game of écarté possible, unless I stop and play with the postillion, the postillion; and the whole country swarming with thieves and rascals and highwaymen.'

'I beg your lordship's pardon,' put in the landlord, who now appeared in the doorway to announce the chaise, 'but this part of the North Road is known for safety. There has not been a robbery, to call a robbery, this five years' time. Further south, of course, it's nearer London, and another story,' he added.

'Well, then, if that's so,' concluded my lord, 'le' 's have t'other bowl and a pack of cards.'

'My lord, you forget,' said Archer, 'I might still gain; but it is hardly possible for me to lose.'

'Think I'm a sharper?' inquired the peer. 'Gen'leman's parole's all I ask.'

But Mr. Archer was proof against these blandishments, and said farewell gravely enough to Lord Windermoor, shaking his hand and at the same time bowing very low. 'You will never know,' says he, 'the service you have done me.' And with that, and before my lord had finally taken up his meaning, he had slipped about the table, touched Nance lightly but imperiously on the arm, and left the room. In face of the outbreak of his lordship's lamentations she made haste to follow the truant.

CHAPTER II—IN WHICH MR. ARCHER IS INSTALLED

The chaise had been driven round to the front door; the courtyard lay all deserted, and only lit by a lantern set upon a window-sill. Through this Nance rapidly led the way, and began to ascend the swellings of the moor with a heart that somewhat fluttered in her bosom. She was not afraid, but in the course of these last passages with Lord Windermoor Mr. Archer had ascended to that pedestal on which her fancy waited to instal him. The reality, she felt, excelled her dreams, and this cold night walk was the first romantic incident in her experience.

It was the rule in these days to see gentlemen unsteady after dinner, yet Nance was both surprised and amused when her companion, who had spoken so soberly, began to stumble and waver by her side with the most airy divagations. Sometimes he would get so close to her that she must edge away; and at others lurch clear out of the track and plough among deep heather. His courtesy and gravity meanwhile remained unaltered. He asked her how far they had to go; whether the way lay all upon the moorland, and when he learned they had to pass a wood expressed his pleasure. 'For,' said he, 'I am passionately fond of trees. Trees and fair lawns, if you consider of it rightly, are the ornaments of nature, as palaces and fine approaches—' And here he stumbled into a patch of slough and nearly fell. The girl had hard work not to laugh, but at heart she was lost in admiration for one who talked so elegantly.

They had got to about a quarter of a mile from the 'Green Dragon,' and were near the summit of the rise, when a sudden rush of wheels arrested them. Turning and looking back, they saw the post-house, now much declined in brightness; and speeding away northward the two tremulous bright dots of my Lord Windermoor's chaise-lamps. Mr. Archer followed these yellow and unsteady stars until they dwindled into points and disappeared.

'There goes my only friend,' he said. 'Death has cut off those that loved me, and change of fortune estranged my flatterers; and but for you, poor bankrupt, my life is as lonely as this moor.'

The tone of his voice affected both of them. They stood there on the side of the moor, and became thrillingly conscious of the void waste of the night, without a feature for the eye, and except for the fainting whisper of the carriage-wheels without a murmur for the ear. And instantly, like a mockery, there broke out, very far away, but clear and jolly, the note of the mail-guard's horn. 'Over the hills' was his air. It rose to the two watchers on the moor with the most cheerful sentiment of human company and travel, and at the same time in and around the 'Green Dragon' it woke up a great bustle of lights running to and fro and clattering hoofs. Presently after, out of the darkness to southward, the mail grew near with a growing rumble. Its lamps were very large and bright, and threw their radiance forward in overlapping cones; the four cantering horses swarmed and steamed; the body of the coach followed like a great shadow; and this lit picture slid with a sort of ineffectual swiftness over the black field of night, and was eclipsed by the buildings of the 'Green Dragon.'

Mr. Archer turned abruptly and resumed his former walk; only that he was now more steady, kept better alongside his young conductor, and had fallen into a silence broken by sighs. Nance waxed very pitiful over his fate, contrasting an imaginary past of courts and great society, and perhaps the King himself, with the tumbledown ruin in a wood to which she was now conducting him.

'You must try, sir, to keep your spirits up,' said she. 'To be sure this is a great change for one like you; but who knows the future?'

Mr. Archer turned towards her in the darkness, and she could clearly perceive that he smiled upon her very kindly. 'There spoke a sweet nature,' said he, 'and I must thank you for these words. But I would not have you fancy that I regret the past for any happiness found in it, or that I fear the simplicity and hardship of the country. I am a man that has been much tossed about in life; now up, now down; and do you think that I shall not be able to support what you support—you who are kind, and therefore know how to feel pain; who are beautiful, and therefore hope; who are young, and therefore (or am I the more mistaken?) discontented?'

'Nay, sir, not that, at least,' said Nance; 'not discontented. If I were to be discontented, how should I look those that have real sorrows in the face? I have faults enough, but not that fault; and I have my merits too, for I have a good opinion of myself. But for beauty, I am not so simple but that I can tell a banter from a compliment.'

'Nay, nay,' said Mr. Archer, 'I had half forgotten; grief is selfish, and I was thinking of myself and not of you, or I had never blurted out so bold a piece of praise. 'Tis the best proof of my sincerity. But come, now, I would lay a wager you are no coward?'

'Indeed, sir, I am not more afraid than another,' said Nance. 'None of my blood are given to fear.'

'And you are honest?' he returned.

'I will answer for that,' said she.

'Well, then, to be brave, to be honest, to be kind, and to be contented, since you say you are so—is not that to fill up a great part of virtue?'

'I fear you are but a flatterer,' said Nance, but she did not say it clearly, for what with bewilderment and satisfaction, her heart was quite oppressed.

There could be no harm, certainly, in these grave compliments; but yet they charmed and frightened her, and to find favour, for reasons however obscure, in the eyes of this elegant, serious, and most unfortunate young gentleman, was a giddy elevation, was almost an apotheosis, for a country maid.

But she was to be no more exercised; for Mr. Archer, disclaiming any thought of flattery, turned off to other subjects, and held her all through the wood in conversation, addressing her with an air of perfect sincerity, and listening to her answers with every mark of interest. Had open flattery continued, Nance would have soon found refuge in good sense; but the more subtle lure she could not suspect, much less avoid. It was the first time she had ever taken part in a conversation illuminated by any ideas. All was then true that she had heard and dreamed of gentlemen; they were a race apart, like deities knowing good and evil. And then there burst upon her soul a divine thought, hope's glorious sunrise: since she could understand, since it seemed that she too, even she, could interest this sorrowful Apollo, might she not learn? or was she not learning? Would not her soul awake and put forth wings? Was she not, in fact, an enchanted princess, waiting but a touch to become royal? She saw herself transformed, radiantly attired, but in the most exquisite taste: her face grown longer and more refined; her tint etherealised; and she heard herself with delighted wonder talking like a book.

Meanwhile they had arrived at where the track comes out above the river dell, and saw in front of them the castle, faintly shadowed on the night, covering with its broken battlements a bold projection of the bank, and showing at the extreme end, where were the habitable tower and wing, some crevices of candle-light. Hence she called loudly upon her uncle, and he was seen to issue, lantern in hand, from the tower door, and, where the ruins did not intervene, to pick his way over the swarded courtyard, avoiding treacherous cellars and winding among blocks of fallen masonry. The arch of the great gate was still entire, flanked by two tottering bastions, and it was here that Jonathan met them, standing at the edge of the bridge, bent somewhat forward, and blinking at them through the glow of his own lantern. Mr. Archer greeted him with civility; but the old man was in no humour of compliance. He guided the newcomer across the court-yard, looking sharply and quickly in his face, and grumbling all the time about the cold, and the discomfort and dilapidation of the castle. He was sure he hoped that Mr. Archer would like it; but in truth he could not think what brought him there. Doubtless he had a good reason—this with a look of cunning scrutiny—but, indeed, the place was quite unfit for any person of repute; he himself was eaten up with the rheumatics. It was the most rheumaticky place in England, and some fine day the whole habitable part (to call it habitable) would fetch away bodily and go down the slope into the river. He had seen the cracks widening; there was a plaguy issue in the bank below; he thought a spring was mining it; it might be to-morrow, it might be next day; but they were all sure of a come-down sooner or later. 'And that is a poor death,' said he, 'for any one, let alone a gentleman, to have a whole old ruin dumped upon his belly. Have a care to your left there; these cellar vaults have all broke down, and the grass and hemlock hide 'em. Well, sir, here is welcome to you, such as it is, and wishing you well away.'

And with that Jonathan ushered his guest through the tower door, and down three steps on the left hand into the kitchen or common room of the castle. It was a huge, low room, as large as a meadow, occupying the whole width of the habitable wing, with six barred windows looking on the court, and two into the river valley. A dresser, a table, and a few chairs stood dotted here and there upon the uneven flags. Under the great chimney a good fire burned in an iron fire-basket; a high old settee, rudely carved with figures and Gothic lettering, flanked it on either side; there was a hinge table and a stone bench in the chimney corner, and above the arch hung guns, axes, lanterns, and great sheaves of rusty keys.

Jonathan looked about him, holding up the lantern, and shrugged his shoulders, with a pitying grimace. 'Here it is,' he said. 'See the damp on the floor, look at the moss; where there's moss you may be sure that it's rheumaticky. Try and get near that fire for to warm yourself; it'll blow the coat off your back. And with a young gentleman with a face like yours, as pale as a tallow-candle, I'd be afeard of a churchyard cough and a galloping decline,' says Jonathan, naming the maladies with gloomy gusto, 'or the cold might strike and turn your blood,' he added.

Mr. Archer fairly laughed. 'My good Mr. Holdaway,' said he, 'I was born with that same tallow-candle face, and the only fear that you inspire me with is the fear that I intrude unwelcomely upon your private hours. But I think I can promise you that I am very little troublesome, and I am inclined to hope that the terms which I can offer may still pay you the derangement.'

'Yes, the terms,' said Jonathan, 'I was thinking of that. As you say, they are very small,' and he shook his head.

'Unhappily, I can afford no more,' said Mr. Archer. 'But this we have arranged already,' he added with a certain stiffness; 'and as I am aware that Miss Holdaway has matter to communicate, I will, if you permit, retire at once. To-night I must bivouac; to-morrow my trunk is to follow from the "Dragon." So if you will show me to my room I shall wish you a good slumber and a better awakening.'

Jonathan silently gave the lantern to Nance, and she, turning and curtseying in the doorway, proceeded to conduct their guest up the broad winding staircase of the tower. He followed with a very brooding face.

'Alas!' cried Nance, as she entered the room, 'your fire black out,' and, setting down the lantern, she clapped upon her knees before the chimney and began to rearrange the charred and still smouldering remains. Mr. Archer looked about the gaunt apartment with a sort of shudder. The great height, the bare stone, the shattered windows, the aspect of the uncurtained bed, with one of its four fluted columns broken short, all struck a chill upon his fancy. From this dismal survey his eyes returned to Nance crouching before the fire, the candle in one hand and artfully puffing at the embers; the flames as they broke forth played upon the soft outline of her cheek—she was alive and young, coloured with the bright hues of life, and a woman. He looked upon her, softening; and then sat down and continued to admire the picture.

'There, sir,' said she, getting upon her feet, 'your fire is doing bravely now. Good-night.'

He rose and held out his hand. 'Come,' said he, 'you are my only friend in these parts, and you must shake hands.'

She brushed her hand upon her skirt and offered it, blushing.

'God bless you, my dear,' said he.

And then, when he was alone, he opened one of the windows, and stared down into the dark valley. A gentle wimpling of the river among stones ascended to his ear; the trees upon the other bank stood very black against the sky; farther away an owl was hooting. It was dreary and cold, and as he turned back to the hearth and the fine glow of fire, 'Heavens!' said he to himself, 'what an unfortunate destiny is mine!'

He went to bed, but sleep only visited his pillow in uneasy snatches. Outbreaks of loud speech came up the staircase; he heard the old stones of the castle crack in the frosty night with sharp reverberations, and the bed complained under his tossings. Lastly, far on into the morning, he awakened from a doze to hear, very far off, in the extreme and breathless quiet, a wailing flourish on the horn. The down mail was drawing near to the 'Green Dragon.' He sat up in bed; the sound was tragical by distance, and the modulation appealed to his ear like human speech. It seemed to call upon him with a dreary insistence—to call him far away, to address him personally, and to have a meaning that he failed to seize. It was thus, at least, in this nodding castle, in a cold, miry woodland, and so far from men and society, that the traffic on the Great North Road spoke to him in the intervals of slumber.

CHAPTER III—JONATHAN HOLDAWAY

Nance descended the tower stair, pausing at every step. She was in no hurry to confront her uncle with bad news, and she must dwell a little longer on the rich note of Mr. Archer's voice, the charm of his kind words, and the beauty of his manner and person. But, once at the stair-foot, she threw aside the spell and recovered her sensible and workaday self.

Jonathan was seated in the middle of the settle, a mug of ale beside him, in the attitude of one prepared for trouble; but he did not speak, and suffered her to fetch her supper and eat of it, with a very excellent appetite, in silence. When she had done, she, too, drew a tankard of home-brewed, and came and planted herself in front of him upon the settle.

'Well?' said Jonathan.

'My lord has run away,' said Nance.

'What?' cried the old man.

'Abroad,' she continued; 'run away from creditors. He said he had not a stiver, but he was drunk enough. He said you might live on in the castle, and Mr. Archer would pay you; but you was to look for no more wages, since he would be glad of them himself.'

Jonathan's face contracted; the flush of a black, bilious anger mounted to the roots of his hair; he gave an inarticulate cry, leapt upon his feet, and began rapidly pacing the stone floor. At first he kept his hands behind his back in a tight knot; then he began to gesticulate as he turned.

'This man—this lord,' he shouted, 'who is he? He was born with a gold spoon in his mouth, and I with a dirty straw. He rolled in his coach when he was a baby. I have dug and toiled and laboured since I was that high—that high.' And he shouted again. 'I'm bent and broke, and full of pains. D' ye think I don't know the taste of sweat? Many's the gallon I've drunk of it—ay, in the midwinter, toiling like a slave. All through, what has my life been? Bend, bend, bend my old creaking back till it would ache like breaking; wade about in the foul mire, never a dry stitch; empty belly, sore hands, hat off to my Lord Redface; kicks and ha'pence; and now, here, at the hind end, when I'm worn to my poor bones, a kick and done with it.' He walked a little while in silence, and then, extending his hand, 'Now you, Nance Holdaway,' says he, 'you come of my blood, and you're a good girl. When that man was a boy, I used to carry his gun for him. I carried the gun all day on my two feet, and many a stitch I had, and chewed a bullet for. He rode upon a horse, with feathers in his hat; but it was him that had the shots and took the game home. Did I complain? Not I. I knew my station. What did I ask, but just the chance to live and die honest? Nance Holdaway, don't let them deny it to me—don't let them do it. I've been as poor as Job, and as honest as the day, but now, my girl, you mark these words of mine, I'm getting tired of it.'

'I wouldn't say such words, at least,' said Nance.

'You wouldn't?' said the old man grimly. 'Well, and did I when I was your age? Wait till your back's broke and your hands tremble, and your eyes fail, and you're weary of the battle and ask no more but to lie down in your bed and give the ghost up like an honest man; and then let there up and come some insolent, ungodly fellow—ah! if I had him in these hands! "Where's my money that you gambled?" I should say. "Where's my money that you drank and diced?" "Thief!" is what I would say; "Thief!"' he roared, '"Thief"'

'Mr. Archer will hear you if you don't take care,' said Nance, 'and I would be ashamed, for one, that he should hear a brave, old, honest, hard-working man like Jonathan Holdaway talk nonsense like a boy.'

'D' ye think I mind for Mr. Archer?' he cried shrilly, with a clack of laughter; and then he came close up to her, stooped down with his two palms upon his knees, and looked her in the eyes, with a strange hard expression, something like a smile. 'Do I mind for God, my girl?' he said; 'that's what it's come to be now, do I mind for God?'

'Uncle Jonathan,' she said, getting up and taking him by the arm; 'you sit down again, where you were sitting. There, sit still; I'll have no more of this; you'll do yourself a mischief. Come, take a drink of this good ale, and I'll warm a tankard for you. La, we'll pull through, you'll see. I'm young, as you say, and it's my turn to carry the bundle; and don't you worry your bile, or we'll have sickness, too, as well as sorrow.'

'D' ye think that I'd forgotten you?' said Jonathan, with something like a groan; and thereupon his teeth clicked to, and he sat silent with the tankard in his hand and staring straight before him.

'Why,' says Nance, setting on the ale to mull, 'men are always children, they say, however old; and if ever I heard a thing like this, to set to and make yourself sick, just when the money's failing. Keep a good heart up; you haven't kept a good heart these seventy years, nigh hand, to break down about a pound or two. Here's this Mr. Archer come to lodge, that you disliked so much. Well, now you see it was a clear Providence. Come, let's think upon our mercies. And here is the ale mulling lovely; smell of it; I'll take a drop myself, it smells so sweet. And, Uncle Jonathan, you let me say one word. You've lost more than money before now; you lost my aunt, and bore it like a man. Bear this.'

His face once more contracted; his fist doubled, and shot forth into the air, and trembled. 'Let them look out!' he shouted. 'Here, I warn all men; I've done with this foul kennel of knaves. Let them look out!'

'Hush, hush! for pity's sake,' cried Nance.

And then all of a sudden he dropped his face into his hands, and broke out with a great hiccoughing dry sob that was horrible to hear. 'O,' he cried, 'my God, if my son hadn't left me, if my Dick was here!' and the sobs shook him; Nance sitting still and watching him, with distress. 'O, if he were here to help his father!' he went on again. 'If I had a son like other fathers, he would save me now, when all is breaking down; O, he would save me! Ay, but where is he? Raking taverns, a thief perhaps. My curse be on him!' he added, rising again into wrath.

'Hush!' cried Nance, springing to her feet: 'your boy, your dead wife's boy—Aunt Susan's baby that she loved—would you curse him? O, God forbid!'

The energy of her address surprised him from his mood. He looked upon her, tearless and confused. 'Let me go to my bed,' he said at last, and he rose, and, shaking as with ague, but quite silent, lighted his candle, and left the kitchen.

Poor Nance! the pleasant current of her dreams was all diverted. She beheld a golden city, where she aspired to dwell; she had spoken with a deity, and had told herself that she might rise to be his equal; and now the earthly ligaments that bound her down had been tightened. She was like a tree looking skyward, her roots were in the ground. It seemed to her a thing so coarse, so rustic, to be thus concerned about a loss in money; when Mr. Archer, fallen from the sky-level of counts and nobles, faced his changed destiny with so immovable a courage. To weary of honesty; that, at least, no one could do, but even to name it was already a disgrace; and she beheld in fancy her uncle, and the young lad, all laced and feathered, hand upon hip, bestriding his small horse. The opposition seemed to perpetuate itself from generation to generation; one side still doomed to the clumsy and the servile, the other born to beauty.

She thought of the golden zones in which gentlemen were bred, and figured with so excellent a grace; zones in which wisdom and smooth words, white linen and slim hands, were the mark of the desired inhabitants; where low temptations were unknown, and honesty no virtue, but a thing as natural as breathing.

CHAPTER IV—MINGLING THREADS

It was nearly seven before Mr. Archer left his apartment. On the landing he found another door beside his own opening on a roofless corridor, and presently he was walking on the top of the ruins. On one hand he could look down a good depth into the green court-yard; on the other his eye roved along the downward course of the river, the wet woods all smoking, the shadows long and blue, the mists golden and rosy in the sun, here and there the water flashing across an obstacle. His heart expanded and softened to a grateful melancholy, and with his eye fixed upon the distance, and no thought of present danger, he continued to stroll along the elevated and treacherous promenade.

A terror-stricken cry rose to him from the courtyard. He looked down, and saw in a glimpse Nance standing below with hands clasped in horror and his own foot trembling on the margin of a gulf. He recoiled and leant against a pillar, quaking from head to foot, and covering his face with his hands; and Nance had time to run round by the stair and rejoin him where he stood before he had changed a line of his position.

'Ah!' he cried, and clutched her wrist; 'don't leave me. The place rocks;

I have no head for altitudes.'

'Sit down against that pillar,' said Nance. 'Don't you be afraid; I won't leave you, and don't look up or down: look straight at me. How white you are!'

'The gulf,' he said, and closed his eyes again and shuddered.

'Why,' said Nance, 'what a poor climber you must be! That was where my cousin Dick used to get out of the castle after Uncle Jonathan had shut the gate. I've been down there myself with him helping me. I wouldn't try with you,' she said, and laughed merrily.

The sound of her laughter was sincere and musical, and perhaps its beauty barbed the offence to Mr. Archer. The blood came into his face with a quick jet, and then left it paler than before. 'It is a physical weakness,' he said harshly, 'and very droll, no doubt, but one that I can conquer on necessity. See, I am still shaking. Well, I advance to the battlements and look down. Show me your cousin's path.'

'He would go sure-foot along that little ledge,' said Nance, pointing as she spoke; 'then out through the breach and down by yonder buttress. It is easier coming back, of course, because you see where you are going. From the buttress foot a sheep-walk goes along the scarp—see, you can follow it from here in the dry grass. And now, sir,' she added, with a touch of womanly pity, 'I would come away from here if I were you, for indeed you are not fit.'

Sure enough Mr. Archer's pallor and agitation had continued to increase; his cheeks were deathly, his clenched fingers trembled pitifully. 'The weakness is physical,' he sighed, and had nearly fallen. Nance led him from the spot, and he was no sooner back in the tower-stair, than he fell heavily against the wall and put his arm across his eyes. A cup of brandy had to be brought him before he could descend to breakfast; and the perfection of Nance's dream was for the first time troubled.

Jonathan was waiting for them at table, with yellow, blood-shot eyes and a peculiar dusky complexion. He hardly waited till they found their seats, before, raising one hand, and stooping with his mouth above his plate, he put up a prayer for a blessing on the food and a spirit of gratitude in the eaters, and thereupon, and without more civility, fell to. But it was notable that he was no less speedily satisfied than he had been greedy to begin. He pushed his plate away and drummed upon the table.

'These are silly prayers,' said he, 'that they teach us. Eat and be thankful, that's no such wonder. Speak to me of starving—there's the touch. You're a man, they tell me, Mr. Archer, that has met with some reverses?'

'I have met with many,' replied Mr. Archer.

'Ha!' said Jonathan. 'None reckons but the last. Now, see; I tried to make this girl here understand me.'

'Uncle,' said Nance, 'what should Mr. Archer care for your concerns? He hath troubles of his own, and came to be at peace, I think.'

'I tried to make her understand me,' repeated Jonathan doggedly; 'and now I'll try you. Do you think this world is fair?'

'Fair and false!' quoth Mr. Archer.

The old man laughed immoderately. 'Good,' said he, 'very good, but what I mean is this: do you know what it is to get up early and go to bed late, and never take so much as a holiday but four: and one of these your own marriage day, and the other three the funerals of folk you loved, and all that, to have a quiet old age in shelter, and bread for your old belly, and a bed to lay your crazy bones upon, with a clear conscience?'

'Sir,' said Mr. Archer, with an inclination of his head, 'you portray a very brave existence.'

'Well,' continued Jonathan, 'and in the end thieves deceive you, thieves rob and rook you, thieves turn you out in your old age and send you begging. What have you got for all your honesty? A fine return! You that might have stole scores of pounds, there you are out in the rain with your rheumatics!'

Mr. Archer had forgotten to eat; with his hand upon his chin he was studying the old man's countenance. 'And you conclude?' he asked.

'Conclude!' cried Jonathan. 'I conclude I'll be upsides with them.'

'Ay,' said the other, 'we are all tempted to revenge.'

'You have lost money?' asked Jonathan.

'A great estate,' said Archer quietly.

'See now!' says Jonathan, 'and where is it?'

'Nay, I sometimes think that every one has had his share of it but me,' was the reply. 'All England hath paid his taxes with my patrimony: I was a sheep that left my wool on every briar.'

'And you sit down under that?' cried the old man. 'Come now, Mr. Archer, you and me belong to different stations; and I know mine—no man better—but since we have both been rooked, and are both sore with it, why, here's my hand with a very good heart, and I ask for yours, and no offence, I hope.'

'There is surely no offence, my friend,' returned Mr. Archer, as they shook hands across the table; 'for, believe me, my sympathies are quite acquired to you. This life is an arena where we fight with beasts; and, indeed,' he added, sighing, 'I sometimes marvel why we go down to it unarmed.'

In the meanwhile a creaking of ungreased axles had been heard descending through the wood; and presently after, the door opened, and the tall ostler entered the kitchen carrying one end of Mr. Archer's trunk. The other was carried by an aged beggar man of that district, known and welcome for some twenty miles about under the name of 'Old Cumberland.' Each was soon perched upon a settle, with a cup of ale; and the ostler, who valued himself upon his affability, began to entertain the company, still with half an eye on Nance, to whom in gallant terms he expressly dedicated every sip of ale. First he told of the trouble they had to get his Lordship started in the chaise; and how he had dropped a rouleau of gold on the threshold, and the passage and doorstep had been strewn with guinea-pieces. At this old Jonathan looked at Mr. Archer. Next the visitor turned to news of a more thrilling character: how the down mail had been stopped again near Grantham by three men on horseback—a white and two bays; how they had handkerchiefs on their faces; how Tom the guard's blunderbuss missed fire, but he swore he had winged one of them with a pistol; and how they had got clean away with seventy pounds in money, some valuable papers, and a watch or two.

'Brave! brave!' cried Jonathan in ecstasy. 'Seventy pounds! O, it's brave!'

'Well, I don't see the great bravery,' observed the ostler, misapprehending him. 'Three men, and you may call that three to one. I'll call it brave when some one stops the mail single-handed; that's a risk.'

'And why should they hesitate?' inquired Mr. Archer. 'The poor souls who are fallen to such a way of life, pray what have they to lose? If they get the money, well; but if a ball should put them from their troubles, why, so better.'

'Well, sir,' said the ostler, 'I believe you'll find they won't agree with you. They count on a good fling, you see; or who would risk it?—And here's my best respects to you, Miss Nance.'

'And I forgot the part of cowardice,' resumed Mr. Archer. 'All men fear.'

'O, surely not!' cried Nance.

'All men,' reiterated Mr. Archer.

'Ay, that's a true word,' observed Old Cumberland, 'and a thief, anyway, for it's a coward's trade.'

'But these fellows, now,' said Jonathan, with a curious, appealing manner—'these fellows with their seventy pounds! Perhaps, Mr. Archer, they were no true thieves after all, but just people who had been robbed and tried to get their own again. What was that you said, about all England and the taxes? One takes, another gives; why, that's almost fair. If I've been rooked and robbed, and the coat taken off my back, I call it almost fair to take another's.'

'Ask Old Cumberland,' observed the ostler; 'you ask Old Cumberland, Miss Nance!' and he bestowed a wink upon his favoured fair one.

170

'Why that?' asked Jonathan.

'He had his coat taken—ay, and his shirt too,' returned the ostler.

'Is that so?' cried Jonathan eagerly. 'Was you robbed too?'

'That was I,' replied Cumberland, 'with a warrant! I was a well-to-do man when I was young.'

'Ay! See that!' says Jonathan. 'And you don't long for a revenge?'

'Eh! Not me!' answered the beggar. 'It's too long ago. But if you'll give me another mug of your good ale, my pretty lady, I won't say no to that.'

'And shalt have! And shalt have!' cried Jonathan. 'Or brandy even, if you like it better.'

And as Cumberland did like it better, and the ostler chimed in, the party pledged each other in a dram of brandy before separating.

As for Nance, she slipped forth into the ruins, partly to avoid the ostler's gallantries, partly to lament over the defects of Mr. Archer. Plainly, he was no hero. She pitied him; she began to feel a protecting interest mingle with and almost supersede her admiration, and was at the same time disappointed and yet drawn to him. She was, indeed, conscious of such unshaken fortitude in her own heart, that she was almost tempted by an occasion to be bold for two. She saw herself, in a brave attitude, shielding her imperfect hero from the world; and she saw, like a piece of heaven, his gratitude for her protection.

CHAPTER V—LIFE IN THE CASTLE

From that day forth the life of these three persons in the ruin ran very smoothly. Mr. Archer now sat by the fire with a book, and now passed whole days abroad, returning late, dead weary. His manner was a mask; but it was half transparent; through the even tenor of his gravity and courtesy profound revolutions of feeling were betrayed, seasons of numb despair, of restlessness, of aching temper. For days he would say nothing beyond his usual courtesies and solemn compliments; and then, all of a sudden, some fine evening beside the kitchen fire, he would fall into a vein of elegant gossip, tell of strange and interesting events, the secrets of families, brave deeds of war, the miraculous discovery of crime, the visitations of the dead. Nance and her uncle would sit till the small hours with eyes wide open: Jonathan applauding the unexpected incidents with many a slap of his big hand; Nance, perhaps, more pleased with the narrator's eloquence and wise reflections; and then, again, days would follow of abstraction, of listless humming, of frequent apologies and long hours of silence. Once only, and then after a week of unrelieved melancholy, he went over to the 'Green Dragon,' spent the afternoon with the landlord and a bowl of punch, and returned as on the first night, devious in step but courteous and unperturbed of speech.

If he seemed more natural and more at his ease it was when he found Nance alone; and, laying by some of his reserve, talked before her rather than to her of his destiny, character and hopes. To Nance these interviews were but a doubtful privilege. At times he would seem to take a pleasure in her presence, to consult her gravely, to hear and to discuss her counsels; at times even, but these were rare and brief, he would talk of herself, praise the qualities that she possessed, touch indulgently on her defects, and lend her books to read and even examine her upon her reading; but far more often he would fall into a half unconsciousness, put her a question and then answer it himself, drop into the veiled tone of voice of one soliloquising, and leave her at last as though he had forgotten her existence. It was odd, too, that in all this random converse, not a fact of his past life, and scarce a name, should ever cross his lips. A profound reserve kept watch upon his most unguarded moments. He spoke continually of himself, indeed, but still in enigmas; a veiled prophet of egoism.

The base of Nance's feelings for Mr. Archer was admiration as for a superior being; and with this, his treatment, consciously or not, accorded happily. When he forgot her, she took the blame upon herself. His formal politeness was so exquisite that this essential brutality stood excused. His compliments, besides, were always grave and rational; he would offer reason for his praise, convict her of merit, and thus disarm suspicion. Nay, and the very hours when he forgot and remembered her alternately could by the ardent fallacies of youth be read in the light of an attention. She might be far from his confidence; but still she was nearer it than any one. He might ignore her presence, but yet he sought it.

Moreover, she, upon her side, was conscious of one point of superiority. Beside this rather dismal, rather effeminate man, who recoiled from a worm, who grew giddy on the castle wall, who bore so helplessly the weight of his misfortunes, she felt herself a head and shoulders taller in cheerful and sterling courage. She could walk head in air along the most precarious rafter; her hand feared neither the grossness nor the harshness of life's web, but was thrust cheerfully, if need were, into the briar bush, and could take hold of any crawling horror. Ruin was mining the walls of her cottage, as already it had mined and subverted Mr. Archer's palace. Well, she faced it with a bright countenance and a busy hand. She had got some washing, some rough seamstress work from the 'Green Dragon,' and from another neighbour ten miles away across the moor. At this she cheerfully laboured, and from that height she could afford to pity the useless talents and poor attitude of Mr. Archer. It did not change her admiration, but it made it bearable. He was above her in all ways; but she was above him in one. She kept it to herself, and hugged it. When, like all young creatures, she made long stories to justify, to nourish, and to forecast the course of her affection, it was this private superiority that made all rosy, that cut the knot, and that, at last, in some great situation, fetched to her knees the dazzling but imperfect hero. With this pretty exercise she beguiled the hours of labour, and consoled herself for Mr. Archer's bearing.

Pity was her weapon and her weakness. To accept the loved one's faults, although it has an air of freedom, is to kiss the chain, and this pity it was which, lying nearer to her heart, lent the one element of true emotion to a fanciful and merely brain-sick love.

Thus it fell out one day that she had gone to the 'Green Dragon' and brought back thence a letter to Mr. Archer. He, upon seeing it, winced like a man under the knife: pain, shame, sorrow, and the most trenchant edge of mortification cut into his heart and wrung the steady composure of his face.

'Dear heart! have you bad news?' she cried.

But he only replied by a gesture and fled to his room, and when, later on, she ventured to refer to it, he stopped her on the threshold, as if with words prepared beforehand. 'There are some pains,' said he, 'too acute for consolation, or I would bring them to my kind consoler. Let the memory of that letter, if you please, be buried.' And then as she continued to gaze at him, being, in spite of herself, pained by his elaborate phrase, doubtfully sincere in word and manner: 'Let it be enough,' he added haughtily, 'that if this matter wring my heart, it doth not touch my conscience. I am a man, I would have you to know, who suffers undeservedly.'

He had never spoken so directly: never with so convincing an emotion; and her heart thrilled for him. She could have taken his pains and died of them with joy.

Meanwhile she was left without support. Jonathan now swore by his lodger, and lived for him. He was a fine talker. He knew the finest sight of stories; he was a man and a gentleman, take him for all in all, and a perfect credit to Old England. Such were the old man's declared sentiments, and sure enough he clung to Mr. Archer's side, hung upon his utterance when he spoke, and watched him with unwearing interest when he was silent. And yet his feeling was not clear; in the partial wreck of his mind, which was leaning to decay, some after-thought was strongly present. As he gazed in Mr. Archer's face a sudden brightness would kindle in his rheumy eyes, his eyebrows would lift as with a sudden thought, his mouth would open as though to speak, and close again on silence. Once or twice he even called Mr. Archer mysteriously forth into the dark courtyard, took him by the button, and laid a demonstrative finger on his chest; but there his ideas or his courage failed him; he would shufflingly excuse himself and return to his position by the fire without a word of explanation. 'The good man was growing old,' said Mr. Archer with a suspicion of a shrug. But the good man had his idea, and even when he was alone the name of Mr. Archer fell from his lips continually in the course of mumbled and gesticulative conversation.

CHAPTER VI—THE BAD HALF-CROWN

However early Nance arose, and she was no sluggard, the old man, who had begun to outlive the earthly habit of slumber, would usually have been up long before, the fire would be burning brightly, and she would see him wandering among the ruins, lantern in hand, and talking assiduously to himself. One day, however, after he had returned late from the market town, she found that she had stolen a march upon that indefatigable early riser. The kitchen was all blackness. She crossed the castle-yard to the wood-cellar, her steps printing the thick hoarfrost. A scathing breeze blew out of the north-east and slowly carried a regiment of black and tattered clouds over the face of heaven, which was already kindled with the wild light of morning, but where she walked, in shelter of the ruins, the flame of her candle burned steady. The extreme cold smote upon her conscience. She could not bear to think this bitter business fell usually to the lot of one so old as Jonathan, and made desperate resolutions to be earlier in the future.

The fire was a good blaze before he entered, limping dismally into the kitchen. 'Nance,' said he, 'I be all knotted up with the rheumatics; will you rub me a bit?' She came and rubbed him where and how he bade her. 'This is a cruel thing that old age should be rheumaticky,' said he. 'When I was young I stood my turn of the teethache like a man! for why? because it couldn't last for ever; but these rheumatics come to live and die with you. Your aunt was took before the time came; never had an ache to mention. Now I lie all night in my single bed and the blood never warms in me; this knee of mine it seems like lighted up with rheumatics; it seems as though you could see to sew by it; and all the strings of my old body ache, as if devils was pulling 'em. Thank you kindly; that's someways easier now, but an old man, my dear, has little to look for; it's pain, pain, pain to the end of the business, and I'll never be rightly warm again till I get under the sod,' he said, and looked down at her with a face so aged and weary that she had nearly wept.

'I lay awake all night,' he continued; 'I do so mostly, and a long walk kills me. Eh, deary me, to think that life should run to such a puddle! And I remember long syne when I was strong, and the blood all hot and good about me, and I loved to run, too—deary me, to run! Well, that's all by. You'd better pray to be took early, Nance, and not live on till you get to be like me, and are robbed in your grey old age, your cold, shivering, dark old age, that's like a winter's morning'; and he bitterly shuddered, spreading his hands before the fire.

'Come now,' said Nance, 'the more you say the less you'll like it, Uncle Jonathan; but if I were you I would be proud for to have lived all your days honest and beloved, and come near the end with your good name: isn't that a fine thing to be proud of? Mr. Archer was telling me in some strange land they used to run races each with a lighted candle, and the art was to keep the candle burning. Well, now, I thought that was like life: a man's good conscience is the flame he gets to carry, and if he comes to the winning-post with that still burning, why, take it how you will, the man's a hero—even if he was low-born like you and me.'

'Did Mr. Archer tell you that?' asked Jonathan.

'No, dear,' said she, 'that's my own thought about it. He told me of the race. But see, now,' she continued, putting on the porridge, 'you say old age is a hard season, but so is youth. You're half out of the battle, I would say; you loved my aunt and got her, and buried her, and some of these days soon you'll go to meet her; and take her my love and tell her I tried to take good care of you; for so I do, Uncle Jonathan.'

Jonathan struck with his fist upon the settle. 'D' ye think I want to die, ye vixen?' he shouted. 'I want to live ten hundred years.'

This was a mystery beyond Nance's penetration, and she stared in wonder as she made the porridge.

'I want to live,' he continued, 'I want to live and to grow rich. I want to drive my carriage and to dice in hells and see the ring, I do. Is this a life that I lived? I want to be a rake, d' ye understand? I want to know what things are like. I don't want to die like a blind kitten, and me seventy-six.'

'O fie!' said Nance.

The old man thrust out his jaw at her, with the grimace of an irreverent schoolboy. Upon that aged face it seemed a blasphemy. Then he took out of his bosom a long leather purse, and emptying its contents on the settle, began to count and recount the pieces, ringing and examining each, and suddenly he leapt like a young man. 'What!' he screamed. 'Bad? O Lord! I'm robbed again!' And falling on his knees before the settle he began to pour forth the most dreadful curses on the head of his deceiver. His eyes were shut, for to him this vile solemnity was prayer. He held up the bad half-crown in his right hand, as though he were displaying it to Heaven, and what increased the horror of the scene, the curses he invoked were those whose efficacy he had tasted—old age and poverty, rheumatism and an ungrateful son. Nance listened appalled; then she sprang forward and dragged down his arm and laid her hand upon his mouth.

'Whist!' she cried. 'Whist ye, for God's sake! O my man, whist ye! If Heaven were to hear; if poor Aunt Susan were to hear! Think, she may be listening.' And with the histrionism of strong emotion she pointed to a corner of the kitchen.

His eyes followed her finger. He looked there for a little, thinking, blinking; then he got stiffly to his feet and resumed his place upon the settle, the bad piece still in his hand. So he sat for some time, looking upon the half-crown, and now wondering to himself on the injustice and partiality of the law, now computing again and again the nature of his loss. So he was still sitting when Mr. Archer entered the kitchen. At this a light came into his face, and after some seconds of rumination he dispatched Nance upon an errand.

'Mr. Archer,' said he, as soon as they were alone together, 'would you give me a guinea-piece for silver?'

'Why, sir, I believe I can,' said Mr. Archer.

And the exchange was just effected when Nance re-entered the apartment. The blood shot into her face.

'What's to do here?' she asked rudely.

'Nothing, my dearie,' said old Jonathan, with a touch of whine.

'What's to do?' she said again.

'Your uncle was but changing me a piece of gold,' returned Mr. Archer.

'Let me see what he hath given you, Mr. Archer,' replied the girl. 'I had a bad piece, and I fear it is mixed up among the good.'

'Well, well,' replied Mr. Archer, smiling, 'I must take the merchant's risk of it. The money is now mixed.'

'I know my piece,' quoth Nance. 'Come, let me see your silver, Mr. Archer. If I have to get it by a theft I'll see that money,' she cried.

'Nay, child, if you put as much passion to be honest as the world to steal, I must give way, though I betray myself,' said Mr. Archer. 'There it is as I received it.'

Nance quickly found the bad half-crown.

'Give him another,' she said, looking Jonathan in the face; and when that had been done, she walked over to the chimney and flung the guilty piece into the reddest of the fire. Its base constituents began immediately to run; even as she watched it the disc crumbled, and the lineaments of the King became confused. Jonathan, who had followed close behind, beheld these changes from over her shoulder, and his face darkened sorely.

'Now,' said she, 'come back to table, and to-day it is I that shall say grace, as I used to do in the old times, day about with Dick'; and covering her eyes with one hand, 'O Lord,' said she with deep emotion, 'make us thankful; and, O Lord, deliver us from evil! For the love of the poor souls that watch for us in heaven, O deliver us from evil.'

CHAPTER VII—THE BLEACHING-GREEN

The year moved on to March; and March, though it blew bitter keen from the North Sea, yet blinked kindly between whiles on the river dell. The mire dried up in the closest covert; life ran in the bare branches, and the air of the afternoon would be suddenly sweet with the fragrance of new grass.

Above and below the castle the river crooked like the letter 'S.' The lower loop was to the left, and embraced the high and steep projection which was crowned by the ruins; the upper loop enclosed a lawny promontory, fringed by thorn and willow. It was easy to reach it from the castle side, for the river ran in this part very quietly among innumerable boulders and over dam-like walls of rock. The place was all enclosed, the wind a stranger, the turf smooth and solid; so it was chosen by Nance to be her bleaching-green.

One day she brought a bucketful of linen, and had but begun to wring and lay them out when Mr. Archer stepped from the thicket on the far side, drew very deliberately near, and sat down in silence on the grass. Nance looked up to greet him with a smile, but finding her smile was not returned, she fell into embarrassment and stuck the more busily to her employment. Man or woman, the whole world looks well at any work to which they are accustomed; but the girl was ashamed of what she did. She was ashamed, besides, of the sun-bonnet that so well became her, and ashamed of her bare arms, which were her greatest beauty.

'Nausicaa,' said Mr. Archer at last, 'I find you like Nausicaa.'

'And who was she?' asked Nance, and laughed in spite of herself, an empty and embarrassed laugh, that sounded in Mr. Archer's ears, indeed, like music, but to her own like the last grossness of rusticity.

'She was a princess of the Grecian islands,' he replied. 'A king, being shipwrecked, found her washing by the shore. Certainly I, too, was shipwrecked,' he continued, plucking at the grass. 'There was never a more desperate castaway—to fall from polite life, fortune, a shrine of honour, a grateful conscience, duties willingly taken up and faithfully discharged; and to fall to this—idleness, poverty, inutility, remorse.' He seemed to have forgotten her presence, but here he remembered her again. 'Nance,' said he, 'would you have a man sit down and suffer or rise up and strive?'

'Nay,' she said. 'I would always rather see him doing.'

'Ha!' said Mr. Archer, 'but yet you speak from an imperfect knowledge. Conceive a man damned to a choice of only evil—misconduct upon either side, not a fault behind him, and yet naught before him but this choice of sins. How would you say then?'

'I would say that he was much deceived, Mr. Archer,' returned Nance. 'I would say there was a third choice, and that the right one.'

'I tell you,' said Mr. Archer, 'the man I have in view hath two ways open, and no more. One to wait, like a poor mewling baby, till Fate save or ruin him; the other to take his troubles in his hand, and to perish or be saved at once. It is no point of morals; both are wrong. Either way this step-child of Providence must fall; which shall he choose, by doing or not doing?'

'Fall, then, is what I would say,' replied Nance. 'Fall where you will, but do it! For O, Mr. Archer,' she continued, stooping to her work, 'you that are good and kind, and so wise, it doth sometimes go against my heart to see you live on here like a sheep in a turnip-field! If you were braver—' and here she paused, conscience-smitten.

'Do I, indeed, lack courage?' inquired Mr. Archer of himself. 'Courage, the footstool of the virtues, upon which they stand? Courage, that a poor private carrying a musket has to spare of; that does not fail a weasel or a rat; that is a brutish faculty? I to fail there, I wonder? But what is courage, then? The constancy to endure oneself or to see others suffer? The itch of ill-advised activity: mere shuttle-wittedness, or to be still and patient? To inquire of the significance of words is to rob ourselves of what we seem to know, and yet, of all things, certainly to stand still is the least heroic. Nance,' he said, 'did you ever hear of Hamlet?'

'Never,' said Nance.

''Tis an old play,' returned Mr. Archer, 'and frequently enacted. This while I have been talking Hamlet. You must know this Hamlet was a Prince among the Danes,' and he told her the play in a very good style, here and there quoting a verse or two with solemn emphasis.

'It is strange,' said Nance; 'he was then a very poor creature?'

'That was what he could not tell,' said Mr. Archer. 'Look at me, am I as poor a creature?'

She looked, and what she saw was the familiar thought of all her hours; the tall figure very plainly habited in black, the spotless ruffles, the slim hands; the long, well-shapen, serious, shaven face, the wide and somewhat thin-lipped mouth, the dark eyes that were so full of depth and change and colour. He was gazing at her with his brows a little knit, his chin upon one hand and that elbow resting on his knee.

'Ye look a man!' she cried, 'ay, and should be a great one! The more shame to you to lie here idle like a dog before the fire.'

'My fair Holdaway,' quoth Mr. Archer, 'you are much set on action. I cannot dig, to beg I am ashamed.' He continued, looking at her with a half-absent fixity, "Tis a strange thing, certainly, that in my years of fortune I should never taste happiness, and now when I am broke, enjoy so much of it, for was I ever happier than to-day? Was the grass softer, the stream pleasanter in sound, the air milder, the heart more at peace? Why should I not sink? To dig—why, after all, it should be easy. To take a mate, too? Love is of all grades since Jupiter; love fails to none; and children'—but here he passed his hand suddenly over his eyes. 'O fool and coward, fool and coward!' he said bitterly; 'can you forget your fetters? You did not know that I was fettered, Nance?' he asked, again addressing her.

But Nance was somewhat sore. 'I know you keep talking,' she said, and, turning half away from him, began to wring out a sheet across her shoulder. 'I wonder you are not wearied of your voice. When the hands lie abed the tongue takes a walk.'

Mr. Archer laughed unpleasantly, rose and moved to the water's edge. In this part the body of the river poured across a little narrow fell, ran some ten feet very smoothly over a bed of pebbles, then getting wind, as it were, of another shelf of rock which barred the channel, began, by imperceptible degrees, to separate towards either shore in dancing currents, and to leave the middle clear and stagnant. The set towards either side was nearly equal; about one half of the whole water plunged on the side of the castle, through a narrow gullet; about one half ran ripping past the margin of the green and slipped across a babbling rapid.

'Here,' said Mr. Archer, after he had looked for some time at the fine and shifting demarcation of these currents, 'come here and see me try my fortune.'

'I am not like a man,' said Nance; 'I have no time to waste.'

'Come here,' he said again. 'I ask you seriously, Nance. We are not always childish when we seem so.'

She drew a little nearer.

'Now,' said he, 'you see these two channels—choose one.'

'I'll choose the nearest, to save time,' said Nance.

'Well, that shall be for action,' returned Mr. Archer. 'And since I wish to have the odds against me, not only the other channel but yon stagnant water in the midst shall be for lying still. You see this?' he continued, pulling up a withered rush. 'I break it in three. I shall put each separately at the top of the upper fall, and according as they go by your way or by the other I shall guide my life.'

'This is very silly,' said Nance, with a movement of her shoulders.

'I do not think it so,' said Mr. Archer.

'And then,' she resumed, 'if you are to try your fortune, why not evenly?'

'Nay,' returned Mr. Archer with a smile, 'no man can put complete reliance in blind fate; he must still cog the dice.'

By this time he had got upon the rock beside the upper fall, and, bidding her look out, dropped a piece of rush into the middle of the intake. The rusty fragment was sucked at once over the fall, came up again far on the right hand, leaned ever more and more in the same direction, and disappeared under the hanging grasses on the castle side.

'One,' said Mr. Archer, 'one for standing still.'

But the next launch had a different fate, and after hanging for a while about the edge of the stagnant water, steadily approached the bleaching-green and danced down the rapid under Nance's eyes.

'One for me,' she cried with some exultation; and then she observed that Mr. Archer had grown pale, and was kneeling on the rock, with his hand raised like a person petrified. 'Why,' said she, 'you do not mind it, do you?'

'Does a man not mind a throw of dice by which a fortune hangs?' said Mr. Archer, rather hoarsely. 'And this is more than fortune. Nance, if you have any kindness for my fate, put up a prayer before I launch the next one.'

'A prayer,' she cried, 'about a game like this? I would not be so heathen.'

'Well,' said he, 'then without,' and he closed his eyes and dropped the piece of rush. This time there was no doubt. It went for the rapid as straight as any arrow.

'Action then!' said Mr. Archer, getting to his feet; 'and then God forgive us,' he added, almost to himself.

'God forgive us, indeed,' cried Nance, 'for wasting the good daylight! But come, Mr. Archer, if I see you look so serious I shall begin to think you was in earnest.'

'Nay,' he said, turning upon her suddenly, with a full smile; 'but is not this good advice? I have consulted God and demigod; the nymph of the river, and what I far more admire and trust, my blue-eyed Minerva. Both have said the same. My own heart was telling it already. Action, then, be mine; and into the deep sea with all this paralysing casuistry. I am happy to-day for the first time.'

CHAPTER VIII—THE MAIL GUARD

Somewhere about two in the morning a squall had burst upon the castle, a clap of screaming wind that made the towers rock, and a copious drift of rain that streamed from the windows. The wind soon blew itself out, but the day broke cloudy and dripping, and when the little party assembled at breakfast their humours appeared to have changed with the change of weather. Nance had been brooding on the scene at the river-side, applying it in various ways to her particular aspirations, and the result, which was hardly to her mind, had taken the colour out of her cheeks. Mr. Archer, too, was somewhat absent, his thoughts were of a mingled strain; and even upon his usually impassive countenance there were betrayed successive depths of depression and starts of exultation, which the girl translated in terms of her own hopes and fears. But Jonathan was the most altered: he was strangely silent, hardly passing a word, and watched Mr. Archer with an eager and furtive eye. It seemed as if the idea that had so long hovered before him had now taken a more solid shape, and, while it still attracted, somewhat alarmed his imagination.

At this rate, conversation languished into a silence which was only broken by the gentle and ghostly noises of the rain on the stone roof and about all that field of ruins; and they were all relieved when the note of a man whistling and the sound of approaching footsteps in the grassy court announced a visitor. It was the ostler from the 'Green Dragon' bringing a letter for Mr. Archer. Nance saw her hero's face contract and then relax again at sight of it; and she thought that she knew why, for the sprawling, gross black characters of the address were easily distinguishable from the fine writing on the former letter that had so much disturbed him. He opened it and began to read; while the ostler sat down to table with a pot of ale, and proceeded to make himself agreeable after his fashion.

'Fine doings down our way, Miss Nance,' said he. 'I haven't been abed this blessed night.'

Nance expressed a polite interest, but her eye was on Mr. Archer, who was reading his letter with a face of such extreme indifference that she was tempted to suspect him of assumption.

'Yes,' continued the ostler, 'not been the like of it this fifteen years: the North Mail stopped at the three stones.'

Jonathan's cup was at his lip, but at this moment he choked with a great splutter; and Mr. Archer, as if startled by the noise, made so sudden a movement that one corner of the sheet tore off and stayed between his finger and thumb. It was some little time before the old man was sufficiently recovered to beg the ostler to go on, and he still kept coughing and crying and rubbing his eyes. Mr. Archer, on his side, laid the letter down, and, putting his hands in his pocket, listened gravely to the tale.

'Yes,' resumed Sam, 'the North Mail was stopped by a single horseman; dash my wig, but I admire him! There were four insides and two out, and poor Tom Oglethorpe, the guard. Tom showed himself a man; let fly his blunderbuss at him; had him covered, too, and could swear to that; but the Captain never let on, up with a pistol and fetched poor Tom a bullet through the body. Tom, he squelched upon the seat, all over blood. Up comes the Captain to the window. "Oblige me," says he, "with what you have." Would you believe it? Not a man says cheep!—not them. "Thy hands over thy head." Four watches, rings, snuff-boxes, seven-and-forty pounds overhead in gold. One Dicksee, a grazier, tries it on: gives him a guinea. "Beg your pardon," says the Captain, "I think too highly of you to take it at your hand. I will not take less than ten from such a gentleman." This Dicksee had his money in his stocking, but there was the pistol at his eye. Down he goes, offs with his stocking, and there was thirty golden guineas. "Now," says the Captain, "you've tried it on with me, but I scorns the advantage. Ten I said," he says, "and ten I take." So, dash my buttons, I call that man a man!' cried Sam in cordial admiration.

'Well, and then?' says Mr. Archer.

'Then,' resumed Sam, 'that old fat fagot Engleton, him as held the ribbons and drew up like a lamb when he was told to, picks up his cattle, and drives off again. Down they came to the "Dragon," all singing like as if they was scalded, and poor Tom saying nothing. You would 'a' thought they had all lost the King's crown to hear them. Down gets this Dicksee. "Postmaster," he says, taking him by the arm, "this is a most abominable thing," he says. Down gets a Major Clayton, and gets the old man by the other arm. "We've been robbed," he cries, "robbed!" Down gets the others, and all around the old man telling their story, and what they had lost, and how they was all as good as ruined; till at last Old Engleton says, says he, "How about Oglethorpe?" says he. "Ay," says the others, "how about the guard?" Well, with that we bousted him down, as white as a rag and all blooded like a sop. I thought he was dead. Well, he ain't dead; but he's dying, I fancy.'

'Did you say four watches?' said Jonathan.

'Four, I think. I wish it had been forty,' cried Sam. 'Such a party of soused herrings I never did see—not a man among them bar poor Tom. But us that are the servants on the road have all the risk and none of the profit.'

'And this brave fellow,' asked Mr. Archer, very quietly, 'this Oglethorpe—how is he now?'

'Well, sir, with my respects, I take it he has a hole bang through him,' said Sam. 'The doctor hasn't been yet. He'd 'a' been bright and early if it had been a passenger. But, doctor or no, I'll make a good guess that Tom won't see to-morrow. He'll die on a Sunday, will poor Tom; and they do say that's fortunate.'

'Did Tom see him that did it?' asked Jonathan.

'Well, he saw him,' replied Sam, 'but not to swear by. Said he was a very tall man, and very big, and had a 'ankerchief about his face, and a very quick shot, and sat his horse like a thorough gentleman, as he is.'

'A gentleman!' cried Nance. 'The dirty knave!'

'Well, I calls a man like that a gentleman,' returned the ostler; 'that's what I mean by a gentleman.'

'You don't know much of them, then,' said Nance. 'A gentleman would scorn to stoop to such a thing. I call my uncle a better gentleman than any thief.'

'And you would be right,' said Mr. Archer.

'How many snuff-boxes did he get?' asked Jonathan.

'O, dang me if I know,' said Sam; 'I didn't take an inventory.'

'I will go back with you, if you please,' said Mr. Archer. 'I should like to see poor Oglethorpe. He has behaved well.'

'At your service, sir,' said Sam, jumping to his feet. 'I dare to say a gentleman like you would not forget a poor fellow like Tom—no, nor a plain man like me, sir, that went without his sleep to nurse him. And excuse me, sir,' added Sam, 'you won't forget about the letter neither?'

'Surely not,' said Mr. Archer.

Oglethorpe lay in a low bed, one of several in a long garret of the inn. The rain soaked in places through the roof and fell in minute drops; there was but one small window; the beds were occupied by servants, the air of the garret was both close and chilly. Mr. Archer's heart sank at the threshold to see a man lying perhaps mortally hurt in so poor a sick-room, and as he drew near the low bed he took his hat off. The guard was a big, blowsy, innocent-looking soul with a thick lip and a broad nose, comically turned up; his cheeks were crimson, and when Mr. Archer laid a finger on his brow he found him burning with fever.

'I fear you suffer much,' he said, with a catch in his voice, as he sat down on the bedside.

'I suppose I do, sir,' returned Oglethorpe; 'it is main sore.'

'I am used to wounds and wounded men,' returned the visitor. 'I have been in the wars and nursed brave fellows before now; and, if you will suffer me, I propose to stay beside you till the doctor comes.'

'It is very good of you, sir, I am sure,' said Oglethorpe. 'The trouble is they won't none of them let me drink.'

'If you will not tell the doctor,' said Mr. Archer, 'I will give you some water. They say it is bad for a green wound, but in the Low Countries we all drank water when we found the chance, and I could never perceive we were the worse for it.'

'Been wounded yourself, sir, perhaps?' called Oglethorpe.

'Twice,' said Mr. Archer, 'and was as proud of these hurts as any lady of her bracelets. 'Tis a fine thing to smart for one's duty; even in the pangs of it there is contentment.'

'Ah, well!' replied the guard, 'if you've been shot yourself, that explains. But as for contentment, why, sir, you see, it smarts, as you say. And then, I have a good wife, you see, and a bit of a brat—a little thing, so high.'

'Don't move,' said Mr. Archer.

'No, sir, I will not, and thank you kindly,' said Oglethorpe. 'At York they are. A very good lass is my wife—far too good for me. And the little rascal—well, I don't know how to say it, but he sort of comes round you. If I were to go, sir, it would be hard on my poor girl—main hard on her!'

'Ay, you must feel bitter hardly to the rogue that laid you here,' said Archer.

'Why, no, sir, more against Engleton and the passengers,' replied the guard. 'He played his hand, if you come to look at it; and I wish he had shot worse, or me better. And yet I'll go to my grave but what I covered him,' he cried. 'It looks like witchcraft. I'll go to my grave but what he was drove full of slugs like a pepper-box.'

'Quietly,' said Mr. Archer, 'you must not excite yourself. These deceptions are very usual in war; the eye, in the moment of alert, is hardly to be trusted, and when the smoke blows away you see the man you fired at, taking aim, it may be, at yourself. You should observe, too, that you were in the dark night, and somewhat dazzled by the lamps, and that the sudden stopping of the mail had jolted you. In such circumstances a man may miss, ay, even with a blunder-buss, and no blame attach to his marksmanship.' . . .

THE YOUNG CHEVALIER

PROLOGUE—THE WINE-SELLER'S WIFE

There was a wine-seller's shop, as you went down to the river in the city of the Anti-popes. There a man was served with good wine of the country and plain country fare; and the place being clean and quiet, with a prospect on the river, certain gentlemen who dwelt in that city in attendance on a great personage made it a practice (when they had any silver in their purses) to come and eat there and be private.

They called the wine-seller Paradou. He was built more like a bullock than a man, huge in bone and brawn, high in colour, and with a hand like a baby for size. Marie-Madeleine was the name of his wife; she was of Marseilles, a city of entrancing women, nor was any fairer than herself. She was tall, being almost of a height with Paradou; full-girdled, point-device in every form, with an exquisite delicacy in the face; her nose and nostrils a delight to look at from the fineness of the sculpture, her eyes inclined a hair's-breadth inward, her colour between dark and fair, and laid on even like a flower's. A faint rose dwelt in it, as though she had been found unawares bathing, and had blushed from head to foot. She was of a grave countenance, rarely smiling; yet it seemed to be written upon every part of her that she rejoiced in life. Her husband loved the heels of her feet and the knuckles of her fingers; he loved her like a glutton and a brute; his love hung about her like an atmosphere; one that came by chance into the wine-shop was aware of that passion; and it might be said that by the strength of it the woman had been drugged or spell-bound. She knew not if she loved or loathed him; he was always in her eyes like something monstrous—monstrous in his love, monstrous in his person, horrific but imposing in his violence; and her sentiment swung back and forward from desire to sickness. But the mean, where it dwelt chiefly, was an apathetic fascination, partly of horror; as of

Europa in mid ocean with her bull.

On the 10th November 1749 there sat two of the foreign gentlemen in the wine-seller's shop. They were both handsome men of a good presence, richly dressed. The first was swarthy and long and lean, with an alert, black look, and a mole upon his cheek. The other was more fair. He seemed very easy and sedate, and a little melancholy for so young a man, but his smile was charming. In his grey eyes there was much abstraction, as of one recalling fondly that which was past and lost. Yet there was strength and swiftness in his limbs; and his mouth set straight across his face, the under lip a thought upon side, like that of a man accustomed to resolve. These two talked together in a rude outlandish speech that no frequenter of that wine-shop understood. The swarthy man answered to the name of Ballantrae; he of the dreamy eyes was sometimes called Balmile, and sometimes my Lord, or my Lord Gladsmuir; but when the title was given him, he seemed to put it by as if in jesting, not without bitterness.

The mistral blew in the city. The first day of that wind, they say in the countries where its voice is heard, it blows away all the dust, the second all the stones, and the third it blows back others from the mountains. It was now come to the third day; outside the pebbles flew like hail, and the face of the river was puckered, and the very building-stones in the walls of houses seemed to be curdled with the savage cold and fury of that continuous blast. It could be heard to hoot in all the chimneys of the city; it swept about the wine-shop, filling the room with eddies; the chill and gritty touch of it passed between the nearest clothes and the bare flesh; and the two gentlemen at the far table kept their mantles loose about their shoulders. The roughness of these outer hulls, for they were plain travellers' cloaks that had seen service, set the greater mark of richness on what showed below of their laced clothes; for the one was in scarlet and the other in violet and white, like men come from a scene of ceremony; as indeed they were.

It chanced that these fine clothes were not without their influence on the scene which followed, and which makes the prologue of our tale. For a long time Balmile was in the habit to come to the wine-shop and eat a meal or drink a measure of wine; sometimes with a comrade; more often alone, when he would sit and dream and drum upon the table, and the thoughts would show in the man's face in little glooms and lightenings, like the sun and the clouds upon a water. For a long time Marie-Madeleine had observed him apart. His sadness, the beauty of his smile when by any chance he remembered her existence and addressed her, the changes of his mind signalled forth by an abstruse play of feature, the mere fact that he was foreign and a thing detached from the local and the accustomed, insensibly attracted and affected her. Kindness was ready in her mind; it but lacked the touch of an occasion to effervesce and crystallise. Now Balmile had come hitherto in a very poor plain habit; and this day of the mistral, when his mantle was just open, and she saw beneath it the glancing of the violet and the velvet and the silver, and the clustering fineness of the lace, it seemed to set the man in a new light, with which he shone resplendent to her fancy.

The high inhuman note of the wind, the violence and continuity of its outpouring, and the fierce touch of it upon man's whole periphery, accelerated the functions of the mind. It set thoughts whirling, as it whirled the trees of the forest; it stirred them up in flights, as it stirred up the dust in chambers. As brief as sparks, the fancies glittered and succeeded each other in the mind of Marie-Madeleine; and the grave man with the smile, and the bright clothes under the plain mantle, haunted her with incongruous explanations. She considered him, the unknown, the speaker of an unknown tongue, the hero (as she placed him) of an unknown romance, the dweller upon unknown memories. She recalled him sitting there alone, so immersed, so stupefied; yet she was sure he was not stupid. She recalled one day when he had remained a long time motionless, with parted lips, like one in the act of starting up, his eyes fixed on vacancy. Any one else must have looked foolish; but not he. She tried to conceive what manner of memory had thus entranced him; she forged for him a past; she showed him to herself in every light of heroism and greatness and misfortune; she brooded with petulant intensity on all she knew and guessed of him. Yet, though she was already gone so deep, she was still unashamed, still unalarmed; her thoughts were still disinterested; she had still to reach the stage at which—beside the image of that other whom we love to contemplate and to adorn—we place the image of ourself and behold them together with delight.

She stood within the counter, her hands clasped behind her back, her shoulders pressed against the wall, her feet braced out. Her face was bright with the wind and her own thoughts; as a fire in a similar day of tempest glows and brightens on a hearth, so she seemed to glow, standing there, and to breathe out energy. It was the first time Ballantrae had visited that wine-seller's, the first time he had seen the wife; and his eyes were true to her.

'I perceive your reason for carrying me to this very draughty tavern,' he said at last.

'I believe it is propinquity,' returned Balmile.

'You play dark,' said Ballantrae, 'but have a care! Be more frank with me, or I will cut you out. I go through no form of qualifying my threat, which would be commonplace and not conscientious. There is only one point in these campaigns: that is the degree of admiration offered by the man; and to our hostess I am in a posture to make victorious love.'

'If you think you have the time, or the game worth the candle,' replied the other with a shrug.

'One would suppose you were never at the pains to observe her,' said Ballantrae.

'I am not very observant,' said Balmile. 'She seems comely.'

'You very dear and dull dog!' cried Ballantrae; 'chastity is the most besotting of the virtues. Why, she has a look in her face beyond singing! I believe, if you was to push me hard, I might trace it home to a trifle of a squint. What matters? The height of beauty is in the touch that's wrong, that's the modulation in a tune. 'Tis the devil we all love; I owe many a conquest to my mole'—he touched it as he spoke with a smile, and his eyes glittered;—'we are all hunchbacks, and beauty is only that kind of deformity that I happen to admire. But come! Because you are chaste, for which I am sure I pay you my respects, that is no reason why you should be blind. Look at her, look at the delicious nose of her, look at her cheek, look at her ear, look at her hand and wrist—look at the whole baggage from heels to crown, and tell me if she wouldn't melt on a man's tongue.'

As Ballantrae spoke, half jesting, half enthusiastic, Balmile was constrained to do as he was bidden. He looked at the woman, admired her excellences, and was at the same time ashamed for himself and his companion. So it befell that when Marie-Madeleine raised her eyes, she met those of the subject of her contemplations fixed directly on herself with a look that is unmistakable, the look of a person measuring and valuing another—and, to clench the false impression, that his glance was instantly and guiltily withdrawn. The blood beat back upon her heart and leaped again; her obscure thoughts flashed clear before her; she flew in fancy straight to his arms like a wanton, and fled again on the instant like a nymph. And at that moment there chanced an interruption, which not only spared her embarrassment, but set the last consecration on her now articulate love.

Into the wine-shop there came a French gentleman, arrayed in the last refinement of the fashion, though a little tumbled by his passage in the wind. It was to be judged he had come from the same formal gathering at which the others had preceded him; and perhaps that he had gone there in the hope to meet with them, for he came up to Ballantrae with unceremonious eagerness.

'At last, here you are!' he cried in French. 'I thought I was to miss you altogether.'

The Scotsmen rose, and Ballantrae, after the first greetings, laid his hand on his companion's shoulder.

'My lord,' said he, 'allow me to present to you one of my best friends and one of our best soldiers, the Lord Viscount Gladsmuir.'

The two bowed with the elaborate elegance of the period.

'Monseigneur,' said Balmile, 'je n'ai pas la prétention de m'affubler d'un titre que la mauvaise fortune de mon roi ne me permet pas de porter comma il sied. Je m'appelle, pour vous servir, Blair de Balmile tout court.' [My lord, I have not the effrontery to cumber myself with a title which the ill fortunes of my king will not suffer me to bear the way it should be. I call myself, at your service, plain Blair of Balmile.]

'Monsieur le Vicomte ou monsieur Blèr' de Balmaïl,' replied the newcomer, 'le nom n'y fait rien, et l'on connaît vos beaux faits.' [The name matters nothing, your gallant actions are known.]

A few more ceremonies, and these three, sitting down together to the table, called for wine. It was the happiness of Marie-Madeleine to wait unobserved upon the prince of her desires. She poured the wine, he drank of it; and that link between them seemed to her, for the moment, close as a caress. Though they lowered their tones, she surprised great names passing in their conversation, names of kings, the names of de Gesvre and Belle-Isle; and the man who dealt in these high matters, and she who was now coupled with him in her own thoughts, seemed to swim in mid air in a transfiguration. Love is a crude core, but it has singular and far-reaching fringes; in that passionate attraction for the stranger that now swayed and mastered her, his harsh incomprehensible language, and these names of grandees in his talk, were each an element.

The Frenchman stayed not long, but it was plain he left behind him matter of much interest to his companions; they spoke together earnestly, their heads down, the woman of the wine-shop totally forgotten; and they were still so occupied when Paradou returned.

This man's love was unsleeping. The even bluster of the mistral, with which he had been combating some hours, had not suspended, though it had embittered, that predominant passion. His first look was for his wife, a look of hope and suspicion, menace and humility and love, that made the over-blooming brute appear for the moment almost beautiful. She returned his glance, at first as though she knew him not, then with a swiftly waxing coldness of intent; and at last, without changing their direction, she had closed her eyes.

There passed across her mind during that period much that Paradou could not have understood had it been told to him in words: chiefly the sense of an enlightening contrast betwixt the man who talked of kings and the man who kept a wine-shop, betwixt the love she yearned for and that to which she had been long exposed like a victim bound upon the altar. There swelled upon her, swifter than the Rhone, a tide of abhorrence and disgust.

She had succumbed to the monster, humbling herself below animals; and now she loved a hero, aspiring to the semi-divine. It was in the pang of that humiliating thought that she had closed her eyes.

Paradou—quick as beasts are quick, to translate silence—felt the insult through his blood; his inarticulate soul bellowed within him for revenge. He glanced about the shop. He saw the two indifferent gentlemen deep in talk, and passed them over: his fancy flying not so high. There was but one other present, a country lout who stood swallowing his wine, equally unobserved by all and unobserving—to him he dealt a glance of murderous suspicion, and turned direct upon his wife. The wine-shop had lain hitherto, a space of shelter, the scene of a few ceremonial passages and some whispered conversation, in the howling river of the wind; the clock had not yet ticked a score of times since Paradou's appearance; and now, as he suddenly gave tongue, it seemed as though the mistral had entered at his heels.

'What ails you, woman?' he cried, smiting on the counter.

'Nothing ails me,' she replied. It was strange; but she spoke and stood at that moment like a lady of degree, drawn upward by her aspirations.

'You speak to me, by God, as though you scorned me!' cried the husband.

The man's passion was always formidable; she had often looked on upon its violence with a thrill, it had been one ingredient in her fascination; and she was now surprised to behold him, as from afar off, gesticulating but impotent. His fury might be dangerous like a torrent or a gust of wind, but it was inhuman; it might be feared or braved, it should never be respected. And with that there came in her a sudden glow of courage and that readiness to die which attends so closely upon all strong passions.

'I do scorn you,' she said.

'What is that?' he cried.

'I scorn you,' she repeated, smiling.

'You love another man!' said he.

'With all my soul,' was her reply.

The wine-seller roared aloud so that the house rang and shook with it.

'Is this the—?' he cried, using a foul word, common in the South; and he seized the young countryman and dashed him to the ground. There he lay for the least interval of time insensible; thence fled from the house, the most terrified person in the county. The heavy measure had escaped from his hands, splashing the wine high upon the wall. Paradou caught it. 'And you?' he roared to his wife, giving her the same name in the feminine, and he aimed at her the deadly missile. She expected it, motionless, with radiant eyes.

But before it sped, Paradou was met by another adversary, and the unconscious rivals stood confronted. It was hard to say at that moment which appeared the more formidable. In Paradou, the whole muddy and truculent depths of the half-man were stirred to frenzy; the lust of destruction raged in him; there was not a feature in his face but it talked murder. Balmile had dropped his cloak: he shone out at once in his finery, and stood to his full stature; girt in mind and body all his resources, all his temper, perfectly in command in his face the light of battle. Neither spoke; there was no blow nor threat of one; it was war reduced to its last element, the spiritual; and the huge wine-seller slowly lowered his weapon. Balmile was a noble, he a commoner; Balmile exulted in an honourable cause. Paradou already perhaps began to be ashamed of his violence. Of a sudden, at least, the tortured brute turned and fled from the shop in the footsteps of his former victim, to whose continued flight his reappearance added wings.

So soon as Balmile appeared between her husband and herself, Marie-Madeleine transferred to him her eyes. It might be her last moment, and she fed upon that face; reading there inimitable courage and illimitable valour to protect. And when the momentary peril was gone by, and the champion turned a little awkwardly towards her whom he had rescued, it was to meet, and quail before, a gaze of admiration more distinct than words. He bowed, he stammered, his words failed him; he who had crossed the floor a moment ago, like a young god, to smite, returned like one discomfited; got somehow to his place by the table, muffled himself again in his discarded cloak, and for a last touch of the ridiculous, seeking for anything to restore his countenance, drank of the wine before him, deep as a porter after a heavy lift. It was little wonder if Ballantrae, reading the scene with malevolent eyes, laughed out loud and brief, and drank with raised glass, 'To the champion of the Fair.'

Marie-Madeleine stood in her old place within the counter; she disdained the mocking laughter; it fell on her ears, but it did not reach her spirit. For her, the world of living persons was all resumed again into one pair, as in the days of Eden; there was but the one end in life, the one hope before her, the one thing needful, the one thing possible—to be his.

CHAPTER I—THE PRINCE

That same night there was in the city of Avignon a young man in distress of mind. Now he sat, now walked in a high apartment, full of draughts and shadows. A single candle made the darkness visible; and the light scarce sufficed to show upon the wall, where they had been recently and rudely nailed, a few miniatures and a copper medal of the young man's head. The same was being sold that year in London, to admiring thousands. The original was fair; he had beautiful brown eyes, a beautiful bright open face; a little feminine, a little hard, a little weak; still full of the light of youth, but already beginning to be vulgarised; a sordid bloom come upon it, the lines coarsened with a touch of puffiness. He was dressed, as for a gala, in peach-colour and silver; his breast sparkled with stars and was bright with ribbons; for he had held a levee in the afternoon and received a distinguished personage incognito. Now he sat with a bowed head, now walked precipitately to and fro, now went and gazed from the uncurtained window, where the wind was still blowing, and the lights winked in the darkness.

The bells of Avignon rose into song as he was gazing; and the high notes and the deep tossed and drowned, boomed suddenly near or were suddenly swallowed up, in the current of the mistral. Tears sprang in the pale blue eyes; the expression of his face was changed to that of a more active misery, it seemed as if the voices of the bells reached, and touched and pained him, in a waste of vacancy where even pain was welcome. Outside in the night they continued to sound on, swelling and fainting; and the listener heard in his memory, as it were their harmonies, joy-bells clashing in a northern city, and the acclamations of a multitude, the cries of battle, the gross voices of cannon, the stridor of an animated life. And then all died away, and he stood face to

197

face with himself in the waste of vacancy, and a horror came upon his mind, and a faintness on his brain, such as seizes men upon the brink of cliffs.

On the table, by the side of the candle, stood a tray of glasses, a bottle, and a silver bell. He went thither swiftly, then his hand lowered first above the bell, then settled on the bottle. Slowly he filled a glass, slowly drank it out; and, as a tide of animal warmth recomforted the recesses of his nature, stood there smiling at himself. He remembered he was young; the funeral curtains rose, and he saw his life shine and broaden and flow out majestically, like a river sunward. The smile still on his lips, he lit a second candle and a third; a fire stood ready built in a chimney, he lit that also; and the fir-cones and the gnarled olive billets were swift to break in flame and to crackle on the hearth, and the room brightened and enlarged about him like his hopes. To and fro, to and fro, he went, his hands lightly clasped, his breath deeply and pleasurably taken. Victory walked with him; he marched to crowns and empires among shouting followers; glory was his dress. And presently again the shadows closed upon the solitary. Under the gilt of flame and candle-light, the stone walls of the apartment showed down bare and cold; behind the depicted triumph loomed up the actual failure: defeat, the long distress of the flight, exile, despair, broken followers, mourning faces, empty pockets, friends estranged. The memory of his father rose in his mind: he, too, estranged and defied; despair sharpened into wrath. There was one who had led armies in the field, who had staked his life upon the family enterprise, a man of action and experience, of the open air, the camp, the court, the council-room; and he was to accept direction from an old, pompous gentleman in a home in Italy, and buzzed about by priests? A pretty king, if he had not a martial son to lean upon! A king at all?

'There was a weaver (of all people) joined me at St. Ninians; he was more of a man than my papa!' he thought. 'I saw him lie doubled in his blood and a grenadier below him—and he died for my papa! All died for him, or risked the dying, and I lay for him all those months in the rain and skulked in heather like a fox; and now he writes me his advice! calls me Carluccio—me, the man of the house, the only king in that king's race.' He ground his teeth. 'The only king in Europe!' Who else? Who has done and suffered except me? who has lain and run and hidden with his faithful subjects, like a second Bruce? Not my accursed cousin, Louis of France, at least, the lewd effeminate traitor!' And filling the glass to the brim, he drank a king's damnation. Ah, if he had the power of Louis, what a king were here!

The minutes followed each other into the past, and still he persevered in this debilitating cycle of emotions, still fed the fire of his excitement with driblets of Rhine wine: a boy at odds with life, a boy with a spark of the heroic, which he was now burning out and drowning down in futile reverie and solitary excess.

From two rooms beyond, the sudden sound of a raised voice attracted him.

'By . . .

HEATHERCAT

CHAPTER I—TRAQUAIRS OF MONTROYMONT

The period of this tale is in the heat of the killing-time; the scene laid for the most part in solitary hills and morasses, haunted only by the so-called Mountain Wanderers, the dragoons that came in chase of them, the women that wept on their dead bodies, and the wild birds of the moorland that have cried there since the beginning. It is a land of many rain-clouds; a land of much mute history, written there in prehistoric symbols. Strange green raths are to be seen commonly in the country, above all by the kirkyards; barrows of the dead, standing stones; beside these, the faint, durable footprints and handmarks of the Roman; and an antiquity older perhaps than any, and still living and active—a complete Celtic nomenclature and a scarce-mingled Celtic population. These rugged and grey hills were once included in the boundaries of the Caledonian Forest. Merlin sat here below his apple-tree and lamented Gwendolen; here spoke with Kentigern; here fell into his enchanted trance. And the legend of his slumber seems to body forth the story of that Celtic race, deprived for so many centuries of their authentic speech, surviving with their ancestral inheritance of melancholy perversity and patient, unfortunate courage.

The Traquairs of Montroymont (Mons Romanus, as the erudite expound it) had long held their seat about the head-waters of the Dule and in the back parts of the moorland parish of Balweary. For two hundred years they had enjoyed in these upland quarters a certain decency (almost to be named distinction) of repute; and the annals of their house, or what is remembered of them, were obscure and bloody. Ninian Traquair was 'cruallie slochtered' by the Crozers at the kirk-door of Balweary, anno 1482. Francis killed Simon Ruthven of Drumshoreland, anno 1540; bought letters of slayers at the widow and heir, and, by a barbarous form of compounding, married (without tocher) Simon's daughter Grizzel, which is the way the Traquairs and Ruthvens came first to an intermarriage. About the last Traquair and Ruthven marriage, it is the business of this book, among many other things, to tell.

The Traquairs were always strong for the Covenant; for the King also, but the Covenant first; and it began to be ill days for Montroymont when the Bishops came in and the dragoons at the heels of them. Ninian (then laird) was an anxious husband of himself and the property, as the times required, and it may be said of him, that he lost both. He was heavily suspected of the Pentland Hills rebellion. When it came the length of Bothwell Brig, he stood his trial before the Secret Council, and was convicted of talking with some insurgents by the wayside, the subject of the conversation not very clearly appearing, and of the reset and maintenance of one Gale, a gardener man, who was seen before Bothwell with a musket, and afterwards, for a continuance of months, delved the garden at Montroymont. Matters went very ill with Ninian at the Council; some of the lords were clear for treason; and even the boot was talked of. But he was spared that torture; and at last, having pretty good friendship among great men, he came off with a fine of seven thousand marks, that caused the estate to groan. In this case, as in so many others, it was the wife that made the trouble. She was a great keeper of conventicles; would ride ten miles to one, and when she was fined, rejoiced greatly to suffer for the Kirk; but it was rather her husband that suffered. She had their only son, Francis, baptized privately by the hands of Mr. Kidd; there was that much the more to pay for! She could neither be driven nor wiled into the parish kirk; as for taking the sacrament at the hands of any Episcopalian curate, and tenfold more at those of Curate Haddo, there was nothing further from her purposes; and Montroymont had to put his hand in his pocket month by month and year by year. Once, indeed, the little lady was cast in prison, and the laird, worthy, heavy, uninterested man, had to ride up and take her place; from which he was not discharged under nine months and a sharp fine. It scarce seemed she had any gratitude to him; she came out of gaol herself, and plunged immediately deeper in conventicles, resetting recusants, and all her old, expensive folly, only with greater vigour and openness, because Montroymont was safe in the Tolbooth and she had no witness to consider. When he was liberated and came back, with his fingers singed, in December 1680, and late in the black night, my lady was from home. He came into the house at his alighting, with a riding-rod yet in his hand; and, on the servant-maid telling him, caught her by the scruff of the neck, beat her violently, flung her down in the passageway, and went upstairs to his bed fasting and without a light. It was three in the morning when my lady returned from that conventicle, and, hearing of the assault (because the maid had sat up for her, weeping), went to their common chamber with a lantern in hand and stamping with her shoes so as to wake the dead; it was supposed, by those that heard her, from a design to have it out with the good man at once. The house-servants gathered on the stair, because it was a main interest with them to know which of these two was the better horse; and for the space of two hours they were heard to go at the matter, hammer and tongs. Montroymont alleged he was at the end of possibilities; it was no longer within his power to pay the annual rents; she had served him basely by keeping conventicles while he lay in prison for her sake; his friends were weary, and there was nothing else before him but the entire loss of the family lands, and to begin life again by the wayside as a common beggar. She took him up very sharp and high: called upon him, if he were a Christian? and which he most considered, the loss of a few dirty, miry glebes, or of his soul? Presently he was heard to weep, and my lady's voice to go on continually like a running burn, only the words indistinguishable; whereupon it was supposed a victory for her ladyship, and the domestics took themselves to bed. The next day Traquair appeared like a man who had gone under the harrows; and his lady wife thenceforward continued in her old course without the least deflection.

Thenceforward Ninian went on his way without complaint, and suffered his wife to go on hers without remonstrance. He still minded his estate, of which it might be said he took daily a fresh farewell, and counted it already lost; looking ruefully on the acres and the graves of his fathers, on the moorlands where the wild-fowl consorted, the low, gurgling pool of the trout, and the high, windy place of the calling curlews—things that were yet his for the day and would be another's to-morrow; coming back again, and sitting ciphering till the dusk at his approaching ruin, which no device of arithmetic could postpone beyond a year or two. He was essentially the simple ancient man, the farmer and landholder; he would have been content to watch the seasons come and go, and his cattle increase, until the limit of age; he would have been content at any time to die, if he could have left the estates undiminished to an heir-male of his ancestors, that duty standing first in his instinctive calendar. And now he saw everywhere the image of the new proprietor come to meet him, and go sowing and reaping, or fowling for his pleasure on the red moors, or eating the very gooseberries in the Place garden; and saw always, on the other hand, the figure of Francis go forth, a beggar, into the broad world.

It was in vain the poor gentleman sought to moderate; took every test and took advantage of every indulgence; went and drank with the dragoons in Balweary; attended the communion and came regularly to the church to Curate Haddo, with his son beside him. The mad, raging, Presbyterian zealot of a wife at home made all of no avail; and indeed the house must have fallen years before if it had not been for the secret indulgence of the curate, who had a great sympathy with the laird, and winked hard at the doings in Montroymont. This curate was a man very ill reputed in the countryside, and indeed in all Scotland. 'Infamous Haddo' is Shield's expression. But Patrick Walker is more copious. 'Curate Hall Haddo,' says he, sub voce Peden, 'or Hell Haddo, as he was more justly to be called, a pokeful of old condemned errors and the filthy vile lusts of the flesh, a published whore-monger, a common gross drunkard, continually and godlessly scraping and skirling on a fiddle, continually breathing flames against the remnant of Israel. But the Lord put an end to his piping, and all these offences were composed into one bloody grave.' No doubt this was written to excuse his slaughter; and I have never heard it claimed for Walker that he was either a just witness or an indulgent judge. At least, in a merely human character, Haddo comes off not wholly amiss in the matter of these Traquairs: not that he showed any graces of the Christian, but had a sort of Pagan decency, which might almost tempt one to be concerned about his sudden, violent, and unprepared fate.

CHAPTER II—FRANCIE

Francie was eleven years old, shy, secret, and rather childish of his age, though not backward in schooling, which had been pushed on far by a private governor, one M'Brair, a forfeited minister harboured in that capacity at

Montroymont. The boy, already much employed in secret by his mother, was the most apt hand conceivable to run upon a message, to carry food to lurking fugitives, or to stand sentry on the skyline above a conventicle. It seemed no place on the moorlands was so naked but what he would find cover there; and as he knew every hag, boulder, and heather-bush in a circuit of seven miles about Montroymont, there was scarce any spot but what he could leave or approach it unseen. This dexterity had won him a reputation in that part of the country; and among the many children employed in these dangerous affairs, he passed under the by-name of Heathercat.

How much his father knew of this employment might be doubted. He took much forethought for the boy's future, seeing he was like to be left so poorly, and would sometimes assist at his lessons, sighing heavily, yawning deep, and now and again patting Francie on the shoulder if he seemed to be doing ill, by way of a private, kind encouragement. But a great part of the day was passed in aimless wanderings with his eyes sealed, or in his cabinet sitting bemused over the particulars of the coming bankruptcy; and the boy would be absent a dozen times for once that his father would observe it.

On 2nd of July 1682 the boy had an errand from his mother, which must be kept private from all, the father included in the first of them. Crossing the braes, he hears the clatter of a horse's shoes, and claps down incontinent in a hag by the wayside. And presently he spied his father come riding from one direction, and Curate Haddo walking from another; and Montroymont leaning down from the saddle, and Haddo getting on his toes (for he was a little, ruddy, bald-pated man, more like a dwarf), they greeted kindly, and came to a halt within two fathoms of the child.

'Montroymont,' the curate said, 'the deil's in 't but I'll have to denunciate your leddy again.'

'Deil's in 't indeed!' says the laird.

'Man! can ye no induce her to come to the kirk?' pursues Haddo; 'or to a communion at the least of it? For the conventicles, let be! and the same for yon solemn fule, M'Brair: I can blink at them. But she's got to come to the kirk, Montroymont.'

'Dinna speak of it,' says the laird. 'I can do nothing with her.'

'Couldn't ye try the stick to her? it works wonders whiles,' suggested Haddo. 'No? I'm wae to hear it. And I suppose ye ken where you're going?'

'Fine!' said Montroymont. 'Fine do I ken where: bankrup'cy and the Bass Rock!'

'Praise to my bones that I never married!' cried the curate. 'Well, it's a grievous thing to me to see an auld house dung down that was here before Flodden Field. But naebody can say it was with my wish.'

'No more they can, Haddo!' says the laird. 'A good friend ye've been to me, first and last. I can give you that character with a clear conscience.'

Whereupon they separated, and Montroymont rode briskly down into the Dule Valley. But of the curate Francis was not to be quit so easily. He went on with his little, brisk steps to the corner of a dyke, and stopped and whistled and waved upon a lassie that was herding cattle there. This Janet M'Clour was a big lass, being taller than the curate; and what made her look the more so, she was kilted very high. It seemed for a while she would not come, and Francie heard her calling Haddo a 'daft auld fule,' and saw her running and dodging him among the whins and hags till he was fairly blown. But at the last he gets a bottle from his plaid-neuk and holds it up to her; whereupon she came at once into a composition, and the pair sat, drinking of the bottle, and daffing and laughing together, on a mound of heather. The boy had scarce heard of these vanities, or he might have been minded of a nymph and satyr, if anybody could have taken long-leggit Janet for a nymph. But they seemed to be huge friends, he thought; and was the more surprised, when the curate had taken his leave, to see the lassie fling stones after him with screeches of laughter, and Haddo turn about and caper, and shake his staff at her, and laugh louder than herself. A wonderful merry pair, they seemed; and when Francie had crawled out of the hag, he had a great deal to consider in his mind. It was possible they were all fallen in error about Mr. Haddo, he reflected—having seen him so tender with Montroymont, and so kind and playful with the lass Janet; and he had a temptation to go out of his road and question her herself upon the matter. But he had a strong spirit of duty on him; and plodded on instead over the braes till he came near the House of Cairngorm. There, in a hollow place by the burnside that was shaded by some birks, he was aware of a barefoot boy, perhaps a matter of three years older than himself. The two approached with the precautions of a pair of strange dogs, looking at each other queerly.

'It's ill weather on the hills,' said the stranger, giving the watchword.

'For a season,' said Francie, 'but the Lord will appear.'

'Richt,' said the barefoot boy; 'wha're ye frae?'

'The Leddy Montroymont,' says Francie.

'Ha'e, then!' says the stranger, and handed him a folded paper, and they stood and looked at each other again. 'It's unco het,' said the boy.

'Dooms het,' says Francie.

'What do they ca' ye?' says the other.

'Francie,' says he. 'I'm young Montroymont. They ca' me Heathercat.'

'I'm Jock Crozer,' said the boy. And there was another pause, while each rolled a stone under his foot.

'Cast your jaiket and I'll fecht ye for a bawbee,' cried the elder boy with sudden violence, and dramatically throwing back his jacket.

'Na, I've nae time the now,' said Francie, with a sharp thrill of alarm, because Crozer was much the heavier boy.

'Ye're feared. Heathercat indeed!' said Crozer, for among this infantile army of spies and messengers, the fame of Crozer had gone forth and was resented by his rivals. And with that they separated.

On his way home Francie was a good deal occupied with the recollection of this untoward incident. The challenge had been fairly offered and basely refused: the tale would be carried all over the country, and the lustre of the name of Heathercat be dimmed. But the scene between Curate Haddo and Janet M'Clour had also given him much to think of: and he was still puzzling over the case of the curate, and why such ill words were said of him, and why, if he were so merry-spirited, he should yet preach so dry, when coming over a knowe, whom should he see but Janet, sitting with her back to him, minding her cattle! He was always a great child for secret, stealthy ways, having been employed by his mother on errands when the same was necessary; and he came behind the lass without her hearing.

'Jennet,' says he.

'Keep me,' cries Janet, springing up. 'O, it's you, Maister Francie! Save us, what a fricht ye gied me.'

'Ay, it's me,' said Francie. 'I've been thinking, Jennet; I saw you and the curate a while back—'

'Brat!' cried Janet, and coloured up crimson; and the one moment made as if she would have stricken him with a ragged stick she had to chase her bestial with, and the next was begging and praying that he would mention it to none. It was 'naebody's business, whatever,' she said; 'it would just start a clash in the country'; and there would be nothing left for her but to drown herself in Dule Water.

'Why?' says Francie.

The girl looked at him and grew scarlet again.

'And it isna that, anyway,' continued Francie. 'It was just that he seemed so good to ye—like our Father in heaven, I thought; and I thought that mebbe, perhaps, we had all been wrong about him from the first. But I'll have to tell Mr. M'Brair; I'm under a kind of a bargain to him to tell him all.'

'Tell it to the divil if ye like for me!' cried the lass. 'I've naething to be ashamed of. Tell M'Brair to mind his ain affairs,' she cried again: 'they'll be hot enough for him, if Haddie likes!' And so strode off, shoving her beasts before her, and ever and again looking back and crying angry words to the boy, where he stood mystified.

By the time he had got home his mind was made up that he would say nothing to his mother. My Lady Montroymont was in the keeping-room, reading a godly book; she was a wonderful frail little wife to make so much noise in the world and be able to steer about that patient sheep her husband; her eyes were like sloes, the fingers of her hands were like tobacco-pipe shanks, her mouth shut tight like a trap; and even when she was the most serious, and still more when she was angry, there hung about her face the terrifying semblance of a smile.

'Have ye gotten the billet, Francie said she; and when he had handed it over, and she had read and burned it, 'Did you see anybody?' she asked.

'I saw the laird,' said Francie.

'He didna see you, though?' asked his mother.

'Deil a fear,' from Francie.

'Francie!' she cried. 'What's that I hear? an aith? The Lord forgive me, have I broughten forth a brand for the burning, a fagot for hell-fire?'

'I'm very sorry, ma'am,' said Francie. 'I humbly beg the Lord's pardon, and yours, for my wickedness.'

'H'm,' grunted the lady. 'Did ye see nobody else?'

'No, ma'am,' said Francie, with the face of an angel, 'except Jock Crozer, that gied me the billet.'

'Jock Crozer!' cried the lady. 'I'll Crozer them! Crozers indeed! What next? Are we to repose the lives of a suffering remnant in Crozers? The whole clan of them wants hanging, and if I had my way of it, they wouldna want it long. Are you aware, sir, that these Crozers killed your forebear at the kirk-door?'

'You see, he was bigger 'n me,' said Francie.

'Jock Crozer!' continued the lady. 'That'll be Clement's son, the biggest thief and reiver in the country-side. To trust a note to him! But I'll give the benefit of my opinions to Lady Whitecross when we two forgather. Let her look to herself! I have no patience with half-hearted carlines, that complies on the Lord's day morning with the kirk, and comes taigling the same night to the conventicle. The one or the other! is what I say: hell or heaven—Haddie's abominations or the pure word of God dreeping from the lips of Mr. Arnot,

> "'Like honey from the honeycomb
>
> That dreepeth, sweeter far.'"

My lady was now fairly launched, and that upon two congenial subjects: the deficiencies of the Lady Whitecross and the turpitudes of the whole Crozer race—which, indeed, had never been conspicuous for respectability. She pursued the pair of them for twenty minutes on the clock with wonderful animation and detail, something of the pulpit manner, and the spirit of one possessed. 'O hellish compliance!' she exclaimed. 'I would not suffer a complier to break bread with Christian folk. Of all the sins of this day there is not one so God-defying, so Christ-humiliating, as damnable compliance': the boy standing before her meanwhile, and brokenly pursuing other thoughts, mainly of Haddo and Janet, and Jock Crozer stripping off his jacket. And yet, with all his distraction, it might be argued that he heard too much: his father and himself being 'compliers'—that is to say, attending the church of the parish as the law required.

Presently, the lady's passion beginning to decline, or her flux of ill words to be exhausted, she dismissed her audience. Francie bowed low, left the room, closed the door behind him: and then turned him about in the passage-way, and with a low voice, but a prodigious deal of sentiment, repeated the name of the evil one twenty times over, to the end of which, for the greater efficacy, he tacked on 'damnable' and 'hellish.' Fas est ab hoste doceri—disrespect is made more pungent by quotation; and there is no doubt but he felt relieved, and went upstairs into his tutor's chamber with a quiet mind. M'Brair sat by the cheek of the peat-fire and shivered, for he had a quartan ague and this was his day. The great night-cap and plaid, the dark unshaven cheeks of the man, and the white, thin hands that held the plaid about his chittering body, made a sorrowful picture. But Francie knew and loved him; came straight in, nestled close to the refugee, and told his story. M'Brair had been at the College with Haddo; the Presbytery had licensed both on the same day; and at this tale, told with so much innocency by the boy, the heart of the tutor was commoved.

'Woe upon him! Woe upon that man!' he cried. 'O the unfaithful shepherd! O the hireling and apostate minister! Make my matters hot for me? quo' she! the shameless limmer! And true it is, that he could repose me in that nasty, stinking hole, the Canongate Tolbooth, from which your mother drew me out—the Lord reward her for it!—or to that cold, unbieldy, marine place of the Bass Rock, which, with my delicate kist, would be fair ruin to me. But I will be valiant in my Master's service. I have a duty here: a duty to my God, to myself, and to Haddo: in His strength, I will perform it.'

Then he straitly discharged Francie to repeat the tale, and bade him in the future to avert his very eyes from the doings of the curate. 'You must go to his place of idolatry; look upon him there!' says he, 'but nowhere else. Avert your eyes, close your ears, pass him by like a three days' corp. He is like that damnable monster Basiliscus, which defiles—yea, poisons!—by the sight.'—All which was hardly claratory to the boy's mind.

Presently Montroymont came home, and called up the stairs to Francie. Traquair was a good shot and swordsman: and it was his pleasure to walk with his son over the braes of the moorfowl, or to teach him arms in the back court, when they made a mighty comely pair, the child being so lean, and light, and active, and the laird himself a man of a manly, pretty stature, his hair (the periwig being laid aside) showing already white with many anxieties, and his face of an even, flaccid red. But this day Francie's heart was not in the fencing.

'Sir,' says he, suddenly lowering his point, 'will ye tell me a thing if I was to ask it?'

'Ask away,' says the father.

'Well, it's this,' said Francie: 'Why do you and me comply if it's so wicked?'

'Ay, ye have the cant of it too!' cries Montroymont. 'But I'll tell ye for all that. It's to try and see if we can keep the rigging on this house, Francie. If she had her way, we would be beggar-folk, and hold our hands out by the

210

wayside. When ye hear her—when ye hear folk,' he corrected himself briskly, 'call me a coward, and one that betrayed the Lord, and I kenna what else, just mind it was to keep a bed to ye to sleep in and a bite for ye to eat.—On guard!' he cried, and the lesson proceeded again till they were called to supper.

'There's another thing yet,' said Francie, stopping his father. 'There's another thing that I am not sure that I am very caring for. She—she sends me errands.'

'Obey her, then, as is your bounden duty,' said Traquair.

'Ay, but wait till I tell ye,' says the boy. 'If I was to see you I was to hide.'

Montroymont sighed. 'Well, and that's good of her too,' said he. 'The less that I ken of thir doings the better for me; and the best thing you can do is just to obey her, and see and be a good son to her, the same as ye are to me, Francie.'

At the tenderness of this expression the heart of Francie swelled within his bosom, and his remorse was poured out. 'Faither!' he cried, 'I said "deil" to-day; many's the time I said it, and damnable too, and hellitsh. I ken they're all right; they're beeblical. But I didna say them beeblically; I said them for sweir words—that's the truth of it.'

'Hout, ye silly bairn!' said the father, 'dinna do it nae mair, and come in by to your supper.' And he took the boy, and drew him close to him a moment, as they went through the door, with something very fond and secret, like a caress between a pair of lovers.

The next day M'Brair was abroad in the afternoon, and had a long advising with Janet on the braes where she herded cattle. What passed was never wholly known; but the lass wept bitterly, and fell on her knees to him among the whins. The same night, as soon as it was dark, he took the road again for Balweary. In the Kirkton, where the dragoons quartered, he saw many lights, and heard the noise of a ranting song and people laughing grossly, which was highly offensive to his mind. He gave it the wider berth, keeping among fields; and came down at last by the water-side, where the manse stands solitary between the river and the road. He tapped at the back door, and the old woman called upon him to come in, and guided him through the house to the study, as they still called it, though there was little enough study there in Haddo's days, and more song-books than theology.

'Here's yin to speak wi' ye, Mr. Haddie!' cries the old wife.

And M'Brair, opening the door and entering, found the little, round, red man seated in one chair and his feet upon another. A clear fire and a tallow dip lighted him barely. He was taking tobacco in a pipe, and smiling to himself; and a brandy-bottle and glass, and his fiddle and bow, were beside him on the table.

'Hech, Patey M'Briar, is this you?' said he, a trifle tipsily. 'Step in by, man, and have a drop brandy: for the stomach's sake! Even the deil can quote Scripture—eh, Patey?'

'I will neither eat nor drink with you,' replied M'Brair. 'I am come upon my Master's errand: woe be upon me if I should anyways mince the same. Hall Haddo, I summon you to quit this kirk which you encumber.'

'Muckle obleeged!' says Haddo, winking.

'You and me have been to kirk and market together,' pursued M'Brair; 'we have had blessed seasons in the kirk, we have sat in the same teaching-rooms and read in the same book; and I know you still retain for me some carnal kindness. It would be my shame if I denied it; I live here at your mercy and by your favour, and glory to acknowledge it. You have pity on my wretched body, which is but grass, and must soon be trodden under: but O, Haddo! how much greater is the yearning with which I yearn after and pity your immortal soul! Come now, let us reason together! I drop all points of controversy, weighty though these be; I take your defaced and damnified kirk on your own terms; and I ask you, Are you a worthy minister? The communion season approaches; how can you pronounce thir solemn words, "The elders will now bring forrit the elements," and not quail? A parishioner may be summoned to-night; you may have to rise from your miserable orgies; and I ask you, Haddo, what does your conscience tell you? Are you fit? Are you fit to smooth the pillow of a parting Christian? And if the summons should be for yourself, how then?'

Haddo was startled out of all composure and the better part of his temper. 'What's this of it?' he cried. 'I'm no waur than my neebours. I never set up to be speeritual; I never did. I'm a plain, canty creature; godliness is cheerfulness, says I; give me my fiddle and a dram, and I wouldna hairm a flee.'

'And I repeat my question,' said M'Brair: 'Are you fit—fit for this great charge? fit to carry and save souls?'

'Fit? Blethers! As fit's yoursel',' cried Haddo.

'Are you so great a self-deceiver?' said M'Brair. 'Wretched man, trampler upon God's covenants, crucifier of your Lord afresh. I will ding you to the earth with one word: How about the young woman, Janet M'Clour?'

'Weel, what about her? what do I ken?' cries Haddo. 'M'Brair, ye daft auld wife, I tell ye as true's truth, I never meddled her. It was just daffing, I tell ye: daffing, and nae mair: a piece of fun, like! I'm no denying but what I'm fond of fun, sma' blame to me! But for onything sarious—hout, man, it might come to a deposeetion! I'll sweir it to ye. Where's a Bible, till you hear me sweir?'

'There is nae Bible in your study,' said M'Brair severely.

And Haddo, after a few distracted turns, was constrained to accept the fact.

'Weel, and suppose there isna?' he cried, stamping. 'What mair can ye say of us, but just that I'm fond of my joke, and so's she? I declare to God, by what I ken, she might be the Virgin Mary—if she would just keep clear of the dragoons. But me! na, deil haet o' me!'

'She is penitent at least,' says M'Brair.

'Do you mean to actually up and tell me to my face that she accused me?' cried the curate.

'I canna just say that,' replied M'Brair. 'But I rebuked her in the name of God, and she repented before me on her bended knees.'

'Weel, I daursay she's been ower far wi' the dragoons,' said Haddo. 'I never denied that. I ken naething by it.'

'Man, you but show your nakedness the more plainly,' said M'Brair. 'Poor, blind, besotted creature—and I see you stoytering on the brink of dissolution: your light out, and your hours numbered. Awake, man!' he shouted with a formidable voice, 'awake, or it be ower late.'

'Be damned if I stand this!' exclaimed Haddo, casting his tobacco-pipe violently on the table, where it was smashed in pieces. 'Out of my house with ye, or I'll call for the dragoons.'

'The speerit of the Lord is upon me,' said M'Brair with solemn ecstasy. 'I sist you to compear before the Great White Throne, and I warn you the summons shall be bloody and sudden.'

And at this, with more agility than could have been expected, he got clear of the room and slammed the door behind him in the face of the pursuing curate. The next Lord's day the curate was ill, and the kirk closed, but for all his ill words, Mr. M'Brair abode unmolested in the house of Montroymont.

CHAPTER III—THE HILL-END OF DRUMLOWE

This was a bit of a steep broken hill that overlooked upon the west a moorish valley, full of ink-black pools. These presently drained into a burn that made off, with little noise and no celerity of pace, about the corner of the hill. On the far side the ground swelled into a bare heath, black with junipers, and spotted with the presence of the standing stones for which the place was famous. They were many in that part, shapeless, white with lichen—you would have said with age: and had made their abode there for untold centuries, since first the heathens shouted for their installation. The ancients had hallowed them to some ill religion, and their neighbourhood had long been avoided by the prudent before the fall of day; but of late, on the upspringing of new requirements, these lonely stones on the moor had again become a place of assembly. A watchful picket on the Hill-end commanded all the northern and eastern approaches; and such was the disposition of the

214

ground, that by certain cunningly posted sentries the west also could be made secure against surprise: there was no place in the country where a conventicle could meet with more quiet of mind or a more certain retreat open, in the case of interference from the dragoons. The minister spoke from a knowe close to the edge of the ring, and poured out the words God gave him on the very threshold of the devils of yore. When they pitched a tent (which was often in wet weather, upon a communion occasion) it was rigged over the huge isolated pillar that had the name of Anes-Errand, none knew why. And the congregation sat partly clustered on the slope below, and partly among the idolatrous monoliths and on the turfy soil of the Ring itself. In truth the situation was well qualified to give a zest to Christian doctrines, had there been any wanted. But these congregations assembled under conditions at once so formidable and romantic as made a zealot of the most cold. They were the last of the faithful; God, who had averted His face from all other countries of the world, still leaned from heaven to observe, with swelling sympathy, the doings of His moorland remnant; Christ was by them with His eternal wounds, with dropping tears; the Holy Ghost (never perfectly realised nor firmly adopted by Protestant imaginations) was dimly supposed to be in the heart of each and on the lips of the minister. And over against them was the army of the hierarchies, from the men Charles and James Stuart, on to King Lewie and the Emperor; and the scarlet Pope, and the muckle black devil himself, peering out the red mouth of hell in an ecstasy of hate and hope. 'One pull more!' he seemed to cry; 'one pull more, and it's done. There's only Clydesdale and the Stewartry, and the three Bailiaries of Ayr, left for God.' And with such an august assistance of powers and principalities looking on at the last conflict of good and evil, it was scarce possible to spare a thought to those old, infirm, debile, ab agendo devils whose holy place they were now violating.

There might have been three hundred to four hundred present. At least there were three hundred horses tethered for the most part in the ring; though some of the hearers on the outskirts of the crowd stood with their bridles in their hand, ready to mount at the first signal. The circle of faces was strangely characteristic; long, serious, strongly marked, the tackle standing out in the lean brown cheeks, the mouth set and the eyes shining with a fierce enthusiasm; the shepherd, the labouring man, and the rarer laird, stood there in their broad blue bonnets or laced hats, and presenting an essential identity of type. From time to time a long-drawn groan of adhesion rose in this audience, and was propagated like a wave to the outskirts, and died away among the keepers of the horses. It had a name; it was called 'a holy groan.'

A squall came up; a great volley of flying mist went out before it and whelmed the scene; the wind stormed with a sudden fierceness that carried away the minister's voice and twitched his tails and made him stagger, and turned the congregation for a moment into a mere pother of blowing plaid-ends and prancing horses; and the rain followed and was dashed straight into their faces. Men and women panted aloud in the shock of that violent shower-bath; the teeth were bared along all the line in an involuntary grimace; plaids, mantles, and riding-coats were proved vain, and the worshippers felt the water stream on their naked flesh. The minister, reinforcing his great and shrill voice, continued to contend against and triumph over the rising of the squall and the dashing of the rain.

'In that day ye may go thirty mile and not hear a crawing cock,' he said; 'and fifty mile and not get a light to your pipe; and an hundred mile and not see a smoking house. For there'll be naething in all Scotland but deid men's banes and blackness, and the living anger of the Lord. O, where to find a bield—O sirs, where to find a bield from the wind of the Lord's anger? Do ye call this a wind? Bethankit! Sirs, this is but a temporary dispensation; this is but a puff of wind, this is but a spit of rain and by with it. Already there's a blue bow in the west, and the sun will take the crown of the causeway again, and your things'll be dried upon ye, and your flesh will be warm upon your bones. But O, sirs, sirs! for the day of the Lord's anger!'

His rhetoric was set forth with an ear-piercing elocution, and a voice that sometimes crashed like cannon. Such as it was, it was the gift of all hill-preachers, to a singular degree of likeness or identity. Their images scarce ranged beyond the red horizon of the moor and the rainy hill-top, the shepherd and his sheep, a fowling-piece, a spade, a pipe, a dunghill, a crowing cock, the shining and the withdrawal of the sun. An occasional pathos of simple humanity, and frequent patches of big Biblical words, relieved the homely tissue. It was a poetry apart; bleak, austere, but genuine, and redolent of the soil.

A little before the coming of the squall there was a different scene enacting at the outposts. For the most part, the sentinels were faithful to their important duty; the Hill-end of Drumlowe was known to be a safe meeting-place; and the out-pickets on this particular day had been somewhat lax from the beginning, and grew laxer during the inordinate length of the discourse. Francie lay there in his appointed hiding-hole, looking abroad between two whin-bushes. His view was across the course of the burn, then over a piece of plain moorland, to a gap between two hills; nothing moved but grouse, and some cattle who slowly traversed his field of view, heading northward: he heard the psalms, and sang words of his own to the savage and melancholy music; for he had his own design in hand, and terror and cowardice prevailed in his bosom alternately, like the hot and the cold fit of an ague. Courage was uppermost during the singing, which he accompanied through all its length with this impromptu strain:

'And I will ding Jock Crozer down

No later than the day.'

Presently the voice of the preacher came to him in wafts, at the wind's will, as by the opening and shutting of a door; wild spasms of screaming, as of some undiscerned gigantic hill-bird stirred with inordinate passion, succeeded to intervals of silence; and Francie heard them with a critical ear. 'Ay,' he thought at last, 'he'll do; he has the bit in his mou' fairly.'

He had observed that his friend, or rather his enemy, Jock Crozer, had been established at a very critical part of the line of outposts; namely, where the burn issues by an abrupt gorge from the semicircle of high moors. If anything was calculated to nerve him to battle it was this. The post was important; next to the Hill-end itself, it might be called the key to the position; and it was where the cover was bad, and in which it was most natural to place a child. It should have been Heathercat's; why had it been given to Crozer? An exquisite fear of what should be the answer passed through his marrow every time he faced the question. Was it possible that Crozer could have boasted? that there were rumours abroad to his—Heathercat's—discredit? that his honour was publicly sullied? All the world went dark about him at the thought; he sank without a struggle into the midnight pool of despair; and every time he so sank, he brought back with him—not drowned heroism indeed, but half-drowned courage by the locks. His heart beat very slowly as he deserted his station, and began to crawl towards that of Crozer. Something pulled him back, and it was not the sense of duty, but a remembrance of Crozer's build and hateful readiness of fist. Duty, as he conceived it, pointed him forward on the rueful path that he was travelling. Duty bade him redeem his name if he were able, at the risk of broken bones; and his bones and every tooth in his head ached by anticipation. An awful subsidiary fear whispered him that if he were hurt, he should disgrace himself by weeping. He consoled himself, boy-like, with the consideration that he was not yet committed; he could easily steal over unseen to Crozer's post, and he had a continuous private idea that he would very probably steal back again. His course took him so near the minister that he could hear some of his words: 'What news, minister, of Claver'se? He's going round like a roaring rampaging lion. . . .

Footnotes:

[0] With special reference to Father Damien, pp. 63–81.

[65] From the Sydney Presbyterian, October 26, 1889.

[85] Theater of Mortality, p. 10; Edin. 1713.

[86] History of My Own Times, beginning 1660, by Bishop Gilbert Burnet, p. 158.

[87a] Wodrow's Church History, Book II. chap. i. sect. I.

[87b] Crookshank's Church History, 1751, second ed. p. 202.

[88] Burnet, p. 348.

[89] Fuller's Historie of the Holy Warre, fourth ed. 1651.

[90] Wodrow, vol. ii. p. 17.

[92] Sir J. Turner's Memoirs, pp. 148–50.

[93] A Cloud of Witnesses, p. 376.

[94a] Wodrow, pp. 19, 20.

[94b] A Hind Let Loose, p. 123.

[95] Turner, p. 163.

[96a] Turner, p. 198.

[96b] Ibid. p. 167.

[97] Wodrow, p. 29.

[98] Turner, Wodrow, and Church History by James Kirkton, an outed minister of the period.

[99] Kirkton, p. 244.

[101a] Kirkton.

[101b] Turner.

[102] Kirkton.

[103] Kirkton.

[104] Cloud of Witnesses, p. 389; Edin. 1765.

[105a] Kirkton, p. 247.

[105b] Ibid. p. 254.

[105c] Ibid. p. 247.

[105d] Ibid. pp. 247, 248.

[106] Kirkton, p. 248.

[107a] Kirkton, p. 249.

[107b] Naphtali, p. 205; Glasgow, 1721.

[107c] Wodrow, p. 59.

[108a] Kirkton, p. 246.

[108b] Defoe's History of the Church of Scotland.

[151] 'This paper was written in collaboration with James Waiter Ferrier, and if reprinted this is to be stated, though his principal collaboration was to lie back in an easy-chair and laugh.'—[R.L.S., Oct. 25, 1894.]

[183] The illustrator was, in fact, a lady, Miss Eunice Bagster, eldest daughter of the publisher, Samuel Bagster; except in the case of the cuts depicting the fight with Apollyon, which were designed by her brother, Mr. Jonathan Bagster. The edition was published in 1845. I am indebted for this information to the kindness of Mr. Robert Bagster, the present managing director of the firm.—[Sir Sidney Colvin's Note.]

[205] See a short essay of De Quincey's.

[206a] Religio Medici, Part ii.

[206b] Duchess of Malfi.

About Author

Childhood and youth

Stevenson was born at 8 Howard Place, Edinburgh, Scotland on 13 November 1850 to Thomas Stevenson (1818–87), a leading lighthouse engineer, and his wife Margaret Isabella (born Balfour, 1829–97). He was christened Robert Lewis Balfour Stevenson. At about age 18, he changed the spelling of "Lewis" to "Louis", and he dropped "Balfour" in 1873.

Lighthouse design was the family's profession; Thomas's father (Robert's grandfather) was civil engineer Robert Stevenson, and Thomas's brothers (Robert's uncles) Alan and David were in the same field. Thomas's maternal grandfather Thomas Smith had been in the same profession. However, Robert's mother's family were gentry, tracing their lineage back to Alexander Balfour who had held the lands of Inchyra in Fife in the fifteenth century. His mother's father Lewis Balfour (1777–1860) was a minister of the Church of Scotland at nearby Colinton, and her siblings included physician George William Balfour and marine engineer James Balfour. Stevenson spent the greater part of his boyhood holidays in his maternal grandfather's house. "Now I often wonder what I inherited from this old minister," Stevenson wrote. "I must suppose, indeed, that he was fond of preaching sermons, and so am I, though I never heard it maintained that either of us loved to hear them."

Lewis Balfour and his daughter both had weak chests, so they often needed to stay in warmer climates for their health. Stevenson inherited a tendency to coughs and fevers, exacerbated when the family moved to a damp, chilly house at 1 Inverleith Terrace in 1851. The family moved again to the sunnier 17 Heriot Row when Stevenson was six years old, but the tendency to extreme sickness in winter remained with him until he was 11. Illness was a recurrent feature of his adult life and left him extraordinarily thin. Contemporaneous views were that he had tuberculosis, but more recent views are that it was bronchiectasis or even sarcoidosis.

Stevenson's parents were both devout Presbyterians, but the household was not strict in its adherence to Calvinist principles. His nurse Alison Cunningham (known as Cummy) was more fervently religious. Her mix of Calvinism and folk beliefs were an early source of nightmares for the child, and he showed a precocious concern for religion. But she also cared for him tenderly in illness, reading to him from John Bunyan and the Bible as he lay sick in bed and telling tales of the Covenanters. Stevenson recalled this time of sickness in "The Land of Counterpane" in A Child's Garden of Verses (1885), dedicating the book to his nurse.

Stevenson was an only child, both strange-looking and eccentric, and he found it hard to fit in when he was sent to a nearby school at age 6, a problem repeated at age 11 when he went on to the Edinburgh Academy; but he mixed well in lively games with his cousins in summer holidays at Colinton. His frequent illnesses often kept him away from his first school, so he was taught for long stretches by private tutors. He was a late reader, learning at age 7 or 8, but even before this he dictated stories to his mother and nurse, and he compulsively wrote stories throughout his childhood. His father was proud of this interest; he had also written stories in his spare time until his own father found them and told him to "give up such nonsense and mind your business." He paid for the printing of Robert's first publication at 16, entitled The Pentland Rising: A Page of History, 1666. It was an account of the Covenanters' rebellion which was published in 1866, the 200th anniversary of the event.

Education

In September 1857, Stevenson went to Mr Henderson's School in India Street, Edinburgh, but because of poor health stayed only a few weeks and did not return until October 1859. During his many absences he was taught by private tutors. In October 1861, he went to Edinburgh Academy, an independent school for boys, and stayed there sporadically for about fifteen months. In the autumn of 1863, he spent one term at an English boarding school at Spring Grove in Isleworth in Middlesex (now an urban area of West London). In October 1864, following an improvement to his health, he

224

was sent to Robert Thomson's private school in Frederick Street, Edinburgh, where he remained until he went to university. In November 1867, Stevenson entered the University of Edinburgh to study engineering. He showed from the start no enthusiasm for his studies and devoted much energy to avoiding lectures. This time was more important for the friendships he made with other students in the Speculative Society (an exclusive debating club), particularly with Charles Baxter, who would become Stevenson's financial agent, and with a professor, Fleeming Jenkin, whose house staged amateur drama in which Stevenson took part, and whose biography he would later write. Perhaps most important at this point in his life was a cousin, Robert Alan Mowbray Stevenson (known as "Bob"), a lively and light-hearted young man who, instead of the family profession, had chosen to study art. Each year during vacations, Stevenson travelled to inspect the family's engineering works—to Anstruther and Wick in 1868, with his father on his official tour of Orkney and Shetland islands lighthouses in 1869, and for three weeks to the island of Erraid in 1870. He enjoyed the travels more for the material they gave for his writing than for any engineering interest. The voyage with his father pleased him because a similar journey of Walter Scott with Robert Stevenson had provided the inspiration for Scott's 1822 novel The Pirate. In April 1871, Stevenson notified his father of his decision to pursue a life of letters. Though the elder Stevenson was naturally disappointed, the surprise cannot have been great, and Stevenson's mother reported that he was "wonderfully resigned" to his son's choice. To provide some security, it was agreed that Stevenson should read Law (again at Edinburgh University) and be called to the Scottish bar. In his 1887 poetry collection Underwoods, Stevenson muses on his having turned from the family profession:

> Say not of me that weakly I declined
>
> The labours of my sires, and fled the sea,
>
> The towers we founded and the lamps we lit,
>
> To play at home with paper like a child.
>
> But rather say: In the afternoon of time

A strenuous family dusted from its hands

The sand of granite, and beholding far

Along the sounding coast its pyramids

And tall memorials catch the dying sun,

Smiled well content, and to this childish task

Around the fire addressed its evening hours.

In other respects too, Stevenson was moving away from his upbringing. His dress became more Bohemian; he already wore his hair long, but he now took to wearing a velveteen jacket and rarely attended parties in conventional evening dress. Within the limits of a strict allowance, he visited cheap pubs and brothels. More importantly, he had come to reject Christianity and declared himself an atheist. In January 1873, his father came across the constitution of the LJR (Liberty, Justice, Reverence) Club, of which Stevenson and his cousin Bob were members, which began: "Disregard everything our parents have taught us". Questioning his son about his beliefs, he discovered the truth, leading to a long period of dissension with both parents:

What a damned curse I am to my parents! As my father said "You have rendered my whole life a failure". As my mother said "This is the heaviest affliction that has ever befallen me". O Lord, what a pleasant thing it is to have damned the happiness of (probably) the only two people who care a damn about you in the world.

Early writing and travels

Stevenson was visiting a cousin in England in late 1873 when he met two people who became very important to him: Sidney Colvin and Fanny (Frances Jane) Sitwell. Sitwell was a 34-year-old woman with a son, who was separated from her husband. She attracted the devotion of many who met her, including Colvin, who married her in 1901. Stevenson was also drawn to her, and they kept up a warm correspondence over several years in which he wavered between the role of a suitor and a son (he addressed

226

her as "Madonna"). Colvin became Stevenson's literary adviser and was the first editor of his letters after his death. He placed Stevenson's first paid contribution in The Portfolio, an essay entitled "Roads".

Stevenson was soon active in London literary life, becoming acquainted with many of the writers of the time, including Andrew Lang, Edmund Gosse, and Leslie Stephen, the editor of the Cornhill Magazine who took an interest in Stevenson's work. Stephen took Stevenson to visit a patient at the Edinburgh Infirmary named William Ernest Henley, an energetic and talkative man with a wooden leg. Henley became a close friend and occasional literary collaborator, until a quarrel broke up the friendship in 1888, and he is often considered to be the model for Long John Silver in Treasure Island.

Stevenson was sent to Menton on the French Riviera in November 1873 to recuperate after his health failed. He returned in better health in April 1874 and settled down to his studies, but he returned to France several times after that. He made long and frequent trips to the neighborhood of the Forest of Fontainebleau, staying at Barbizon, Grez-sur-Loing, and Nemours and becoming a member of the artists' colonies there. He also traveled to Paris to visit galleries and the theatres. He qualified for the Scottish bar in July 1875, and his father added a brass plate to the Heriot Row house reading "R.L. Stevenson, Advocate". His law studies did influence his books, but he never practised law; all his energies were spent in travel and writing. One of his journeys was a canoe voyage in Belgium and France with Sir Walter Simpson, a friend from the Speculative Society, a frequent travel companion, and the author of The Art of Golf (1887). This trip was the basis of his first travel book An Inland Voyage (1878).

Marriage

The canoe voyage with Simpson brought Stevenson to Grez in September 1876 where he met Fanny Van de Grift Osbourne (1840–1914), born in Indianapolis. She had married at age 17 and moved to Nevada to rejoin husband Samuel after his participation in the American Civil War. Their children were Isobel (or "Belle"), Lloyd, and Hervey (who died in 1875). But anger over her husband's infidelities led to a number of separations. In 1875, she had taken her children to France where she and Isobel studied art.

Stevenson returned to Britain shortly after this first meeting, but Fanny apparently remained in his thoughts, and he wrote the essay "On falling in love" for the Cornhill Magazine. They met again early in 1877 and became lovers. Stevenson spent much of the following year with her and her children in France. In August 1878, she returned to San Francisco and Stevenson remained in Europe, making the walking trip that formed the basis for Travels with a Donkey in the Cévennes (1879). But he set off to join her in August 1879, against the advice of his friends and without notifying his parents. He took second-class passage on the steamship Devonia, in part to save money but also to learn how others traveled and to increase the adventure of the journey. He then traveled overland by train from New York City to California. He later wrote about the experience in The Amateur Emigrant. It was good experience for his writing, but it broke his health.

He was near death when he arrived in Monterey, California, where some local ranchers nursed him back to health. He stayed for a time at the French Hotel located at 530 Houston Street, now a museum dedicated to his memory called the "Stevenson House". While there, he often dined "on the cuff," as he said, at a nearby restaurant run by Frenchman Jules Simoneau which stood at what is now Simoneau Plaza; several years later, he sent Simoneau an inscribed copy of his novel Strange Case of Dr Jekyll and Mr Hyde (1886), writing that it would be a stranger case still if Robert Louis Stevenson ever forgot Jules Simoneau. While in Monterey, he wrote an evocative article about "the Old Pacific Capital" of Monterey.

By December 1879, Stevenson had recovered his health enough to continue to San Francisco where he struggled "all alone on forty-five cents a day, and sometimes less, with quantities of hard work and many heavy thoughts," in an effort to support himself through his writing. But by the end of the winter, his health was broken again and he found himself at death's door. Fanny was now divorced and recovered from her own illness, and she came to his bedside and nursed him to recovery. "After a while," he wrote, "my spirit got up again in a divine frenzy, and has since kicked and spurred my vile body forward with great emphasis and success." When his father heard of his condition, he cabled him money to help him through this period.

Fanny and Robert were married in May 1880, although he said that he was "a mere complication of cough and bones, much fitter for an emblem of mortality than a bridegroom." He travelled with his new wife and her son Lloyd north of San Francisco to Napa Valley and spent a summer honeymoon at an abandoned mining camp on Mount Saint Helena. He wrote about this experience in The Silverado Squatters. He met Charles Warren Stoddard, co-editor of the Overland Monthly and author of South Sea Idylls, who urged Stevenson to travel to the South Pacific, an idea which returned to him many years later. In August 1880, he sailed with Fanny and Lloyd from New York to Britain and found his parents and his friend Sidney Colvin on the wharf at Liverpool, happy to see him return home. Gradually, his wife was able to patch up differences between father and son and make herself a part of the family through her charm and wit.

Attempted settlement in Europe and the US

Stevenson searched in vain between 1880 and 1887 for a residence suitable to his health. He spent his summers at various places in Scotland and England, including Westbourne, Dorset, a residential area in Bournemouth. It was during his time in Bournemouth that he wrote the story Strange Case of Dr Jekyll and Mr Hyde, naming the character Mr. Poole after the town of Poole which is situated next to Bournemouth. In Westbourne, he named his house Skerryvore after the tallest lighthouse in Scotland, which his uncle Alan had built (1838–44). In the wintertime, Stevenson travelled to France and lived at Davos Platz and the Chalet de Solitude at Hyères, where he was very happy for a time. "I have so many things to make life sweet for me," he wrote, "it seems a pity I cannot have that other one thing—health. But though you will be angry to hear it, I believe, for myself at least, what is is best." In spite of his ill health, he produced the bulk of his best-known work during these years. Treasure Island was published under the pseudonym "Captain George North" and became his first widely popular book; he wrote it during this time, along with Kidnapped, Strange Case of Dr Jekyll and Mr Hyde (which established his wider reputation), The Black Arrow: A Tale of the Two Roses, A Child's Garden of Verses, and Underwoods. He gave a copy of Kidnapped to his friend and frequent Skerryvore visitor Henry James.

His father died in 1887 and Stevenson felt free to follow the advice of his physician to try a complete change of climate, so he headed for Colorado with his mother and family. But after landing in New York, they decided to spend the winter in the Adirondacks at a cure cottage now known as Stevenson Cottage at Saranac Lake, New York. During the intensely cold winter, Stevenson wrote some of his best essays, including Pulvis et Umbra. He also began The Master of Ballantrae and lightheartedly planned a cruise to the southern Pacific Ocean for the following summer.

Politics

Stevenson believed in Conservatism for most of his life. His cousin and biographer Sir Graham Balfour said that "he probably throughout life would, if compelled to vote, have always supported the Conservative candidate." In 1866, Stevenson voted for Benjamin Disraeli, future Conservative Prime Minister of the United Kingdom, over Thomas Carlyle for the Lord Rectorship of the University of Edinburgh. During his college years, he briefly identified himself as a "red-hot socialist". He wrote at age 26: "I look back to the time when I was a Socialist with something like regret.... Now I know that in thus turning Conservative with years, I am going through the normal cycle of change and travelling in the common orbit of men's opinions."

Journey to the Pacific

In June 1888, Stevenson chartered the yacht Casco and set sail with his family from San Francisco. The vessel "plowed her path of snow across the empty deep, far from all track of commerce, far from any hand of help." The sea air and thrill of adventure for a time restored his health, and for nearly three years he wandered the eastern and central Pacific, stopping for extended stays at the Hawaiian Islands where he became a good friend of King Kalākaua. He befriended the king's niece Princess Victoria Kaiulani, who also had Scottish heritage. He spent time at the Gilbert Islands, Tahiti, New Zealand, and the Samoan Islands. During this period, he completed The Master of Ballantrae, composed two ballads based on the legends of the islanders, and wrote The Bottle Imp. He preserved the experience of these years in his various letters and in his In the South Seas (which was published posthumously). He made a voyage in 1889 with Lloyd on the trading schooner Equator, visiting Butaritari, Mariki, Apaiang, and Abemama in the Gilbert Islands. They spent several months on Abemama with tyrant-chief Tem Binoka, whom Stevenson described in In the South Seas.

Stevenson left Sydney on the Janet Nicoll in April 1890 for his third and final voyage among the South Seas islands. He intended to produce another book of travel writing to follow his earlier book In the South Seas, but it was his wife who eventually published her journal of their third voyage. (Fanny misnames the ship in her account The Cruise of the Janet Nichol.) A fellow passenger was Jack Buckland, whose stories of life as an island trader became the inspiration for the character of Tommy Hadden in The Wrecker (1892), which Stevenson and Lloyd Osbourne wrote together. Buckland visited the Stevensons at Vailima in 1894.

Last years

In 1890, Stevenson purchased a tract of about 400 acres (1.6 km²) in Upolu, an island in Samoa where he established himself on his estate in the village of Vailima after two aborted attempts to visit Scotland. He took the native name Tusitala (Samoan for "Teller of Tales"). His influence spread among the Samoans, who consulted him for advice, and he soon became involved in local politics. He was convinced that the European officials who had been appointed to rule the Samoans were incompetent, and he published A Footnote to History after many futile attempts to resolve the matter. This was such a stinging protest against existing conditions that it resulted in the recall of two officials, and Stevenson feared for a time that it would result in his own deportation. He wrote to Colvin, "I used to think meanly of the plumber; but how he shines beside the politician!"

He also found time to work at his writing, although he felt that "there was never any man had so many irons in the fire". He wrote The Beach of Falesa, Catriona (titled David Balfour in the US), The Ebb-Tide, and the Vailima Letters during this period.

Stevenson grew depressed and wondered if he had exhausted his creative vein, as he had been "overworked bitterly" and that the best he could write was "ditch-water". He even feared that he might again become a helpless invalid. He rebelled against this idea: "I wish to die in my boots; no more Land of Counterpane for me. To be drowned, to be shot, to be thrown from a horse — ay, to be hanged, rather than pass again through that slow dissolution." He then suddenly had a return of energy and he began work on Weir of Hermiston. "It's so good that it frightens me," he is reported to have exclaimed. He felt that this was the best work he had done.

On 3 December 1894, Stevenson was talking to his wife and straining to open a bottle of wine when he suddenly exclaimed, "What's that?", asked his wife "does my face look strange?", and collapsed. He died within a few hours, probably of a cerebral haemorrhage. He was 44 years old. The Samoans insisted on surrounding his body with a watch-guard during the night and on bearing him on their shoulders to nearby Mount Vaea, where they buried him on a spot overlooking the sea on land donated by British Acting Vice Consul Thomas Trood. Stevenson had always wanted his Requiem inscribed on his tomb:

Under the wide and starry sky,

Dig the grave and let me lie.

Glad did I live and gladly die,

And I laid me down with a will.

This be the verse you grave for me:

Here he lies where he longed to be;

Home is the sailor, home from sea,

And the hunter home from the hill.

Stevenson was loved by the Samoans, and his tombstone epigraph was translated to a Samoan song of grief. (Source: Wikipedia)